Farm Journal's
Meal & Menu
Planner
Cookbook

Other Farm Journal Cookbooks

Farm Journal's
Meal & Menu Planner
Cookbook

By ELISE W. MANNING

FARM JOURNAL, INC.
Philadelphia, Pennsylvania

Distributed to the trade by
E.P. Dutton, New York, New York

Book Design by Michael P. Durning

Library of Congress Cataloging in Publication Data

Manning, Elise W.
  Farm journal's meal & menu planner cookbook.

  Includes index.
  1. Cookery.   2. Menus.   I. Farm journal
(Philadelphia, 1956-   )   II. Title.
III. Title: Meal & menu planner cookbook.
TX7115.M284   641.5   80-18106
ISBN 0-525-93116-3

Contents

Color Photographs

Meal & Menu Planner Cookbook Food Photographs by William Hazzard/Hazzard Studios, except: Spicy Sugar Loaf and Fruit Honeys by Ted Hoffman/ Chas. P. Mills & Son; Super Cyder Float by Photographic Illustrators, Ltd.; Turkey Curry with Rice by Richard Tomlinson; and Three Baked Goods by Fred Carbone.

Jacket photograph by William Hazzard Studios.

Farm Journal's
Meal & Menu
Planner
Cookbook

Introduction

It takes a lot of effort to keep yourself and your family happily fed without repeating the same recipes week after week—after all, every year you may plan more than a thousand meals. That's why we decided to produce a book of meals and menus that can be your kitchen companion throughout the year.

We've selected over 400 great country recipes for every season—recipes from farm and ranch women experienced in cooking meals their families love to come home to all year round.

Even if your family prefers the reliable stand-bys, you can vary your menus by seasoning them with a little imagination. Hamburger doesn't always have to be made into a round patty; it can arrive at the table as miniature loaves, in a casserole snow-capped with mashed potatoes, or even baked in a ring and filled with fresh vegetables of the season.

For good nutrition, our menus have been planned around the building blocks of a good diet—meats, vegetables and fruits, breads and cereals, and dairy products—with emphasis on the fresh produce of each season.

Once you're sure you are providing your family with a nutritionally sound diet, the next step in menu planning is to balance flavor, texture and color. These menus have been carefully balanced so that they're as pretty to look at as they are good to eat. Parsley, pimiento, paprika, watercress, toasted almonds and jeweled-toned jellies add a lot to a meal even if they're used only as trimmings. A roast of beef with rich brown gravy alongside leafy green spinach salad and surrounded by sunny circles of carrot is a joy to look at even before you begin to eat.

At the beginning of each season's menus, there's an introduction offering hints on how to look for the perfect produce and how to take care of it once you bring it home to your kitchen. Our recipes emphasize seasonal foods that are plentiful and low in price, to help you keep costs down when preparing both family and company meals. We've also included suggestions for holiday menus to help you celebrate those special occasions.

As you look through our daily lunch and dinner menus, you'll notice that they include one underlined item and one or more starred ones. The recipe for the underlined item—whether it be a main dish, vegetable, soup, salad, bread or dessert—is given in its entirety right on that same page. The recipes for each one of the starred items appear elsewhere in the book, and you can find them easily by consulting the index.

On weekends, most of us enjoy a leisurely morning meal, so at the end of each section we've included four additional menus for extra-special breakfasts and brunches—enough for a month of Sundays.

It's often the little things in life that mean a lot, and that applies to meal and menu planning, too. To conclude each section, we've added a page called "Shortcuts and Seasonings," filled with hints to make cooking easier and tips on how to add special touches to your menu without a lot of effort.

Even if you don't follow these menus step by step, we hope that we've given you a wealth of recipes and new ideas to make your meals more memorable, 365 days of the year.

March 20 -
June 20

Spring

S P R I N G

Spring is a mixture of seasons with its blustery, biting winds in March, heavy showers in April and then the warm glow of sunshine in May and early June.

The menus in this section are designed to help you take advantage of the abundant produce of the season: the first tender young asparagus, emerald-green scallions, crisp red radishes, early lettuce, juicy golden pineapple and new potatoes and peas.

To protect you from the chilly winds of March, we offer recipes for robust Herbed Onion Soup, our Famous Clam Chowder and a deliciously different Chicken Lima Bean Stew topped with fluffy buttermilk dumplings.

For April, we feature the first delicacies of spring—strawberries, rhubarb and veal, plus a stuffed ham for a regal Easter Sunday dinner.

To celebrate May's gifts from the garden, we suggest our Vegetable-Egg Combo. Served with fresh asparagus, this handsome dish tastes every bit as good as it looks. Your family or guests will know it's springtime when you serve them Rhubarb Cherry Pie or delicate Raspberry-Vanilla Cloud for dessert. We've also included easy recipes for breads and rolls that go well with springtime meals. Our Herbed Batter Bread tastes so good that you really don't need to lather it with butter, and the Cottage Cheese Rolls are light, high, and puffy.

In early June, many of our menus reflect the emergence of asparagus, strawberries, watercress and other greens.

If you must purchase your spring bounty instead of gathering it from the garden, shop carefully to get the best value for your money. That means choosing the finest and freshest of the spring fruits and vegetables.

When you buy rhubarb, look for firm stems with a bright, glossy appearance and a rich, rosy color. Be sure that the stems are tender and not fibrous, and avoid thick, large stems.

After you buy that lovely, fragile-looking bunch of watercress with its delicate peppery flavor, store it in the refrigerator in a glass of water, like a bouquet—it will keep much longer.

When buying asparagus, look for tightly closed tips and bright green stalks. Try to buy asparagus loose rather than tied in bundles, so that you can choose stalks that are uniform in size and thus will cook evenly.

Look for bright red, plump strawberries with fresh green caps. The berries should have a bright, natural shine to them; if they are dull or have limp green caps, don't buy them. It's best to refrigerate them with the caps intact, stored in the original basket or spread on a tray. Strawberries are very perishable, so use them as soon as possible. They also can be frozen in airtight containers; of course, they won't have the same texture when thawed, but they'll taste great spooned over angel food cake.

New potatoes boiled in their jackets and liberally doused with butter make a fine vegetable for any spring meal. For a change of flavor, season them with garden-fresh herbs—parsley, chives, green onions, basil or tarragon. For a pretty effect, don't pare the whole potato; simply pare a narrow strip around the middle of each potato and cook until tender.

The menus that follow are a mix of family and special-occasion meals with good nutrition and a balance of colors and textures. Included are menus and recipes perfect for Mother's Day, graduation parties, the bridal showers that always abound in early June and all the other celebrations of the season.

In each menu, we offer the fresh taste of spring.

Lunch

Herbed Onion Soup
Crusty Hard Rolls
Curly Endive Salad
Baked Apples Stuffed with Raisins and Almonds
Coffee   Tea   Milk

Dinner

Pork Kabobs*
Hot Fluffy Rice   Buttered Peas
Corn Relish in Pimiento Cups
Strawberry Tarts
Coffee   Tea   Milk

Herbed Onion Soup

4 large onions, thinly sliced
½ c. butter or regular margarine
4 (13¾-oz.) cans chicken broth
1 c. dry white wine
⅛ tsp. dried marjoram leaves, crushed
8 slices French bread
2 c. shredded Cheddar cheese (8 oz.)

Cook onions in butter in Dutch oven until soft. Add chicken broth, wine and marjoram; cover and simmer 15 minutes.

Meanwhile, toast bread under broiler on one side. Turn slices over and sprinkle with cheese. Broil just until cheese melts.

Place one slice bread, cheese side up, in each soup plate or bowl. Ladle hot soup over. Makes 2¾ quarts or 8 servings.

March 21

Lunch

Pasta and Bean Soup*
Corn Muffins
Date and Nut Cookies
Tea   Milk

Dinner

Swiss Steak

<u>*Mushroom Pilaf*</u>   *Carrot and Celery Sticks*

Spinach Salad

Vanilla Ice Cream with Hot Fudge Sauce

Coffee   Tea   Milk

Mushroom Pilaf

1 (4-oz.) can mushrooms
1 c. chopped onion
¼ c. butter or regular margarine
¼ c. cooking oil
2 c. raw regular rice
3 (10½-oz.) cans condensed beef
  broth
½ tsp. salt
2 tsp. dried oregano leaves
Fresh chopped parsley

Drain mushrooms; reserve liquid. Add enough water to make 2 c.; set aside.

Sauté mushrooms and onion in melted butter and oil in large saucepan until tender, but not brown. Stir in rice and brown slightly, stirring occasionally. Stir in reserved liquid, beef broth, salt and oregano. Bring mixture to a boil. Pour into 3-qt. casserole; cover.

Bake in 375° oven 25 minutes, or until rice is tender. Garnish with parsley. Makes 8 to 10 servings.

*See Index for recipe

Lunch

Espanola Valley Soup*
Egg Salad in Lettuce Cups
Custard Pie
Tea   Milk

Dinner

Pan-Fried Fish Fillets with Toasted Almonds
Baked Potatoes   Buttered Broccoli Spears
Tangy Slaw
Chocolate Cookies
Tea   Milk

Tangy Slaw

10 c. shredded cabbage
1½ c. chopped green pepper
1½ c. shredded pared carrots
¼ c. chopped onion
1 c. salad dressing or mayonnaise
½ c. vinegar
½ c. sugar
½ tsp. salt
¼ tsp. pepper

Combine cabbage, green pepper, carrots and onion in large bowl. Combine salad dressing, vinegar, sugar, salt and pepper in small bowl; stir to blend. Add to cabbage mixture; toss lightly. Serve immediately. Makes 12 to 14 servings.

Lunch

Beef Broth

Luncheon Meat-Cheese Sandwiches*

Fresh Fruit   Oatmeal Cookies

Tea   Milk

Dinner

Chicken Lima Bean Stew

Hot Biscuits

Hearts of Lettuce with Russian Dressing

Sponge Cake

Coffee   Milk

Chicken Lima Bean Stew

1 (3-lb.) broiler-fryer, cut up
4 c. water
2 tblsp. minced fresh parsley
¾ tsp. poultry seasoning
¼ tsp. pepper
4 chicken bouillon cubes
¼ c. cornstarch
½ c. water
1 (17-oz.) can whole kernel corn
1½ c. thinly sliced, pared carrots
2 c. thinly sliced onion
1 (10-oz.) pkg. frozen lima beans
Dumplings (recipe follows)

Place first 6 ingredients in 4-qt. Dutch oven. Cover; simmer 1 hour, or until chicken is tender. Remove chicken from broth. Cool; remove chicken from bones. Cut chicken into large pieces.

Blend together cornstarch and ½ c. water. Stir into simmering broth; cook 1 minute. Add undrained corn, carrots, onion, lima beans and chicken. Drop dumplings in 12 spoonfuls on simmering stew. Cook 10 minutes. Cover; cook 10 more minutes. Makes 8 servings.

Dumplings: Combine 2 c. buttermilk baking mix, 2 tblsp. chopped fresh parsley and ⅔ c. milk. Stir until moistened.

* See Index for recipe

Lunch

Cream of Tomato Soup

Swiss Salmon Sandwiches

Assorted Pickles   Black Olives

Chocolate Nut Cupcakes

Tea   Milk

Dinner

Corned Beef Hash

Buttered Sliced Beets   Hot Applesauce

Tossed Salad

Amish Vanilla Pie*

Coffee   Tea   Milk

Swiss Salmon Sandwiches

1 (8-oz.) can salmon, drained and
   flaked
4 oz. shredded Swiss cheese (1 c.)
2 tblsp. chopped dill pickle
2 tblsp. chopped onion
2 tblsp. sliced stuffed green olives
¼ c. mayonnaise or salad dressing
1 tblsp. lemon juice
6 hamburger buns, split

Combine salmon, cheese, pickle, onion, olives, mayonnaise and lemon juice. Spread between buns. Wrap individually in aluminum foil. Chill. When ready to eat, place wrapped sandwiches in unheated oven. Turn oven to 400° and bake 20 minutes. Makes 6 sandwiches.

* See Index for recipe

Lunch

Tuna Carrot Salad
Cucumber Sandwiches with Chive Butter
Pineapple Chunks with Mint
Tea   Milk

Dinner

Broiled Calves' Liver
Cauliflower Casserole*
Broiled Tomatoes
Brownies à la Mode
Coffee   Milk

Tuna Carrot Salad

1 (7-oz.) can tuna, drained and flaked
1 c. coarsely grated carrots
1 c. chopped celery
¼ c. finely chopped onion
½ c. mayonnaise
½ c. milk
1 tsp. prepared mustard
¼ tsp. pepper
1 (1¾-oz.) can shoestring potatoes

Combine tuna, carrots, celery and onion in bowl; set aside.

Mix together mayonnaise, milk, mustard and pepper. Add to tuna mixture; toss gently. Cover and chill until serving time.

Add shoestring potatoes and toss. Makes 6 servings.

*See Index for recipe

Lunch

Hearty Split Pea Soup*

Pumpernickel Bread

Grapefruit and Orange Sections

Coffee   Milk

Dinner

Lamb Chop Marinade

Creamed Potatoes   Peas and Small White Onions

Blueberry Tarts

Coffee   Milk

Lamb Chop Marinade

6 lamb chops (loin or rib, 1″ thick)
¼ c. salad oil
1 tblsp. lemon juice
1 tsp. salt
½ tsp. pepper
1 small bay leaf
1 tsp. chopped parsley
1 clove garlic, minced
1 small onion, sliced

Place chops in glass baking dish or pan.

Combine oil, lemon juice, salt, pepper, bay leaf, parsley, garlic and onion.

Pour marinade over chops. Cover with plastic wrap and chill at least 3 hours. Turn once or twice.

Arrange meat on oiled broiler rack. Broil about 3″ from source of heat about 12 minutes, turning once during broiling. To test doneness, make slit with knife in one chop near bone. Note if color inside indicates the desired doneness. Makes 6 servings.

Lunch

Famous Clam Chowder

Sliced Tongue Sandwiches   Olives

Chocolate Chip Cookies

Tea   Milk

Dinner

Veal in Sour Cream*

Buttered Noodles   Steamed Spinach

Shredded Lettuce Salad

Fresh Fruit over Lemon Yogurt

Coffee   Milk

Famous Clam Chowder

2 (6½-oz.) cans minced clams
1 c. finely chopped onion
1 c. finely diced celery
2 c. very finely diced potatoes
¾ c. butter or regular margarine
¾ c. flour
1 qt. dairy half-and-half
1½ tsp. salt
Few grains white pepper
2 tblsp. red wine vinegar

Drain juice from clams. Add juice to vegetables in small saucepan.

Add enough water to barely cover vegetables. Simmer, covered, over medium heat until just tender.

In the meantime, melt butter; add flour, blend and cook, stirring for 2 to 3 minutes. Add dairy half-and-half; cook and stir with wire whisk until smooth and thick.

Add undrained vegetables and clams; heat through. Add salt, pepper and vinegar. Makes 8 servings.

*See Index for recipe

Lunch

Macaroni-Sausage Casserole*

Sliced Tomatoes   Hot Rolls

Fruit Cocktail

Coffee   Milk

Dinner

Grilled Halibut Steaks

Julienne Green Beans   Buttered Corn

Tossed Salad with Garlic Dressing

Vanilla Pudding with Sliced Oranges

Coffee   Milk

Grilled Halibut Steaks

8 halibut steaks (about ¼ lb. each)
2 small cloves garlic, cut in halves
6 tblsp. salad oil
6 tblsp. lemon juice
Salt
Paprika
4 to 6 tblsp. toasted sesame seeds
Lemon wedges
Chopped parsley

Rub halibut on both sides with cut garlic cloves; brush with salad oil. Sprinkle with lemon juice (bottled lemon juice is easy to use) and salt. Place on grill about 4″ above medium-hot coals.

Cook about 5 minutes; turn. Sprinkle top of steaks with paprika and toasted sesame seeds. Cook 5 minutes longer, or until the fish is done. Test for doneness with a fork; if the fish flakes easily, it is ready to serve. Serve at once with lemon wedges and chopped parsley. Makes 8 servings.

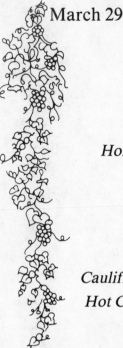

March 29

Lunch

Maine Corn Chowder*
Toasted Sesame Crackers
Watercress and Sliced Radish Salad
Honeydew Melon Balls in Raspberry Gelatin
Tea   Milk

Dinner

Rolled Stuffed Flank Steak
Cauliflower with Cheese Sauce   Romaine Salad
Hot Cherry Turnovers with Brandied Hard Sauce
Coffee   Tea   Milk

Rolled Stuffed Flank Steak

1 (1½- to 2-lb.) flank steak
1 tsp. salt
⅛ tsp. pepper
1 tblsp. prepared mustard
1½ c. day-old bread, cut in ½″ cubes
1 tsp. poultry seasoning
1 medium onion, chopped
½ c. chopped celery
¼ c. melted shortening or salad oil
2 tblsp. flour
Fat for browning
1 c. water or beef broth

Have steak scored (or do it yourself by crisscrossing shallow diamond-shaped cuts on both sides of meat to tenderize).

Sprinkle both sides with salt and pepper; spread mustard over top.

Toss bread, poultry seasoning, onion and celery with shortening.

Spoon mixture evenly over top of steak. Roll up, beginning with narrow end; fasten with skewers, and lace with string, if necessary. Sprinkle with flour.

Brown well on all sides in hot fat in Dutch oven over medium heat.

Add water. Cover tightly; cook over low heat 1½ hours, or until tender. Or cover and bake in 350° oven 2 hours. Remove meat; make gravy. Makes 6 to 8 servings.

See Index for recipe

Lunch

Cold Asparagus Vinaigrette

Rye Melba Toast with Cottage Cheese

Walnut Applesauce Cake*

Tea   Milk

Dinner

Roast Loin of Pork*

Oven-Browned Potatoes   Whipped Squash

Broccoli Egg Ring

Lemon Soufflé with Fresh Strawberry Sauce

Coffee   Milk

Broccoli Egg Ring

1 env. unflavored gelatin
¼ c. cold water
1 c. boiling chicken broth
¼ tsp. salt
⅛ tsp. pepper
2 tblsp. lemon juice
¾ c. mayonnaise
1 (10-oz.) pkg. frozen chopped broccoli, cooked and drained
2 hard-cooked eggs, chopped

Soften gelatin in cold water in bowl 5 minutes. Add hot chicken broth, salt, pepper and lemon juice; stir until dissolved. Gradually stir some of hot gelatin mixture into mayonnaise, blending well. Add mayonnaise mixture to remaining gelatin, stirring to blend. Cover and chill until thick and syrupy.

Fold in broccoli and eggs. Pour into lightly oiled 4-c. ring mold. Cover; chill until set. Makes 6 to 8 servings.

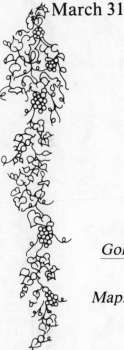

Lunch

Beef Consommé with Lemon Slices
Tuna Club Sandwiches*
Sugar-Frosted Vanilla Wafers
Tea   Milk

Dinner

Boiled Knockwurst
Golden Potato Squares   *Buttered Spinach*
Sliced Tomatoes with Basil
Maple Walnut Ice Cream with Hot Maple Syrup
Coffee   Tea   Milk

Golden Potato Squares

5 lb. potatoes
1½ c. chopped onion
⅔ c. melted butter or regular
  margarine
1 (13-oz.) can evaporated milk
4 eggs, beaten
2½ tsp. salt
¼ tsp. pepper
¼ c. minced fresh parsley
1 c. shredded Cheddar cheese
½ c. shredded Cheddar cheese

Pare potatoes and place immediately in cold water to cover.

Sauté onion in butter in skillet until tender. Add evaporated milk; bring to a boil. Remove from heat.

Combine eggs, salt and pepper in large glass bowl; beat until frothy. Shred potatoes using medium blade of shredder. Place immediately into egg mixture, turning to coat well. (Helps prevent discoloration of potatoes.) Add parsley, 1 c. cheese and milk mixture; mix well. Turn into greased 13x9x2″ (3-qt.) glass baking dish.

Bake in 350° oven 1 hour. Top with ½ c. cheese. Bake 30 minutes more, or until done. Cut in squares. Makes 12 servings.

*See Index for recipe

Lunch

Cheese and Mushroom Omelets

Tossed Salad

Caramel Bread Pudding*

Tea   Milk

Dinner

Hearty Supper Soup

Red and Green Cabbage Salad

Bread Sticks

Fresh Pineapple Spears

Coffee   Tea   Milk

Hearty Supper Soup

1 lb. ground beef
½ c. chopped onion
1 clove garlic, minced
2 (10¾-oz.) cans condensed
   minestrone
1 (1-lb.) can pork and beans in
   tomato sauce
3 c. water
1 c. chopped celery
½ tsp. salt
¼ tsp. dried oregano leaves
1 tsp. Worcestershire sauce

Cook beef, onion and garlic in large saucepan until beef is browned and onion is soft. Drain off excess fat. Add remaining ingredients. Bring to a boil; reduce heat, cover and simmer 15 to 20 minutes. Makes about 2 quarts.

*See Index for recipe

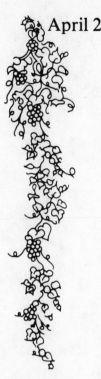

April 2

Lunch

Ham Sandwiches

Shredded Carrot and Apple Salad

Black Olives

Spicy Raisin Cupcakes*

Coffee   Tea   Milk

Dinner

Roast Turkey Thighs

Spring Vegetables à la King

Escarole and Onion Salad

Whole Strawberries with Whipped Cream

Coffee   Tea   Milk

Spring Vegetables à la King

⅓ c. butter or regular margarine
⅓ c. flour
2 c. light cream
1 c. chicken stock or broth
2 tsp. salt
⅛ tsp. pepper
1 (6-oz.) can broiled mushrooms,
  drained and sliced
2 c. cooked asparagus tips
2 c. cooked peas
1 c. cooked sliced carrots
2 to 3 tblsp. chopped green onions
1 egg yolk, slightly beaten

Melt butter in 3-qt. saucepan; add flour and blend. Stir in cream and chicken stock; cook over low heat until thick, stirring constantly. Add salt and pepper.

Add remaining ingredients and heat thoroughly. Serve on toast, fluffy rice or Chinese noodles. Makes 6 servings.

*See Index for recipe

Lunch

Cold Turkey Sandwiches on Brown Bread
<u>*Double Dairy Salad*</u>
Oatmeal Cookies
Coffee   Tea   Milk

Dinner

Oven-Fried Fish*
Creamed Potatoes   Buttered Lima Beans
Canned Plums Topped with Grated Lemon Rind
Coffee   Milk

Double Dairy Salad

2 c. large curd cottage cheese
2 c. dairy sour cream
1 c. diced, pared cucumber
½ c. sliced radishes
¼ c. sliced green onions
¾ tsp. salt
¼ tsp. pepper
Lettuce wedges or tomato slices

Mix together cottage cheese, sour cream, cucumber, radishes, onions, salt and pepper in bowl. Cover and chill well.

Serve over wedges of lettuce or tomato slices. Makes 6 to 8 servings.

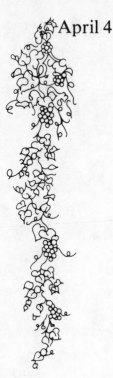

Lunch

Beef Noodle Soup

Prune-Bran Bread

Wedges of Assorted Cheeses

Fruit Cocktail

Coffee   Tea   Milk

Dinner

Golden Broiled Chicken*

Asparagus with Hollandaise Sauce

Parslied Potatoes

Watercress and Endive Salad

Chocolate Mousse

Coffee   Milk

Prune-Bran Bread

1½ c. milk
⅓ c. shortening
1½ c. whole bran cereal
1 c. cut-up cooked prunes
½ c. dark corn syrup
5 to 5½ c. all-purpose flour
2 pkg. active dry yeast
1 tblsp. salt
2 eggs

Scald milk. Remove from heat and add shortening, stirring until it is dissolved. Stir in bran, prunes and corn syrup. Cool to warm.

In large mixer bowl, combine 3 c. flour, yeast and salt. Add bran mixture and eggs. Beat at low speed ½ minute, scraping sides and bottom of bowl constantly. Beat at high speed 3 minutes, scraping bowl occasionally.

By hand stir in enough of remaining flour to make a stiff dough. Turn out on lightly floured surface. Knead dough until smooth and elastic, about 5 minutes.

Place in greased bowl, turning to grease all sides. Cover and let rise in a warm place until doubled, about 2 hours.

Punch down. Divide dough in half, cover and let rest 10 minutes. Shape each half into a loaf and place in 2 greased 9x5x3″ loaf pans. Cover and let rise in warm place until doubled, 1 to 1½ hours.

Bake in 350° oven 40 to 45 minutes, or until loaves sound hollow when tapped. Remove from pans; cool on racks. Makes 2 loaves.

*See Index for recipe

Lunch

Chicken Bouillon

Orange Date Muffins* with Cream Cheese

Marinated Raw Vegetables

Peaches and Grapes in Lime Gelatin

Coffee   Tea   Milk

Dinner

Broiled Lamb Chops with Mushroom Caps

Puffy Carrot Soufflé

Buttered Peas

Romaine Salad

Cherry Tarts

Coffee   Milk

Puffy Carrot Soufflé

2 tblsp. minced onion
¼ c. butter or regular margarine
¼ c. flour
¼ tsp. salt
⅛ tsp. ground nutmeg
1 c. milk
3 eggs, separated
¼ tsp. cream of tartar
1 c. sieved, cooked carrots

Sauté onion in melted butter in 1-qt. saucepan until tender (do not brown). Stir in flour, salt and nutmeg. Gradually stir in milk. Cook, stirring constantly, until mixture thickens. Add some of the hot mixture to the egg yolks. Mix well. Pour all of egg mixture back into hot mixture. Cook for 2 minutes, stirring constantly.

Beat egg whites with cream of tartar until stiff peaks form. Fold in carrots and cooked mixture. Pour into well-buttered 1½-qt. casserole. Place casserole in pan of hot water.

Bake in 350° oven 50 minutes, or until puffed and golden. Makes 4 to 6 servings.

April 6

Lunch

Shrimp Salad in Lettuce Cups

Corn Sticks

<u>*Banana-Strawberry Pudding*</u>

Coffee   Milk

Dinner

Grated Vegetable Meat Loaf*

Crumb-Topped Broiled Tomato Halves

Buttered Cauliflower with Toasted Almonds

Tossed Salad

Pecan Pie

Coffee   Milk

Banana-Strawberry Pudding

1 c. sugar
¼ c. flour
2½ c. milk
3 eggs, beaten
2 tblsp. butter or regular margarine
1 tsp. vanilla
1 (3-oz.) pkg. ladyfingers, cut in thirds (12)
1 pt. fresh strawberries, sliced
3 bananas, sliced
1 env. whipped topping mix
⅓ c. toasted flaked coconut

Combine sugar and flour in 2-qt. saucepan. Slowly stir in milk. Add eggs slowly to mixture. Cook over medium heat, stirring, until thick. (Do not boil.) Remove from heat; add butter and vanilla. Cool.

Layer cooled custard, ladyfingers, strawberries and bananas in 2-qt. glass bowl. Cover and chill well. Prepare whipped topping mix according to package directions. Spread topping on pudding; sprinkle with coconut. Makes 8 servings.

* See Index for recipe

Lunch

Meatball and Lentil Soup*

Toasted French Bread

Apple Yogurt Dusted with Cinnamon

Tea   Milk

Dinner

Broiled Knockwurst Wrapped in Bacon Strips

Corn 'n' Celery Sauté   Whipped Potatoes

Escarole and Bean Sprout Salad

Angel Food Cake

Coffee   Tea   Milk

Corn 'n' Celery Sauté

¼ c. butter or regular margarine
2 c. diagonally sliced celery
   (very thin)
1 (10-oz.) pkg. frozen whole kernel
   corn
2 tblsp. sliced pimiento
½ tsp. salt

Melt butter in saucepan. Add celery; cover and cook 5 minutes. Add remaining ingredients and cook until corn is tender, about 10 minutes. Stir to combine. Makes 6 servings.

*See Index for recipe

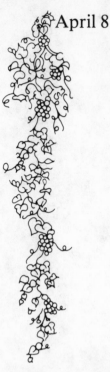

Lunch

*Timballo with Cheese Sauce**

Lettuce Salad with Green Pepper Rings

Baked Custard with Honey

Coffee   Tea   Milk

Dinner

Turkey Hash

Steamed Cabbage Wedges   Diced Beets

Chicory and Sliced Radish Salad

Rhubarb Surprise Pie

Coffee   Tea   Milk

Rhubarb Surprise Pie

1 c. sifted flour
1 tsp. baking powder
½ tsp. salt
2 tblsp. butter or regular margarine
1 egg, beaten
2 tblsp. milk
3 c. diced fresh rhubarb
1 (3-oz.) pkg. strawberry flavor
  gelatin
½ c. unsifted flour
1 c. sugar
½ tsp. ground cinnamon
¼ c. melted butter or regular
  margarine

Sift together 1 c. flour, baking powder and salt in bowl. Cut in 2 tblsp. butter until mixture is crumbly. Add egg and milk; mix well. Press into greased 9″ pie plate.

Arrange rhubarb in pie shell. Sprinkle with gelatin. Combine ½ c. flour, sugar, cinnamon and ¼ c. butter; mix until crumbly. Sprinkle mixture on top of pie.

Bake in 350° oven 50 minutes, or until rhubarb is tender and top is golden. Cool on rack. Makes 6 to 8 servings.

* See Index for recipe

Lunch

Scotch Chicken Soup
Sliced Tomatoes and Shredded Lettuce in Pita Bread
Fig Bars
Tea   Milk

Dinner

Broiled Halibut Steaks with Lemon Butter
Corn Custard Pudding*
Buttered Green Beans
Avocado Salad
Sliced Strawberries with Sour Cream
Coffee   Milk

Scotch Chicken Soup

Wings, backs and giblets from
  3 broiler-fryers
2 qt. water
1 tblsp. salt
1 tsp. garlic salt
¼ tsp. pepper
2 c. chopped onion
1 c. sliced, pared carrots
1 c. sliced celery
¼ c. chopped parsley
⅓ c. barley

Combine chicken, water and seasonings in Dutch oven or kettle. Bring to a boil. Reduce heat; cover and simmer, about 50 minutes, until chicken is tender. Lift chicken from broth, cool slightly, then remove meat from bones. Remove skin and return meat to broth. Add remaining ingredients; cover and simmer 30 minutes. Makes about 3 quarts.

*See Index for recipe

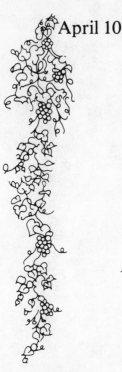

Lunch

*Smothered Burgers**

Potato Sticks   Celery Curls

Stewed Rhubarb

Coffee   Milk

Dinner

Herb-Stuffed Pork Chops

Baked Potatoes   Sautéed Mushrooms

Overnight Tossed Salad

Lemon Soufflé

Coffee   Tea   Milk

Overnight Tossed Salad

6 c. chopped lettuce
½ tsp. salt
½ tsp. sugar
⅛ tsp. pepper
6 hard-cooked eggs, sliced
1 (10-oz.) pkg. frozen peas, thawed
½ lb. bacon, crisp-cooked and
    crumbled
½ c. sliced green onions and tops
½ c. sliced celery
2 c. shredded process Swiss cheese
    (8 oz.)
1¼ c. mayonnaise or salad dressing

Place half the lettuce in a large bowl. Sprinkle with salt, sugar and pepper. Top with layer of eggs, then peas, bacon, remaining lettuce, green onions, celery and cheese.

Spread mayonnaise evenly over the top to cover. Place tight cover on bowl and chill 24 hours. Toss just before serving. Makes 12 servings.

Lunch

Cauliflower-Cheese Soup
Deviled Ham and Chopped Pickle Sandwiches
Green Grapes   Sugar Cookies
Tea   Milk

Dinner

Sausages and Potatoes*
Steamed Spinach
Romaine with Blue Cheese Dressing
Orange Layer Cake
Coffee   Tea   Milk

Cauliflower-Cheese Soup

1 small head cauliflower, broken into flowerets (about 1 lb.)
1 carrot, grated
¼ c. chopped celery
2 chicken bouillon cubes
3 c. water
3 tblsp. butter or regular margarine
3 tblsp. flour
¾ tsp. salt
⅛ tsp. pepper
2 c. milk
1 c. grated Cheddar cheese (4 oz.)

Combine cauliflower, carrot, celery, bouillon cubes and water in large saucepan. Bring to a boil. Reduce heat; cover and simmer 20 minutes, or until vegetables are tender.

Meanwhile, in small saucepan, melt butter. Blend in flour, salt and pepper. Add milk and cook, stirring, until mixture comes to a boil. Add cheese; cook and stir just until it melts. Stir cheese sauce into cauliflower mixture. Makes about 1½ quarts.

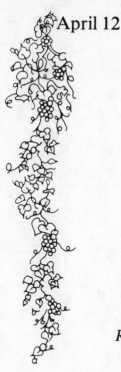

Lunch

Jambalaya*
Watercress and Endive Salad
Crusty French Bread
Blueberry Turnovers
Coffee   Milk

Dinner

Lamb Patties
Brussels Sprouts   Broiled Eggplant
Pineapple Muffins
Raspberry and Vanilla Ice Cream Parfaits
Coffee   Tea   Milk

Pineapple Muffins

2 c. sifted flour
3 tsp. baking powder
½ tsp. salt
½ c. sugar
¼ c. shortening
1 egg, beaten
1 c. crushed pineapple, undrained

Sift together flour, baking powder and salt in small bowl; set aside.

Cream sugar and shortening in bowl until light and fluffy. Add egg and beat well. Stir in undrained pineapple. Add dry ingredients and stir just enough to moisten flour. Do not beat.

Fill greased muffin-pan cups two-thirds full. Bake in 400° oven 20 to 25 minutes, or until golden. Remove from pans at once. Makes 12 to 15 medium muffins.

*See Index for recipe

Lunch

Molded Corned Beef Ring

Cucumber Sandwiches on Toasted Pumpernickel Bread

Green Olives

Coffee Ice Cream with Chocolate Sauce

Coffee   Tea   Milk

Dinner

Honey-Glazed Baked Canadian Bacon

Buttered Broccoli Spears   Carrot Patties*

Lettuce Wedges with Herbed Dressing

Apple Crisp

Coffee   Tea   Milk

Molded Corned Beef Ring

2 env. unflavored gelatin
1 c. cold water
1 (10½-oz.) can condensed beef broth
1 c. mayonnaise
1½ tblsp. lemon juice
1½ tblsp. horseradish
1 tsp. salt
2 c. diced cooked corned beef
1 c. finely chopped cabbage
½ c. diced gherkin pickles
¼ c. diced green pepper

Soften gelatin in cold water in small saucepan 5 minutes. Stir in beef broth. Cook over low heat, stirring constantly, until gelatin is dissolved.

Combine mayonnaise, lemon juice, horseradish and salt. Gradually stir in hot gelatin mixture, blending well. Cover; chill until thick and syrupy.

Fold in corned beef, cabbage, gherkin pickles and green pepper. Pour into lightly oiled 5-c. ring mold. Cover and chill until set. Makes 6 to 8 servings.

*See Index for recipe

Lunch

Chili Beef Soup
Cheddar Cheese Snack Bread*
Carrot and Celery Sticks
Pineapple Chunks Rolled in Coconut
Coffee   Milk

Dinner

Crispy Baked Chicken
Parslied Potatoes   Buttered Lima Beans
Escarole, Sliced Radishes and Onion Salad
Vanilla Pudding with Chocolate Curls
Macaroons
Coffee   Tea   Milk

Crispy Baked Chicken

2 c. dry bread crumbs
2 tsp. onion salt
1¼ tsp. garlic salt
1 tsp. pepper
1 tsp. dried savory leaves
1 tsp. curry powder
2 (2½-lb.) broiler-fryers, cut in
   serving pieces
¾ c. mayonnaise

Combine bread crumbs, onion salt, garlic salt, pepper, savory and curry powder in bowl. Coat chicken pieces with crumb mixture. Place skin side up in 15½ x 10½ x 1″ jelly roll pan.

Bake in 400° oven 15 minutes. Remove from oven. Brush chicken pieces with mayonnaise. Reduce oven temperature to 300° and bake 1 hour, or until chicken is tender and golden. Makes 8 servings.

Lunch

Cold Roast Beef

Sunflower Wheat Muffins

Cottage Cheese

Rhubarb Cobbler

Coffee   Milk

Dinner

Roast Veal

Hot Fluffy Rice   Spinach with Sliced Mushrooms

Cucumber-Cabbage Mold*

Butterscotch Sundaes with Toasted Pecans

Tea   Milk

Sunflower Wheat Muffins

¾ c. sifted all-purpose flour
2½ tsp. baking powder
½ tsp. salt
1¼ c. stirred whole-wheat flour
½ c. coarsely chopped, roasted
  sunflower seeds
1 egg, beaten
¾ c. milk
⅓ c. vegetable oil
⅓ c. honey

Sift together all-purpose flour, baking powder and salt in bowl. Stir in whole-wheat flour and sunflower seeds; set aside.

Blend together egg, milk, oil and honey in small bowl.

Make a well in dry ingredients. Add egg mixture, stirring just enough to moisten (batter will be lumpy). Spoon batter into 12 greased 2½" muffin cups.

Bake in 400° oven 20 to 25 minutes, or until golden brown. Makes 12 muffins.

*See Index for recipe

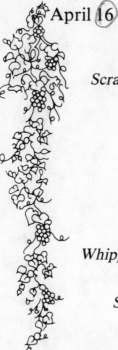

Lunch

Scrambled Eggs and Chives on English Muffins
Sautéed Cherry Tomatoes
*Molasses-Ginger Cookies**
Tea   Milk

Dinner

Succulent Sirloin Steak

Whipped Potatoes   Buttered Asparagus Spears

Endive and Onion Salad

Sliced Strawberries on Angel Food Cake

Coffee   Tea   Milk

Succulent Sirloin Steak

3 lb. sirloin steak, 2" thick
Meat tenderizer
3 tblsp. melted butter or regular
  margarine
2 tblsp. cooking oil
¼ c. soy sauce
2 tblsp. butter or regular margarine
1½ tblsp. lemon juice
1 tsp. sugar
½ tsp. ground ginger
1 clove garlic, minced

Sprinkle meat with meat tenderizer following package directions. Slice in ¼" slices. Sauté meat in 3 tblsp. melted butter and oil in skillet, for about 30 seconds on each side. Place browned meat in 12x8x2" (2-qt.) glass baking dish.

Combine soy sauce, 2 tblsp. butter, lemon juice, sugar, ginger and garlic in small saucepan. Simmer, uncovered, for 5 minutes. Pour over meat slices.

Bake in 350° oven 7 minutes. Makes 6 servings.

See Index for recipe

Lunch

Welsh Rarebit*
Broiled Tomato Slices
Sliced Bananas in Black Raspberry Gelatin
Chocolate Chip Cookies
Tea   Milk

Dinner

Broiled Cod
Buttered Noodles   Mixed Vegetables
Hot Cross Buns
Lime Sherbet
Coffee   Milk

Hot Cross Buns

½ c. sugar
1 pkg. active dry yeast
½ tsp. ground cinnamon
¼ tsp. salt
4½ c. sifted flour
1 c. milk
½ c. butter or regular margarine
¼ c. water
1 egg
1 c. raisins
¼ c. candied orange peel
1 egg yolk, beaten
2 tsp. water

Combine sugar, yeast, cinnamon, salt and 1 c. flour in bowl.

Heat milk, butter and ¼ c. water until lukewarm. Gradually pour liquid into dry ingredients, beating with electric mixer at low speed about 2 minutes, scraping bowl occasionally. Add egg and 1 c. flour; beat for 2 minutes, scraping bowl occasionally.

Gradually add enough remaining flour to make a soft dough. Turn out on floured surface and knead 5 minutes. Add raisins and orange peel and continue kneading until smooth and satiny, about 5 minutes.

Place dough in lightly greased bowl. Cover; let rise in warm place until doubled, about 2 hours.

Punch down. Shape into a ball; let rest 15 minutes.

Shape dough into 12 balls. Place balls in greased 13x9x2″ baking pan. Brush with combined egg yolk and 2 tsp. water. Snip a cross on top of each bun with scissors. Let rise until doubled, about 30 minutes.

Bake in 350° oven 30 minutes, or until golden brown. Remove from pan; cool on rack. Prepare a confectioners' sugar icing and spread on crosses. Makes 12 rolls.

April 18

Lunch

Peanut Butter, Bacon and Lettuce Sandwiches
Radishes   Green Pepper Strips
Oatmeal Refrigerator Cookies*
Coffee   Milk

Dinner

Turkey and Mushroom à la King on Toast Points
Peas and Small White Onions
Rosy Spring Salad
Chocolate Cake
Coffee   Milk

Rosy Spring Salad

4 c. diced rhubarb
1½ c. water
½ c. sugar
2 (3-oz.) pkg. strawberry flavor
  gelatin
1 c. orange juice
1 tsp. grated orange rind
1 c. sliced fresh strawberries

Combine rhubarb, water and sugar in saucepan. Cook until tender, for about 4 to 5 minutes. Pour over gelatin, stirring until dissolved. Add orange juice and rind. Cover and chill until thick and syrupy.

Fold in strawberries. Pour into lightly oiled 6-c. mold; chill until set. Makes 6 to 8 servings.

Lunch

Tomato Bouillon*

Assorted Crackers   Sliced Salami

Raisin Cookies

Tea   Milk

Dinner

Stuffed Easter Ham

Golden Potato Squares*   *Buttered Green Beans*

Tangy Slaw*

Poppy Seed Torte*

Coffee   Tea   Milk

Stuffed Easter Ham

1 (5-lb.) canned ham
¾ c. chopped onion
¾ c. chopped celery
6 tblsp. butter or regular margarine
4½ c. soft bread cubes (¼")
1½ c. chopped, pared apples
⅓ c. raisins
1 c. chicken broth
2 tblsp. minced fresh parsley
½ tsp. ground cinnamon
1 (10-oz.) jar pineapple preserves

Cut ham into 20 (⅜") slices using electric or sharp kitchen knife. Place ham, keeping slices upright in original shape, on aluminum foil-lined jelly roll pan or shallow roasting pan.

Sauté onion and celery in melted butter in skillet until tender (do not brown). Combine sautéed vegetables, bread cubes, apples, raisins, chicken broth, parsley and cinnamon in bowl. Mix lightly, but well.

Place stuffing between ham slices, leaving 2 slices between stuffing layers. Tie stuffed ham securely with string. Cover ham loosely with aluminum foil.

Bake in 350° oven 1 hour.

Meanwhile, melt pineapple preserves in small saucepan over low heat. Remove aluminum foil. Continue baking 1 more hour. Baste with melted pineapple preserves several times during last 30 minutes. Bake until stuffing registers 165° on meat thermometer. Remove from oven. Let stand 10 minutes before serving. Makes 12 servings.

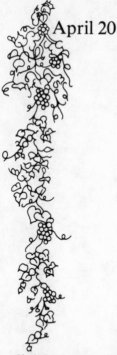

April 20

Lunch

Grilled Tortilla Sandwiches
Refried Beans
Lemon Ice
Coffee   Tea   Milk

Dinner

Knockwurst   Hot Applesauce
Sauerkraut Salad*
Minted Grapefruit
Coffee   Tea   Milk

Grilled Tortilla Sandwiches

1 (9-oz.) pkg. frozen tortillas, thawed (12)

6 tblsp. butter or regular margarine, softened

6 oz. Monterey Jack cheese, sliced ⅛" thick

2 tblsp. chopped canned green chilies

For each sandwich, spread one side of tortilla with butter. Place butter side down in skillet. Cook until lightly browned. Cover with cheese slices; sprinkle with 1 tsp. chopped chilies. Butter second tortilla and place over cheese, butter side up. Turn immediately. Cook until second side is lightly browned and cheese is melted. Makes 6 sandwiches.

*See Index for recipe

Lunch

*Tuna Bisque**

Cream Cheese and Olive Sandwiches

Frozen Peaches   Pound Cake

Coffee   Tea   Milk

Dinner

Teriyaki Steak

Fluffy Buttered Rice   Sautéed Mushrooms

Escarole Salad

Cherry Tarts

Coffee   Tea   Milk

Teriyaki Steak

½ c. soy sauce
⅓ c. water
1 tblsp. brown sugar
½ tsp. ground ginger
1 clove garlic, minced
1 (3- to 4-lb.) boneless bottom round,
    chuck or rump pot roast, cut
    2 to 2½ " thick

Combine soy sauce, water, brown sugar, ginger and garlic. Pour over pot roast in glass or ceramic dish; cover and refrigerate 12 to 24 hours, turning roast occasionally.

Remove meat from marinade, place on broiler rack and broil 5 to 6" from source of heat about 15 minutes, or until very crusty. Turn and broil on other side until inside is desired doneness (usually rather rare). To serve, cut meat across grain at slanted angle into thin slices. Serve with drippings and, if desired, additional teriyaki sauce, made as for marinade. Makes 8 servings.

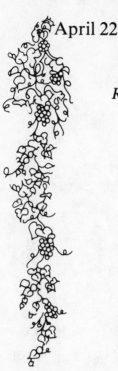

Lunch

Raisin-Carrot Salad in Green Pepper Cups

Crusty Hard Rolls   Potato Chips

Coconut Custard Pie*

Tea   Milk

Dinner

Ham and Broccoli Soufflé

Broiled Tomato Halves

Cheese Muffins

Lettuce Wedges with Russian Dressing

Baked Apples

Coffee   Tea   Milk

Cheese Muffins

2 c. sifted flour
3 tsp. baking powder
½ tsp. salt
¼ c. sugar
1 egg, beaten
1 c. milk
¼ c. salad oil
¼ c. grated sharp Cheddar cheese

Sift flour, baking powder, salt and sugar into a big bowl. Make a well in the center.

Combine egg, milk and salad oil; stir to mix. Pour all at once into the well in flour mixture. Mix quickly with fork or spoon until flour is moistened, but do not beat. The batter will contain some lumps. Fold in cheese with a few strokes.

Pour into greased muffin-pan cups, filling them two-thirds full. Bake in 400° oven 20 to 25 minutes, until muffins are golden. Serve at once. Makes 12 medium muffins.

*See Index for recipe

Lunch

Chicken Bouillon

Scandinavian Egg Salad*

Canned Pears with Raspberry Sauce

Coffee   Tea   Milk

Dinner

Corned Beef Hash

Corn Niblets   Minted Carrots and Peas

Tossed Salad

Banana Cream Pie

Coffee   Tea   Milk

Minted Carrots and Peas

8 small carrots
3 c. fresh or frozen peas
¼ c. butter or regular margarine
½ tsp. salt
3 tblsp. chopped fresh mint leaves

Cook whole carrots in small amount of boiling salted water, covered, 15 minutes, or until tender. Cook peas in boiling salted water until tender. Drain vegetables; reserve liquids for soup or sauce.

Brown butter slightly; add vegetables, salt and mint. Toss lightly. Makes 6 to 8 servings.

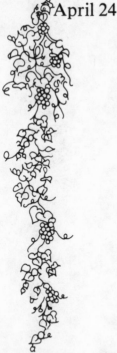

April 24

Lunch

Turkey Vegetable Soup

Buttered Sesame Rolls

Coffee-Iced Brownies*

Coffee   Milk

Dinner

Fish Sticks   French Fried Potatoes

Vegetable Trio Loaf

Pineapple Upside-down Cake

Coffee   Tea   Milk

Vegetable Trio Loaf

2 (3-oz.) pkg. lemon flavor gelatin
1½ tsp. salt
2 c. boiling water
1 c. cold water
2 tblsp. vinegar
1⅓ c. shredded carrots
1½ c. shredded cabbage
1⅓ c. finely chopped fresh spinach
1 tsp. minced green onions

Dissolve gelatin and salt in boiling water in saucepan. Stir in cold water and vinegar. Divide gelatin into 3 portions. Fold carrots into 1 portion. Pour into lightly oiled 9x5x3″ loaf pan. Cover and chill until just set, but not firm. (Let remaining gelatin stand at room temperature.)

Fold cabbage into 1 portion of gelatin. Pour over first layer. Cover and chill until just set, but not firm. Fold spinach and onions into 1 portion. Pour over second layer. Cover and chill until set. Makes 6 to 8 servings.

*See Index for recipe

Lunch

Cottage Cheese Sandwiches*
Assorted Raw Vegetables
Gingerbread with Whipped Cream and Nutmeg
Coffee   Tea   Milk

Dinner

Roast Veal with Sweet Onions
Pasta Shells with Garlic and Oil
Tomato and Lettuce Salad
Layered Lemon and Lime Gelatin
Coffee   Tea   Milk

Roast Veal with Sweet Onions

1 (4-lb.) boneless veal roast
  (rolled shoulder or leg)
⅔ c. salad oil
6 tblsp. wine vinegar
1½ tsp. salt
½ tsp. pepper
1 sweet onion, very thinly sliced

Place meat on rack in roasting pan; insert meat thermometer. Roast in 300° to 325° oven until meat thermometer registers 170°, or about 40 to 45 minutes per pound. Remove from oven and allow to stand about 20 minutes, then slice, saving juices.

Shake or beat together oil, vinegar, salt and pepper. Remove any excess fat and burned drippings from roasting pan; loosen drippings. Add meat juices and the oil-vinegar mixture; stir to blend.

Arrange meat slices, slightly overlapping, in roasting pan; spoon on juices to moisten well. Cover with foil. Before serving, place in 350° oven 10 minutes, or until heated through. Arrange meat slices on a warm serving platter; top with onion slices separated into rings.

Quickly heat remaining roasting pan juice mixture; pass as a sauce. Makes about 8 servings.

Lunch

Cold Sliced Veal

Pickled Cucumbers with Dill*

Apricot and Prune Compote with Slivered Almonds

Coffee   Tea   Milk

Dinner

Baked Ham Slice

Cabbage au Gratin   Buttered Peas

Orange-Watercress Salad

Peppermint Ice Cream   Coconut Cookies

Coffee   Tea   Milk

Baked Ham Slice

1 (3-lb.) ham steak, cut 2″ thick
¼ tsp. ground nutmeg
¼ tsp. dry mustard
Dash of ground cloves
½ c. apple cider or juice
¼ c. maple-flavored syrup

Place ham in 12x8x2″ (2-qt.) glass baking dish. Sprinkle nutmeg, mustard and cloves over top. Pour cider and syrup over ham.

Bake in 325° oven 1 hour, basting 2 or 3 times. Makes 8 to 10 servings.

     *See Index for recipe

Lunch

Tomato Juice

Chicken Tostadas*

Escarole Salad

Orange Sherbet

Coffee   Tea   Milk

Dinner

Miniature Cheese Loaves

Braised Leeks   Buttered Brussels Sprouts

Lettuce and Sliced Red Onion

Chocolate Eclairs

Coffee   Tea   Milk

Miniature Cheese Loaves

2 lb. ground beef
2¾ c. soft bread crumbs
¾ c. chopped onion
½ c. chopped green pepper
2 tblsp. chopped fresh parsley
1 tsp. salt
¼ tsp. dried basil leaves
¼ tsp. pepper
1 (10½-oz.) can condensed vegetable
   or vegetarian vegetable soup
¼ c. milk
½ c. cubed Swiss cheese
1 (1-lb.) jar meatless spaghetti sauce

Combine ground beef, soft bread crumbs, onion, green pepper, parsley, salt, basil, pepper, soup and milk in bowl. Mix lightly, but well. Shape in 8 small meat loaves. Place in 15½x10½x1″ jelly roll pan. Press cheese cubes into each loaf, covering with meat mixture. Bake in 400° oven 35 minutes, or until brown.

Cool, cover and refrigerate. To serve, heat in spaghetti sauce. Makes 8 servings.

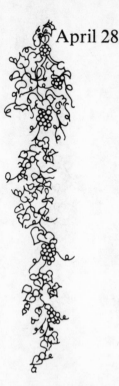

April 28

Lunch

Chilled Beef Consommé
Liverwurst on Brown Bread
<u>*Sugar-Crusted Rhubarb Squares*</u>
Tea   Milk

Dinner

Broiled Sausages
Buttered Noodles   Asparagus Spears
Romaine and Sliced Radish Salad
French Chocolate Pie*
Coffee   Tea   Milk

Sugar-Crusted Rhubarb Squares

2½ c. sifted flour
1 tsp. baking soda
1 tsp. salt
1½ c. brown sugar, firmly packed
1 egg, beaten
⅔ c. cooking oil
1 c. sour milk
1 tsp. vanilla
1½ c. finely diced fresh rhubarb
½ c. chopped walnuts
½ c. sugar
1 tblsp. melted butter or
    regular margarine
½ tsp. ground cinnamon

Sift together flour, baking soda and salt into large bowl. Gradually mix in brown sugar.

Combine egg, oil, sour milk and vanilla. Add to dry ingredients, blending well. Stir in rhubarb and walnuts. Spread batter in greased 9″ square baking pan.

Combine sugar, butter and cinnamon; mix well. Sprinkle over batter.

Bake in 325° oven 55 minutes, or until done. Cut in squares and serve warm or cold. Makes 9 servings.

See Index for recipe

Lunch

Sliced Chicken and Water Chestnuts
on Toasted Frankfurter Buns
Dilly Cheese-Stuffed Celery
Candied Apricots with Toasted Coconut
Tea   Milk

Dinner

Pot Roast with Vegetable Gravy*
Whipped Potatoes   Buttered Carrot Strips
Endive Salad
Strawberry Shortcake
Coffee   Milk

Dilly Cheese-Stuffed Celery

1 c. creamed cottage cheese
1 tblsp. finely chopped green onion
1/8 tsp. dried dill weed
Celery branches, cut in 3″ lengths
Seasoned salt

Place cheese in blender container. Whirl until smooth. Stir in onion and dill weed. Cover and chill at least ½ hour. Spread in celery branches. Sprinkle with seasoned salt. Makes 1 cup spread.

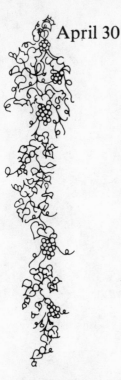

April 30

Lunch

Sloppy Joes on Toasted Buns
Green Pepper Strips
Company Dessert Bowl*
Tea   Milk

Dinner

Broiled Shad
Butter-Crumb Potatoes   Sliced Beets
Spinach Salad
Rhubarb Cobbler
Tea   Milk

Butter-Crumb Potatoes

6 medium potatoes, pared
3 tblsp. melted butter or
   regular margarine
½ c. bread crumbs
1 tsp. salt
¼ tsp. pepper

Roll potatoes in melted butter, then in mixture of remaining ingredients.

Place in greased 2½-qt. casserole. Pour any remaining butter over top.

Cover and bake in 400° oven 45 minutes. Uncover; bake until tender, 15 to 20 minutes. Makes 6 servings.

*See Index for recipe

Lunch

Mexican Salad Bowl*
Tortilla Chips
Strawberry Ice Cream with Strawberries
Lemonade

Dinner

Broiled Lamb Chops with Mint Jelly

Hot Fluffy Rice   Lima Beans with Pimientos

Herbed Batter Bread

Raspberry Jelly Roll

Coffee   Milk

Herbed Batter Bread

1½ c. milk, scalded
3 tblsp. sugar
2 tblsp. butter or
    regular margarine
1 tblsp. salt
¼ c. minced onion
2 pkg. active dry yeast
½ c. lukewarm water
4½ c. sifted flour
1½ tsp. caraway seeds
½ tsp. ground nutmeg
½ tsp. ground sage

Combine milk, sugar, butter, salt and onion in bowl. Let cool.

Sprinkle yeast on lukewarm water; stir to dissolve. Add yeast mixture, 2 c. flour, caraway seeds, nutmeg and sage to milk mixture. Beat with electric mixer at medium speed until smooth, about 2 minutes, scraping bowl occasionally. Or beat with a spoon until batter is smooth.

Gradually stir in remaining flour. (Dough will be sticky.) Cover and let rise in warm place until dough is doubled, about 1 hour.

Stir batter down by beating with spoon about 25 strokes. Spread in greased 9x5x3" loaf pan. Let rise until doubled, about 45 minutes.

Bake in 375° oven 1 hour, or until loaf sounds hollow when tapped. Remove from pan; cool on rack. Makes 1 loaf.

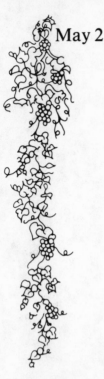

May 2

Lunch

Frankfurters and Coleslaw on Toasted Buns
Tomato Wedges with Garlic Salt
Easy Rice Pudding
Tea   Milk

Dinner

English Fish and Chips*
Broiled Zucchini Strips
Shredded Carrot and Apple Salad
Gingerbread with Whipped Cream
Coffee   Milk

Easy Rice Pudding

2 eggs, slightly beaten
2¼ c. milk, scalded
⅓ c. sugar
¾ c. cooked regular rice
¼ c. raisins
1 tsp. vanilla
½ tsp. grated lemon rind
¼ tsp. salt
½ tsp. ground cinnamon

Beat together eggs and milk in large bowl. Stir in sugar, rice, raisins, vanilla, lemon rind and salt. Pour into greased 1½-qt. casserole. Sprinkle with cinnamon. Set casserole in pan of hot water (½" deep).

Bake in 350° oven 45 minutes, or until set around the edges. Makes 6 servings.

*See Index for recipe

Lunch

Chili with Cheese Soufflé*
Taco Chips
Apple Spice Sherbet
Tea   Milk

Dinner

Glazed Beef Balls
Buttered Noodles   Peas and Water Chestnuts
Tossed Salad
Brownies à la Mode
Coffee   Milk

Glazed Beef Balls

½ c. fine bread crumbs
1 tsp. salt
¼ tsp. pepper
1 tblsp. grated onion
½ tsp. prepared horseradish
1 tblsp. Worcestershire sauce
1 egg, beaten
½ c. tomato juice
2 tblsp. salad oil
1 lb. lean ground beef
Glaze (recipe follows)

Combine all ingredients, except glaze, in large bowl; mix well. Cover and chill at least 1 hour.

Shape meat mixture in balls about the size of walnuts. Place in shallow baking pan; bake in 500° oven 10 to 12 minutes, or until browned. Add to Glaze and heat. Makes 6 servings.

Glaze: Combine in saucepan, ¼ c. brown sugar (firmly packed), 2 tblsp. flour, 1 tsp. dry mustard, ¼ c. chili sauce, ¼ c. dark corn syrup, ½ tsp. salt, dash of Tabasco sauce and ¼ c. orange juice. Cook and stir until slightly thickened.

Lunch

Green Soup

Hot Biscuits with Honey

Ambrosia   Pound Cake

Tea   Milk

Dinner

Fried Chicken

Potato Cakes   Golden Carrots Supreme*

Watercress and Radish Salad

Blueberry Turnovers

Iced Coffee

Green Soup

2 c. frozen peas, thawed
2 (14-oz.) cans chicken broth
2 tsp. onion juice
Dash of curry powder (optional)

Put peas through a sieve or food mill, or whirl in blender. Pour into saucepan. Add broth and heat to simmering point. Add onion juice and curry powder. Season to taste. Makes 8 servings.

*See Index for recipe

Lunch

Guacamole Burgers*
Lettuce Wedges with Oil and Vinegar
Sliced Oranges with Shredded Coconut
Tea   Milk

Dinner

Pork Steaks
Small Glazed Whole Onions
Broccoli with Cheese Sauce
Endive Salad
Rhubarb Cherry Pie
Coffee   Tea

Rhubarb Cherry Pie

3 c. diced rhubarb
2 (1-lb.) cans pitted tart cherries, drained
1¼ c. sugar
¼ c. quick-cooking tapioca
¼ tsp. almond flavoring
10 drops red food coloring
Pastry for 2-crust 9″ pie

Combine rhubarb, cherries, sugar, tapioca, almond flavoring and red food coloring in bowl. Let stand for 15 minutes.

Pour into pastry-lined pie plate. Adjust top crust, flute edges and cut steam vents.

Bake in 400° oven 45 minutes, or until rhubarb is tender and pie is golden brown. Cool on rack. Makes 6 to 8 servings.

*See Index for recipe

May 6

Lunch

Tuna-Cheese Buns
Carrot Curls   Radishes
Chocolate Cookies
Mocha Milkshakes

Dinner

Toad-in-the-Hole*
Sliced Tomatoes   Green Beans with Mushrooms
Avocado Salad
Riced Cherry Gelatin with Banana Chunks
Tea   Milk

Tuna-Cheese Buns

1 (9¼-oz.) can tuna, drained
 and flaked
5 hard-cooked eggs, chopped
3 tblsp. sweet pickle relish
2 tblsp. chopped onion
1 tsp. seasoned salt
½ c. mayonnaise
8 long buns, split and buttered
1 (8-oz.) pkg. sliced process
 American cheese

Combine tuna, eggs, pickle relish, onion, salt and mayonnaise in bowl. Spread between split buns. Cut each cheese slice in half. Put 2 halves, end to end, in bun on top of tuna filling.

Place buns on large sheet of foil and wrap. Arrange on baking sheet. Bake in 350° oven 20 minutes. Makes 8 servings.

*See Index for recipe

Lunch

Chicken Noodle Soup

Egg and Tomato Salad on Toasted Frankfurter Buns

Pineapple Sherbet*

Tea   Milk

Dinner

Roast Duckling

Rice with Almonds   Asparagus with Lemon Butter

Chicory and Cauliflower Salad

Elegant Strawberry Torte

Coffee   Milk

Elegant Strawberry Torte

3 c. sifted cake flour
2 c. brown sugar, firmly packed
½ tsp. salt
1 c. butter or regular margarine
1 egg, slightly beaten
1 c. sour milk
1 tsp. baking soda
½ c. chopped nuts
1 pt. heavy cream, whipped
   and sweetened
1 pt. fresh strawberries, sliced

Mix together flour, brown sugar, salt and butter in bowl until crumbly. Reserve 1 c. crumb mixture; set aside.

Combine egg, milk and baking soda. Add to remaining crumb mixture; stir well. Pour into 2 greased, paper-lined 9″ layer pans. Sprinkle with reserved crumb mixture, then with nuts.

Bake in 375° oven 25 to 30 minutes, or until cake tests done. Cool.

Place one layer, nut side up, on serving plate. Spread with half of the whipped cream. Top with sliced strawberries. Place other layer on top. Spoon remaining whipped cream into puffs around cake. Garnish with sliced strawberries. Serve immediately. Makes 12 servings.

Lunch

Marinated Artichoke Hearts on Lettuce

Sesame Bread Sticks

<u>Orange Cupcakes</u>

Iced Tea

Dinner

Chinese Pepper Steak*

Broiled Eggplant   Braised Celery

Sliced Tomato and Escarole Salad

Butterscotch Pudding with Whipped Cream and Walnuts

Coffee   Milk

Orange Cupcakes

2 c. sifted cake flour
1 tsp. baking soda
½ tsp. baking powder
¼ tsp. salt
1 c. sugar
½ c. shortening
1 egg
1 tsp. grated orange rind
⅔ c. buttermilk
1 c. sugar
½ c. orange juice

Sift together cake flour, baking soda, baking powder and salt.

Cream together 1 c. sugar and shortening in large bowl until light and fluffy. Add egg and orange rind; blend well.

Add dry ingredients alternately with buttermilk, beating well after each addition. Pour batter into paper-lined 2½ " muffin-pan cups, filling two-thirds full.

Bake in 350° oven 20 to 25 minutes, or until done.

Meanwhile, combine 1 c. sugar and orange juice. Stir over medium heat until sugar dissolves. Remove cupcakes from pans. Spoon hot syrup over each. Cool on racks. Makes 18 cupcakes.

Spring

Enjoy Spicy Sugar Loaf (p. 70) with a
cup of hot cocoa on a cool spring
morning. Or, serve piping hot as a
light luncheon or dinner dessert.

This handsome Molded Chicken Salad (p. 66), wreathed with bright carrot curls, radish roses and parsley, is the perfect centerpiece for a special lunch.

Here's a favorite holiday dinner:
Stuffed Easter Ham (p. 37), with a
savory apple dressing; Tangy Slaw
(p. 9); and Poppy Seed Torte (p. 58).

Strawberries and rhubarb offer a taste of spring. From top: Elegant Strawberry Torte (p. 55); Rosy Spring Salad (p. 36); Rhubarb Surprise Pie (p. 26).

Lunch

Open-Faced Cream Cheese and Sliced Radishes
on Pumpernickel Bread
Black Raspberry Gelatin with Grapes
<u>*Coconut Squares*</u>
Tea   Milk

Dinner

Red Flannel Hash*
Sautéed Green Pepper Strips   Tomato Wedges
Coleslaw
Sponge Cake
Coffee   Milk

Coconut Squares

1¼ c. sifted flour
½ tsp. baking powder
¼ tsp. salt
1 c. brown sugar, firmly packed
¼ c. butter or
   regular margarine
2 eggs
1 tsp. vanilla
½ tsp. almond extract
1 c. flaked coconut
½ c. chopped walnuts
Lemon Glaze (recipe follows)

Sift together flour, baking powder and salt in small bowl; set aside.

Cream together brown sugar and butter in large bowl until light and fluffy. Add eggs, one at a time, beating well after each addition. Beat in vanilla and almond extract.

Gradually add flour mixture, beating well after each addition. Stir in coconut and walnuts. Spread mixture in greased 9″ square pan.

Bake in 325° oven 30 minutes, or until golden brown. Spread with Lemon Glaze while warm. Cool in pan on rack. Cut in 1½″ squares. Makes 1½ dozen.

Lemon Glaze: Combine 1 c. sifted confectioners' sugar, ½ tsp. grated lemon rind and 1 tblsp. hot milk. Blend until smooth.

Lunch

*Chicken Corn Soup**

Buttered Toasted Crackers

Celery Sticks

Lemon-Frosted Cupcakes

Tea   Milk

Dinner

Prime Ribs of Beef

Stuffed Baked Potatoes   Broccoli with Cheese Sauce

Watercress Salad with Herbed Dressing

Poppy Seed Torte

Coffee   Milk

Poppy Seed Torte

½ c. graham cracker crumbs
½ c. unsifted flour
¼ c. finely chopped walnuts
¼ c. melted butter or
  regular margarine
2 tblsp. cornstarch
2 tblsp. poppy seeds
1 c. sugar
¼ tsp. salt
5 eggs, separated
1½ c. milk
1 env. unflavored gelatin
¼ c. cold water
1 tsp. vanilla
½ tsp. cream of tartar
½ c. sugar

Combine graham cracker crumbs, flour, walnuts and butter in bowl; mix well. Pat crumb mixture into bottom and up sides, about 1", in 8" springform pan.

Bake in 325° oven 12 minutes, or until golden brown. Cool on rack.

Combine cornstarch, poppy seeds, 1 c. sugar and salt in double boiler top. Beat egg yolks in bowl. Stir in milk. Slowly stir milk mixture into dry ingredients. Cook over simmering water until thickened, stirring constantly, about 10 minutes. Meanwhile, soften gelatin in cold water 5 minutes. Add to hot custard; remove from heat. Let cool to room temperature. Add vanilla.

Beat egg whites and cream of tartar in bowl until frothy. Gradually add ½ c. sugar, beating until soft peaks form. Fold custard into egg whites. Pour into cooled crust. Refrigerate until set, about 6 hours or overnight.

Can be decorated with puffs of whipped cream and jelly beans, if you wish. Makes 12 servings.

Lunch

Vegetable-Egg Combo
Asparagus with French Dressing
Brown Sugar Cookies
Coffee   Tea   Milk

Dinner

Veal Loaf*
Buttered Corn Niblets
Cauliflower with White Sauce
Romaine Salad
Baked Individual Custards
Coffee   Tea   Milk

Vegetable-Egg Combo

½ c. chopped onion
¼ c. butter or regular margarine
3 c. diced fresh tomatoes
⅓ c. chopped green pepper
1 tblsp. sugar
2 tsp. salt
¼ tsp. pepper
¼ tsp. ground nutmeg
2 tblsp. vinegar
½ c. grated Parmesan cheese
2 tsp. chopped chives
2 tsp. chopped fresh parsley
6 eggs, slightly beaten
6 slices buttered toast
Chopped fresh parsley

Sauté onion in melted butter in large skillet until tender (do not brown). Add tomatoes, green pepper, sugar, salt, pepper, nutmeg and vinegar. Cook until tender, for about 8 minutes, stirring occasionally. Blend in cheese, chives and parsley; cook for 2 minutes. Stir in eggs. Cook slowly, for about 2 to 3 minutes, stirring occasionally. Do not overcook. Serve on buttered toast. Garnish with parsley. Makes 6 servings.

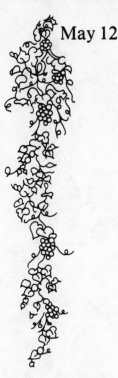

May 12

Lunch

Tuna Salad Sandwiches

Pickles Potato Sticks

Lemon Slices*

Iced Tea

Dinner

Broiled Chicken Breasts

Basque Potatoes Diced Carrots

Lettuce Wedges with French Dressing

Strawberry Tarts

Coffee Tea Milk

Basque Potatoes

½ c. finely chopped onion
½ c. chopped celery
½ c. shredded carrot
1 clove garlic, minced
2 tblsp. butter or
 regular margarine
1 (10½-oz.) can condensed
 chicken broth
2 lb. potatoes, pared and cut in
 1″ cubes (about 4 c.)
½ tsp. salt
⅛ tsp. pepper
Chopped fresh parsley

Sauté onion, celery, carrot and garlic in melted butter in 10″ skillet until tender (do not brown). Combine chicken broth with enough water to make 2 c. Add chicken broth, potatoes, salt and pepper to sautéed vegetables. Cover; simmer for 10 minutes. Remove cover. Simmer, stirring occasionally, for 20 minutes or until broth is thickened. Sprinkle with parsley. Makes 4 to 6 servings.

  *See Index for recipe

Lunch

Sliced Corned Beef Sandwiches with Russian Dressing

Cucumber Strips   Olives

Chunky Cider Applesauce*

Vanilla Milkshakes

Dinner

Sweet Italian Sausage with Green Peppers

Buttered Spaghetti

Cottage Cheese Rolls

Tossed Salad

Orange Sherbet with Mandarin Oranges

Coffee   Milk

Cottage Cheese Rolls

2 pkg. active dry yeast
½ c. lukewarm water
2 c. cottage cheese
¼ c. sugar
2 tsp. salt
½ tsp. baking soda
2 eggs
4½ c. sifted flour

Sprinkle yeast on lukewarm water; stir to dissolve.

Heat cottage cheese until lukewarm. Combine cottage cheese, sugar, salt, baking soda, eggs, yeast and 1 c. flour in bowl. Beat with electric mixer at medium speed until smooth, about 2 minutes, scraping bowl occasionally. Or beat with spoon until batter is smooth.

Gradually add enough flour to make a soft dough that leaves the sides of the bowl.

Place dough in greased bowl; turn over to grease top. Cover and let rise in warm place until doubled, about 1½ hours.

Turn dough onto lightly floured surface. Divide dough into 24 equal pieces. Shape each piece into a ball. Place 24 balls in 2 greased 9″ round baking pans. Let rise until doubled, about 45 minutes.

Bake in 350° oven 20 minutes, or until golden brown. Remove from pans; cool on racks. Makes 24 rolls.

Lunch

Roast Beef and Spinach Sandwiches
Potato Chips   Dill Pickles
Vanilla Ice Cream with Rhubarb-Pineapple Sauce
Tea   Milk

Dinner

Broiled Haddock
Creamed Potatoes   Peas and Small White Onions
Country-style Beet Salad*
Apple Pie with Sharp Cheddar Cheese
Coffee   Milk

Rhubarb-Pineapple Sauce

3 c. diced fresh rhubarb
1 (8½-oz.) can crushed pineapple
½ c. sugar
½ c. water
¼ c. red cinnamon candies
2 tblsp. cornstarch
2 tblsp. water
¼ tsp. salt
2 tblsp. lemon juice
2 tblsp. butter or regular margarine

Combine rhubarb, undrained pineapple, sugar, ½ c. water and cinnamon candies in 2-qt. saucepan; mix well. Cook over medium heat until mixture comes to a boil, stirring occasionally.

Combine cornstarch and 2 tblsp. water; mix to blend. Gradually stir into hot mixture. Reduce heat to low; simmer 5 minutes. Remove from heat. Stir in salt, lemon juice and butter. Cool slightly before serving. Delicious served over ice cream or squares of cake. Or pour slightly cooked sauce into jars or bottles; cover with lids. Store in refrigerator. Makes 4 cups.

*See Index for recipe

Lunch

May 15

Sloppy Joes on Toasted Buns

Potato Salad

Fruit Preserves Cake*

Tea   Milk

Dinner

Broiled Ham Slice with Hot Mustard

American-Chinese Asparagus   Noodles with Parmesan

Cucumber and Scallion Salad

Butterscotch Meringue Pie

Coffee   Milk

American-Chinese Asparagus

2 lb. asparagus
⅓ c. butter or
 regular margarine
⅓ c. water
½ tsp. salt
⅛ tsp. pepper

Break off each asparagus stalk as far down as it snaps easily. Cut off scales with a knife. Scrub with soft brush to remove all sand. Lay 1 or 2 stalks together on a cutting board; cut diagonally, making bias slices about 1″ long and ¼″ thick. You will have about 4 c. asparagus.

Heat butter and water to boiling in heavy skillet with tight-fitting lid. Add asparagus and seasonings. Cover and cook over high heat 5 minutes, shaking skillet occasionally. Check with fork to see if asparagus is tender-crisp. If not, cook 1 or 2 minutes longer, adding 1 tblsp. water, if necessary. Water should be evaporated at end of cooking. Makes 6 servings.

*See Index for recipe

May 16

Lunch

Sliced Smoked Sausage
Whole-Wheat Protein Bread*
Coconut Cream Pudding
Tea   Milk

Dinner

Party Crab Bake

Julienne Green Beans   Sautéed Cherry Tomatoes
Endive and Sliced Mushroom Salad
Peach Halves Filled with Vanilla Ice Cream
Coffee   Milk

Party Crab Bake

6 oz. shell macaroni
1 (8-oz.) pkg. cream cheese
½ c. dairy sour cream
½ c. cottage cheese
¼ c. sliced green onions and tops
1 (7½-oz.) can crab meat, flaked
2 medium tomatoes, peeled and sliced
¼ tsp. salt
1½ c. shredded sharp Cheddar cheese

Cook macaroni as directed on package.

Combine cream cheese, sour cream, cottage cheese and onions.

Arrange half of macaroni in bottom of greased 2-qt. casserole. Dip half of cream-cheese mixture by spoonfuls over macaroni. Spread to cover. Top with half of crab meat. Repeat these layers. Top crab meat with sliced tomatoes. Sprinkle with salt and with shredded cheese.

Bake in 350° oven 30 minutes. Makes 4 to 6 servings.

*See Index for recipe

Lunch

Slimmers' Deviled Eggs
Sliced Ham
Sweet Pickles   *Tomato Wedges*
Grapefruit Sections and Fresh Mint in Orange Cups
Tea   *Milk*

Dinner

Frankfurters Stuffed with Cheese
Baked Kidney Beans*   *Coleslaw*
Toasted Corn Muffins
Applesauce and Whipped Cream Parfaits
Coffee   *Milk*

Slimmers' Deviled Eggs

6 hard-cooked eggs
¼ c. creamed cottage cheese
2 tblsp. skim milk
1 tblsp. finely chopped green onion
   and tops
1 tsp. prepared mustard
2 tsp. vinegar
¼ tsp. salt
Dash of pepper
Sprinkling of paprika

Cut eggs in half lengthwise; remove yolks. With fork mash yolks and cottage cheese together until blended; beat in milk. Stir in onion, mustard, vinegar, salt and pepper. Spoon yolk mixture into egg whites. Sprinkle with paprika. Cover and chill. Makes 12.

*See Index for recipe

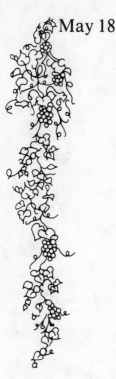

May 18

Lunch

Molded Chicken Salad

Marinated Raw Vegetables

Hot Rolls

Raspberry Sherbet

Iced Tea

Dinner

Lamb Curry with Chutney

Hot Fluffy Rice with Almonds

Spinach and Tomato Salad

Pecan Meringue Pie*

Coffee   Milk

Molded Chicken Salad

1 (3-oz.) pkg. lemon flavor gelatin
1 c. boiling water
½ c. cold water
2 tblsp. vinegar
½ tsp. salt
⅛ tsp. pepper
½ c. salad dressing
2 c. diced cooked chicken
½ c. chopped celery
2 tblsp. minced onion
1 tblsp. minced fresh parsley

Dissolve gelatin in boiling water in bowl. Stir in cold water, vinegar, salt and pepper.

Gradually add some of hot gelatin to salad dressing, stirring until smooth. Stir salad dressing mixture into gelatin, mixing well. Cover and chill until thick and syrupy.

Fold in chicken, celery, onion and parsley. Pour into lightly oiled 4-c. mold or individual molds. Cover and chill until set. Makes 6 servings.

*See Index for recipe

Lunch

Barbecued Beef Buns*
Raw Vegetable Strips   Crackers
Riced Peach Gelatin with Sliced Bananas
Iced Coffee

Dinner

Fried Chicken with Cream Gravy
Sautéed Mushrooms   Peas and Small White Onions
Mile-High Biscuits
Tossed Salad
Whole Strawberries with Powdered Sugar
Tea   Milk

Mile-High Biscuits

3 c. sifted flour
2 tblsp. sugar
4½ tsp. baking powder
¾ tsp. cream of tartar
¾ tsp. salt
¾ c. shortening
1 egg, beaten
1 c. milk

Sift together flour, sugar, baking powder, cream of tartar and salt into mixing bowl.

Cut in shortening with pastry blender or two knives until mixture resembles coarse meal.

Combine egg and milk. Add to flour mixture all at once, stirring just enough with fork to make a soft dough that sticks together.

Turn onto lightly floured surface and knead lightly 15 times. Roll to 1″ thickness. Cut with floured 2″ cutter and place about 1″ apart on ungreased baking sheet.

Bake in 450° oven 12 to 15 minutes, or until golden brown. Serve immediately. Makes 16.

May 20

Lunch

*Skillet Salmon Chowder**

Toasted Corn Muffins

Watermelon

Tea   Milk

Dinner

Broiled Sirloin Tips

Golden Parmesan Potatoes

Diced Asparagus in Tomato Cups

Carrot and Cabbage Salad

Green Grapes with Sour Cream and Cinnamon

Coffee   Milk

Golden Parmesan Potatoes

6 large potatoes (about 3 lb.)
¼ c. sifted flour
¼ c. grated Parmesan cheese
¾ tsp. salt
⅛ tsp. pepper
⅓ c. butter or regular margarine
Chopped fresh parsley

Pare potatoes; cut into quarters. Combine flour, cheese, salt and pepper in a bag. Moisten potatoes with water and shake a few at a time in bag, coating potatoes well with cheese mixture.

Melt butter in 13x9x2″ baking pan. Place potatoes in a layer in pan.

Bake in 375° oven about 1 hour, turning once during baking. When golden brown, sprinkle with parsley. Makes 6 to 8 servings.

*See Index for recipe

Lunch

Thinly Sliced Roast Beef with Horseradish

Delicious Health Bread*

Fresh Fruit Cup

Limeade

Dinner

Stuffed Meat Loaf

Steamed Spinach   *Buttered Onions*

Lettuce Wedges with Roquefort Dressing

Ice Cream-Filled Cream Puffs with Hot Fudge Sauce

Coffee   *Tea*

Stuffed Meat Loaf

1 lb. lean ground beef
1 lb. ground pork
1 c. dry bread crumbs
½ c. grated carrots
¼ c. finely chopped onion
2 eggs, beaten
½ c. milk
2 tsp. salt
1 tsp. Worcestershire sauce
⅛ tsp. pepper
1 (4-oz.) can mushrooms, drained
   and chopped
1 tblsp. finely chopped onion
2 tblsp. butter or regular
   margarine
2 c. soft bread crumbs
1 tblsp. chopped fresh parsley
½ tsp. poultry seasoning
¼ tsp. salt

Mix together ground beef, ground pork, dry bread crumbs, carrots, ¼ c. onion and eggs in bowl. Add milk, 2 tsp. salt, Worcestershire sauce and pepper. Mix lightly, but well.

Place on a double-thick square of greased aluminum foil. Shape into a 14x8″ rectangle.

Sauté mushrooms and 1 tblsp. onion in melted butter in small skillet over medium heat. Combine with soft bread crumbs, chopped parsley, poultry seasoning and ¼ tsp. salt.

Spread stuffing over meat mixture; roll up, starting with long side. Press overlapping edge into roll to seal. Bring foil edges together in a tight double fold on top. Fold ends up, using tight double folds. Place wrapped meat loaf on rack in shallow pan.

Bake in 375° oven 1 hour. Open foil; continue baking for 15 minutes, or until loaf browns. Makes 4 to 6 servings.

*See Index for recipe

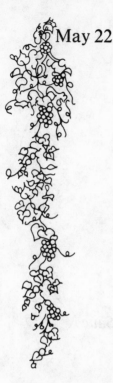

Lunch

Mushroom Omelets
Sautéed Green Pepper Strips
Spicy Sugar Loaf
Tea   Milk

Dinner

Chicken-Fried Rice*
Sautéed Cherry Tomatoes and Zucchini
Shredded Lettuce Salad
Fortune Cookies   Lemon Sherbet
Iced Coffee

Spicy Sugar Loaf

1 (1-lb.) loaf white bread
¼ c. butter, softened
⅔ c. sugar
1 tsp. cinnamon
½ c. sifted confectioners' sugar
1½ to 2 tblsp. light cream
2 tblsp. finely chopped nuts

Spread bread slices on one side with softened butter; sprinkle with combined sugar and cinnamon. Put back in shape of loaf. If desired, cut in lengthwise halves and tie with string. Wrap loaf securely in foil and heat in 375° oven 20 to 25 minutes, or until golden. Unwrap, cut and remove string.

Make glaze with confectioners' sugar and cream; pour glaze over top and sprinkle with nuts. Serve piping hot. Makes 10 to 12 servings.

*See Index for recipe

Lunch

Country Asparagus Pie

Sliced Tomatoes   *Potato Sticks*

Cherry Gelatin   *Oatmeal Cookies*

Tea   *Milk*

Dinner

Fish Piquant*

Peas and Mushrooms   *Parslied Potatoes*

Sliced Beets

Yellow Cake with Fudge Frosting

Coffee   *Milk*

Country Asparagus Pie

Baked 9″ pie shell
4 c. asparagus, cut in 1″ pieces
    (about 2 lb.)
3 tblsp. butter or regular margarine
3 tblsp. flour
1 c. milk
1 chicken bouillon cube
1 tsp. instant minced onion
¾ tsp. salt
⅛ tsp. pepper
4 hard-cooked eggs
½ c. grated Cheddar cheese

Cook asparagus in boiling salted water until tender. Drain thoroughly (in sieve).

Melt butter in 2-qt. saucepan; blend in flour. Add milk and cook, stirring constantly, until mixture bubbles and is thickened. Add bouillon cube, onion, salt and pepper. Stir until bouillon cube is dissolved.

Remove from heat and add asparagus. Chop 3 eggs and add to creamed mixture.

Turn into baked pie shell. Sprinkle with grated cheese. Bake in 350° oven until cheese melts, about 7 minutes. Remove from oven. Cut remaining egg in 6 wedges; arrange on center of pie with points of one end together, petal-fashion. Serve at once. Makes 6 servings.

Lunch

Hot Dog Curls*
Coleslaw   Black Olives
Vanilla Pudding with Sliced Raspberries
Tea   Milk

Dinner

Beef Chuck Roast Supreme
Braised Leeks   Buttered Whole Carrots
Tossed Salad
Chocolate Cake à la Mode
Tea   Milk

Beef Chuck Roast Supreme

2- to 3-lb. beef chuck roast
1 tblsp. dry mustard
1 tsp. salt
¼ tsp. pepper
⅛ tsp. garlic powder
⅔ c. cooking oil
½ c. sherry wine or wine vinegar
1 tblsp. Worcestershire sauce
¼ tsp. soy sauce

Place beef in 13x9x2″ (3-qt.) glass baking dish. Combine remaining ingredients; pour over meat. Cover; chill 8 hours, turning occasionally.

Remove meat from marinade. Place in roasting pan. Cover and cook in 350° oven 1 to 1½ hours, or until tender. Makes 4 to 6 servings.

*See Index for recipe

Lunch

Assorted Luncheon Meats

Crusty Rolls

Green Beans with Garlic Dressing*

Chocolate Chip Ice Cream

Tea   Milk

Dinner

Meat Balls in Brown Gravy

Buttered Noodles   Corn with Pimientos

Escarole and Bean Sprout Salad

3-Layer Lemon Meringue Pie

Coffee   Milk

3-Layer Lemon Meringue Pie

1⅓ c. sugar
½ c. flour
⅛ tsp. salt
2 c. water
⅓ c. lemon juice
3 eggs, separated
3 drops yellow food coloring
1 tsp. grated lemon rind
1 tblsp. butter or regular margarine
¼ tsp. cream of tartar
6 tblsp. sugar
Baked 9″ pie shell

Combine 1⅓ c. sugar, flour and salt in a medium saucepan. Gradually stir in water and lemon juice. Cook over medium heat, stirring constantly, until thickened. Stir a small amount of hot mixture into beaten egg yolks. Stir back into remaining hot mixture. Cook, stirring, for 2 minutes. Remove from heat. Stir in yellow food coloring, lemon rind and butter.

Beat egg whites and cream of tartar in small bowl until frothy. Gradually add 6 tblsp. sugar, beating until stiff glossy peaks form.

Reserve 1 c. of filling. Pour remaining filling into pie shell. Fold ¾ c. meringue into reserved filling. Spread evenly over filling in pie shell. Top with remaining meringue, sealing edges.

Bake in 400° oven 8 to 10 minutes, or until top is golden brown. Cool on rack. Makes 6 to 8 servings.

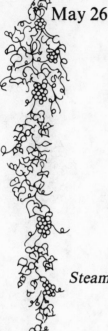

May 26

Lunch

Jellied Consommé
Cucumber and Cream Cheese Sandwiches
Carrot Curls
*Coconut Crown Coffee Cake**
Iced Tea

Dinner

Chicken Breasts Cordon Bleu
Steamed New Potatoes   *Sautéed Cherry Tomatoes*
Watercress and Sliced Mushroom Salad
Sliced Peaches with Whipped Cream
Coffee   Milk

Chicken Breasts Cordon Bleu

3 whole chicken breasts, skinned,
  boned and halved
6 slices boiled ham
6 slices mozzarella cheese (3x1½x½″)
1 medium tomato, seeded and
  chopped
½ tsp. dried sage leaves
⅓ c. fine dry bread crumbs
2 tblsp. grated Parmesan cheese
2 tblsp. minced fresh parsley
¼ c. melted butter or regular
  margarine

Pound each chicken breast half between two pieces of waxed paper with meat mallet to 8x5″ oval. Place 1 ham slice and 1 cheese slice on each flattened chicken breast. Place ⅙ of tomato and sage in center of each. Fold ends over filling and roll up like a jelly roll from 8″ side. Secure with toothpicks.

Combine bread crumbs, Parmesan cheese and parsley. Dip rolls in melted butter; then coat with crumb mixture. Place in 9″ square baking pan. Drizzle with remaining butter.

Bake in 350° oven 40 to 45 minutes, or until chicken is tender. Remove toothpicks. Makes 6 servings.

*See Index for recipe

Lunch

Welsh Rarebit*

Romaine, Black Olive and Radish Salad

Applesauce à la Mode

Tea   Milk

Dinner

Baked Veal Chops with Lemon Slices

<u>*Baked Almond Rice*</u>   *Buttered Brussels Sprouts*

Spinach Salad

Rhubarb Cobbler

Coffee   Milk

Baked Almond Rice

3 c. boiling chicken broth or water
1½ c. regular rice, uncooked
1¼ tsp. salt
¾ c. slivered almonds
3 tblsp. butter or regular margarine

Mix broth, rice and salt in un-greased 3-qt. casserole (or a 13x9x2″ baking pan). Cover tightly—use aluminum foil. Bake in 350° oven 25 to 30 minutes, until liquid is absorbed and rice is tender.

Meanwhile, lightly brown almonds in butter. Add to hot, cooked rice and toss to mix. Makes 6 to 8 servings.

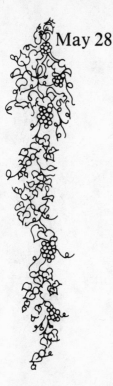

May 28

Lunch

Vichyssoise
Light Puffy Rolls*
Blueberry Turnovers
Coffee   Tea   Milk

Dinner

Roast Lamb
Whipped Potatoes   Minted Carrots
Avocado and Tomato Salad
Raspberry-Vanilla Cloud
Coffee   Milk

Raspberry-Vanilla Cloud

1⅔ c. graham cracker crumbs
¼ c. sugar
1 tsp. ground cinnamon
⅓ c. melted butter or regular
  margarine
½ c. sugar
¼ c. flour
1 pkg. unflavored gelatin
½ tsp. salt
1¾ c. milk
3 egg whites
¼ tsp. cream of tartar
½ c. sugar
1 tsp. vanilla
½ c. heavy cream, whipped
Raspberry Sauce (recipe follows)

Mix together graham cracker crumbs, ¼ c. sugar, cinnamon and butter. Press in 9″ square pan. Bake in 375° oven 4 minutes. Cool.

Combine ½ c. sugar, flour, gelatin and salt in 2-qt. saucepan. Slowly stir in milk. Bring to a boil, stirring constantly. Boil for 1 minute. Cool.

Beat egg whites with cream of tartar until stiff peaks form. Gradually beat in ½ c. sugar. Add vanilla.

Fold egg whites and whipped cream into cooled mixture. Turn into crust. Cover and chill well. Cut in squares and serve topped with Raspberry Sauce. Makes 9 servings.

Raspberry Sauce: Drain 2 (10-oz.) pkg. frozen raspberries, thawed. Add water to juice to make 1½ c. Combine juice, ¼ c. sugar, 2 tblsp. cornstarch and 1 tblsp. lemon juice. Cook, stirring, until mixture boils for 1 minute. Add raspberries and cool thoroughly.

* See Index for recipe

Lunch

Sliced Turkey Sandwiches
Lettuce Wedges with Creamy Thousand Island Dressing*
Sugar Cookies
Coffee Ice Cream Floats

Dinner

Baked Ham
<u>Baked Orange Slices</u>
Scalloped Potatoes   Mixed Vegetables
Endive and Radish Salad
Angel Food Cake with Strawberries
Coffee   Milk

Baked Orange Slices

2 medium oranges
1 c. sugar
½ c. water
¹/₁₆ tsp. cream of tartar
1 stick cinnamon

Cut unpeeled oranges into ¼″ slices. Arrange orange slices in 12x8x2″ (2-qt.) glass baking dish. Combine sugar, water, cream of tartar and cinnamon stick in a saucepan. Simmer for 5 minutes. Remove cinnamon stick. Pour hot syrup over orange slices.

Bake in 300° oven 1 hour. Turn slices once during baking. Cool.

Store in covered jar. Refrigerate overnight or at least 8 hours. Serve as a garnish/relish with meats or poultry. Makes 8 servings.

Lunch

Chicken Broth

Sliced Egg and Watercress Sandwiches

Tomato Wedges　　Black Olives

Creamy Cheesecake*

Tea　　Milk

Dinner

Spaghetti with White Clam Sauce

Tossed Salad

Coolrise French Bread

Fresh Pineapple Spears

Coffee　　Milk

Coolrise French Bread

5½ to 6½ c. sifted flour
2 pkg. active dry yeast
1 tblsp. sugar
1 tblsp. salt
2 tblsp. softened butter or regular
　margarine
2¼ c. hot water (120 to 130°)
Cooking oil

Stir together 2 c. of the flour, un-dissolved yeast, sugar and salt in large bowl. Add butter and hot water all at once. Beat with electric mixer at medium speed 2 minutes, scraping bowl occasionally.

Add 1 c. flour. Beat at high speed 1 minute or until thick and elastic, scraping bowl occasionally.

Gradually stir in enough remaining flour to make a soft dough. Turn out on floured surface.

Knead dough until smooth and elastic, about 10 minutes. Cover with plastic wrap, then a towel. Let rest 20 minutes. Punch down.

Divide dough in half. Roll out each half to 15x8″ rectangle on lightly greased surface. Roll up like a jelly roll, starting with long side. Seal edges and tuck ends under. Taper ends by rolling gently with hand. Place, seam side down, on greased baking sheets. Cover loosely with plastic wrap.

Refrigerate 2 to 24 hours. Let stand 10 minutes at room temperature while preheating oven. Brush gently with cold water. Slash tops of loaves diagonally at 2″ intervals with sharp knife.

Bake in 400° oven 30 to 40 minutes, or until golden brown. Remove from baking sheets immediately. Cool on racks. Makes 2 long loaves.

　　　*See Index for recipe

Lunch

Sloppy Joes on Toasted Buns
Green Pepper Strips
Caramel Bread Pudding*
Tea   Milk

Dinner

Broiled Shad
Buttered Lima Beans   Honey-Glazed Onions
Spinach Salad
Minted Fruit Cup
Tea   Milk

Minted Fruit Cup

2 oranges
1 (20-oz.) can unsweetened pineapple
  chunks
1 banana, peeled and sliced
1 unpared apple, cored and chopped
1 tblsp. honey
1 tsp. dried mint

Peel and section oranges over a bowl, reserving juice. Combine with remaining ingredients. Cover and chill at least ½ hour. Will keep up to 8 hours. Makes 1 quart or 8 servings.

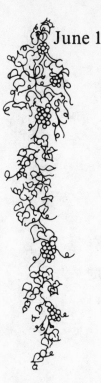

June 1

Lunch

Hot Corned Beef on Toasted Buns
Assorted Pickles
Diced Watermelon
<u>*Brown-Rim Butter Cookies*</u>
Tea   Milk

Dinner

Chicken Fricassee
Brown Rice   Fresh Peas with Mint
Romaine Salad with Blue Cheese Dressing
*Special Corn Meal Muffins**
Whole Strawberries in White Wine
Coffee   Milk

Brown-Rim Butter Cookies

2½ c. sifted flour
1 tsp. salt
½ c. butter or regular margarine
½ c. shortening
⅔ c. sugar
2 eggs
1 tsp. vanilla

Sift together flour and salt into small bowl; set aside.

Cream together butter, shortening and sugar in bowl until light and fluffy, using electric mixer at medium speed. Add eggs, one at a time, beating well after each addition. Blend in vanilla.

Gradually stir dry ingredients into creamed mixture, blending well. Drop mixture by teaspoonfuls, about 3″ apart, on greased baking sheets. Flatten each with bottom of drinking glass dipped in water to 2¾″ rounds.

Bake in 375° oven 8 minutes, or until lightly browned around the edges. Remove from baking sheets; cool on racks. Makes 4 dozen.

     *See Index for recipe

Lunch

Tuna-Macaroni Salad in Tomato Shells
Pumpernickel Bread
Green Grapes and Vanilla Yogurt
Tea   Milk

Dinner

Broiled Sirloin Patties
Patio-Baked Beans*   Coleslaw
Apple Pie with Cheddar Cheese
Coffee   Tea   Milk

Tuna-Macaroni Salad

8 oz. elbow macaroni
1 (7-oz.) can solid pack tuna, drained
½ c. chopped onion
½ c. chopped celery
4 hard-cooked eggs, chopped
½ c. sliced pimiento-stuffed olives
1 large tomato, cut up
¼ tsp. pepper
1½ c. salad dressing or mayonnaise
1 tblsp. sugar
3 tblsp. milk
3 tblsp. lemon juice
1 tsp. prepared mustard
1 tsp. salt

Cook macaroni in boiling salted water in Dutch oven until tender. Drain, then rinse with cold water. Drain well.

Combine macaroni, tuna, onion, celery, eggs, olives, tomato and pepper in large mixing bowl.

Combine salad dressing and sugar in bowl. Gradually stir in milk and lemon juice; blend well. Add mustard and salt; blend well. Pour over macaroni mixture; toss gently to mix. Cover with plastic wrap. Refrigerate until thoroughly chilled. Makes 8 servings.

Lunch

Sliced Chicken

Popovers*

Sliced Oranges Rolled in Fresh Chopped Mint

Tea   Milk

Dinner

Pan-Fried Calves' Liver

Buttered New Potatoes   Shredded Zucchini

Sliced Tomatoes and Escarole Salad

Miniature Cheesecake Jewels

Coffee   Milk

Miniature Cheesecake Jewels

3 (8-oz.) pkg. cream cheese, softened
1 c. sugar
¼ tsp. salt
1 tsp. vanilla
5 eggs
1 pt. dairy sour cream
Assorted canned fruits
Walnut halves or sliced almonds

Beat cream cheese in bowl with electric mixer at medium speed until smooth. Gradually beat in sugar. Blend in salt and vanilla. Add eggs, one at a time, beating well after each addition. Spoon mixture into paper-lined 1¼" muffin-pan cups, filling almost full.

Bake in 325° oven 30 minutes, or until set. Cool in pans 5 minutes. Remove. When cool, cover and refrigerate. Can be stored up to 5 days.

Spread each cheesecake with sour cream. Decorate with cut-up fruits and nuts. Refrigerate. Makes 60.

Lunch

Creamy Bologna and Potato Salad
Marinated Tomatoes and Green Peppers
Chocolate Layer Cake
Iced Coffee

Dinner

Grilled Veal Steak

Buttered Noodles   Tiny Glazed Carrots

Skillet Corn Bread*

Fresh Fruit Cup

Coffee   Milk

Creamy Bologna and Potato Salad

1 env. unflavored gelatin
½ c. cold water
1½ c. minced bologna
2 tblsp. minced onion
½ c. mayonnaise
½ c. chili sauce
2 tsp. prepared mustard
1 env. unflavored gelatin
½ c. cold water
2 c. diced cooked potatoes
½ c. chopped celery
⅓ c. minced onion
2 hard-cooked eggs, chopped
½ c. mayonnaise
½ c. dairy sour cream
1 tblsp. vinegar
2 tblsp. pickle relish
¼ c. chopped fresh parsley
1¼ tsp. salt
⅛ tsp. pepper

Soften 1 env. gelatin in ½ c. cold water in small saucepan 5 minutes. Heat over low heat, stirring constantly, until gelatin is dissolved. Remove from heat.

Combine bologna, 2 tblsp. onion, ½ c. mayonnaise, chili sauce, mustard and dissolved gelatin; mix lightly. Pour into lightly oiled 6½-c. ring mold. Cover and chill until set.

Soften 1 env. gelatin in ½ c. cold water in small saucepan 5 minutes. Heat over low heat, stirring constantly until gelatin is dissolved. Combine potatoes, celery, ⅓ c. onion, eggs, ½ c. mayonnaise, sour cream, vinegar, pickle relish, parsley, salt and pepper in bowl. Stir in dissolved gelatin; mix lightly. Pour over bologna layer. Cover and chill in refrigerator until set. Makes 8 servings.

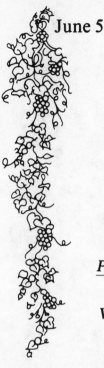

June 5

Lunch

Sliced Egg and Tomato Sandwiches

Radishes and Carrot Strips

Orange Frost*

Tea   Milk

Dinner

Broiled Canadian Bacon

Pie-Pan Asparagus   Broiled Eggplant Slices

Lettuce Wedges with Oil and Vinegar

Vanilla Cream Pie Topped with Sliced Peaches

Coffee   Milk

Pie-Pan Asparagus

¼ c. butter or regular margarine
¼ c. flour
¾ c. chicken broth
¾ c. milk
½ c. grated Cheddar cheese
¼ c. grated Parmesan cheese
½ tsp. salt
⅛ tsp. pepper
2 lb. hot, freshly cooked medium
  asparagus spears (about 32 to 36)
2 tblsp. grated Parmesan cheese

Melt butter in saucepan; blend in flour. Add chicken broth and milk and cook, stirring constantly, until mixture is thick and bubbly. Add Cheddar cheese, ¼ c. Parmesan cheese, salt and pepper; stir until cheeses melt.

Place asparagus in 10″ pie pan. Pour sauce over. Sprinkle with 2 tblsp. Parmesan cheese. Broil until bubbly. Makes 6 servings.

See Index for recipe

Lunch

Fish Chowder

Crackers

Tossed Salad

Apricot Pie à la Mode*

Coffee   Tea   Milk

Dinner

Assorted Cold Cuts with Mustard

Macaroni Salad   Coleslaw

<u>Refrigerator Bran Muffins</u>

Fresh Raspberries with Custard Sauce

Coffee   Milk

Refrigerator Bran Muffins

5 c. sifted flour
5 tsp. baking soda
2 tsp. salt
2 c. boiling water
2 c. whole bran cereal
2 c. sugar
1 c. shortening
4 eggs, well beaten
1 qt. buttermilk
4 c. whole bran cereal buds

Sift together flour, baking soda and salt.

Pour boiling water over whole bran cereal; set aside.

Cream together sugar and shortening in 6-qt. bowl until light and fluffy. Add eggs and beat well. Blend in buttermilk, bran buds and the soaked whole bran cereal. Add sifted dry ingredients; mix well. Store in tightly covered container in refrigerator. Batter will keep up to 6 weeks.

To make muffins, fill greased muffin-pan cups two-thirds full. Bake in 400° oven about 20 minutes. Makes 5 dozen muffins.

June 7

Lunch

Vegetable Soup

Graham Muffins*

Chocolate Ice Cream Sandwich Bars

Iced Tea

Dinner

Gingered Chicken with Grapes

Rice with Toasted Pecans   *Buttered Spinach*

Endive and Watercress Salad

Napoleons

Coffee   Milk

Gingered Chicken with Grapes

2 (3-lb.) broiler-fryers, quartered
1 tsp. salt
1/8 tsp. pepper
1/2 c. cooking oil
1/2 c. finely chopped onion
1/4 lb. fresh mushrooms, sliced
1 clove garlic, minced
1 (13 3/4-oz.) can chicken broth
1 tblsp. lemon juice
1 tsp. sugar
2 tblsp. chopped crystallized ginger
1 c. halved seedless green grapes
6 tblsp. water
1/4 c. flour
3/4 tsp. salt

Season chicken with 1 tsp. salt and pepper. Brown chicken on all sides in hot oil in 12″ skillet. Remove chicken as it browns. Arrange chicken in 15 1/2 x 10 1/2 x 2 1/2 ″ roasting pan.

Sauté onion, mushrooms and garlic in pan drippings until tender (do not brown). Stir in chicken broth, lemon juice, sugar and ginger. Bring to a boil. Pour over chicken. Cover with aluminum foil.

Bake in 350° oven 45 minutes, or until chicken is tender. Remove foil. Add grapes; bake 5 more minutes. Remove from oven. Arrange chicken on hot platter.

Combine water, flour and 1/4 tsp. salt; mix well. Gradually stir into pan juices. Bring to a boil; boil 1 minute. Serve sauce over chicken. Makes 8 servings.

See Index for recipe

Lunch

Cottage Cheese-Stuffed Tomatoes

Green Pepper Strips

*Four-Grain Bread**

Fruit Cocktail

Tea   Milk

Dinner

Salmon Mousse with Marinated Cucumbers

Corn Bread Sticks

Green Beans with Almonds

Fresh Cherries   Pound Cake Fingers

Iced Coffee

Salmon Mousse with Marinated Cucumbers

1 (1-lb.) can red salmon
¼ c. vinegar
¼ c. dairy sour cream
1 tblsp. horseradish
1 tsp. prepared mustard
½ tsp. salt
1 env. unflavored gelatin
¼ c. lemon juice
¼ c. cold water
1 c. heavy cream, whipped
Marinated Cucumbers (recipe
  follows)

Drain salmon. Discard skin and bones. Flake salmon with fork. Place salmon and vinegar in blender jar, ⅓ at a time, blending until smooth. Fold in sour cream, horseradish, mustard and salt.

Soften gelatin in combined lemon juice and cold water 5 minutes. Place in pan of boiling water, stirring until gelatin is completely dissolved.

Stir gelatin into salmon mixture. Fold in whipped cream. Pour into lightly oiled individual molds or 4-c. mold. Cover and chill until set.

Unmold and serve with Marinated Cucumbers. Makes 6 to 8 servings.

Marinated Cucumbers: Combine ¼ c. vinegar, ¼ c. lemon juice, ¼ c. salad oil, ½ tsp. salt, ¼ tsp. Worcestershire sauce and ⅛ tsp. pepper; blend well. Pour dressing over 2 c. thinly sliced, unpared cucumbers and 1 c. green pepper strips; toss lightly to mix. Chill, covered, at least 1 hour. Drain and serve with Salmon Mousse.

*See Index for recipe

Lunch

Salami and Lettuce Sandwiches

Potato Chips   Olives

Cherry-Topped Cheesecake

Coffee   Tea   Milk

Dinner

Mustard Ham Loaf*

Candied Sweet Potatoes

Broccoli with Toasted Almonds

Asparagus Salad

Vanilla-Fudge Ice Cream with Crushed Peanut Brittle

Coffee   Milk

Cherry-Topped Cheesecake

18 graham crackers, crushed
3 tblsp. sugar
½ c. melted butter or regular
 margarine
1 (8-oz.) pkg. cream cheese
½ c. sifted confectioners' sugar
1 tsp. vanilla
1 env. whipped topping mix
1 (1-lb. 8-oz.) jar prepared cherry pie
 filling

Combine graham cracker crumbs, sugar and butter in bowl; mix until crumbly. Press into 8″ springform pan.

Beat together cream cheese, confectioners' sugar and vanilla in another bowl. Prepare whipped topping mix according to package directions. Fold into cream-cheese mixture. Pour into crust. Spread pie filling on top. Cover and chill several hours. Makes 10 servings.

* See Index for recipe

Lunch

Tuna Aspic Mold
Buttered Rolls
Marinated Vegetables
Petits Fours
Iced Coffee

Dinner

Swiss Steak

Sautéed Onions   *Baked Potatoes with Sour Cream*

Romaine Salad with Russian Dressing

Luscious Lime Pie*

Tea   Milk

Tuna Aspic Mold

1 env. unflavored gelatin
½ c. cold water
¼ c. lemon juice
1 c. salad dressing
¹⁄₁₆ tsp. salt
¹⁄₁₆ tsp. pepper
1 (7-oz.) can solid-pack tuna, drained and flaked
¼ c. chopped celery
¼ c. chopped green pepper
3 tblsp. chopped pimiento
1 tblsp. minced green onions
2 env. unflavored gelatin
½ c. cold tomato juice
2½ c. tomato juice
1½ tblsp. grated onion

Soften 1 env. gelatin in ½ c. cold water in small saucepan 5 minutes. Heat over low heat, stirring constantly, until gelatin is dissolved.

Gradually add gelatin and lemon juice to salad dressing, blending well. Stir in salt, pepper, tuna, celery, green pepper, pimiento and green onions. Pour into lightly oiled 6-c. ring mold. Cover and chill until partially set.

Soften 2 env. gelatin in ½ c. cold tomato juice in small saucepan 5 minutes. Heat over low heat, stirring constantly, until gelatin is dissolved. Stir in 2½ c. tomato juice and onion. Pour over first layer in mold. Cover; chill until set. Makes 8 to 10 servings.

*See Index for recipe

June 11

Lunch

Chilled Tomato Juice

Bologna   Swiss Cheese

Onion Buttermilk Biscuits*

Spice Cupcakes

Tea   Milk

Dinner

Broiled Lamb Chops with Tarragon

Green Peas Lorraine   Whipped Potatoes

Coleslaw-Stuffed Tomatoes

Rhubarb Crisp

Iced Coffee

Green Peas Lorraine

3 tblsp. butter or regular margarine
⅓ c. water
2 c. shelled fresh peas (about 2 lb. in pods)
2 tblsp. finely chopped onion
1 tblsp. finely chopped fresh parsley
1 tsp. sugar
½ tsp. salt
⅛ tsp. pepper
¼ tsp. ground nutmeg (optional)
4 to 6 outside lettuce leaves, finely shredded
½ c. light cream

Heat butter, water and peas in saucepan. Add onion, parsley, sugar and seasonings. Cover and simmer until peas are almost tender.

Stir in lettuce. Continue cooking 5 minutes longer. Blend in cream. Heat and serve. Makes 6 servings.

*See Index for recipe

Lunch

Hot Scrambled Eggs and Bacon Strips on Toasted Buns
Celery Sticks
Peanut Butter Fingers*
Tea   Milk

Dinner

Polynesian-style Liver
Hot Fluffy Rice   Asparagus Spears
Escarole and Sliced Cucumber Salad
Chocolate Pudding with Chocolate Curls
Coffee   Milk

Polynesian-style Liver

1 (8-oz.) can pineapple chunks
2 c. tomato juice
2 tblsp. vinegar
1 tblsp. soy sauce
2 tblsp. brown sugar
1 tsp. instant beef bouillon, or 1 beef
  bouillon cube
1½ lb. beef or pork liver, cut in
  1″ strips
3 tblsp. cornstarch
¼ c. water
1 green pepper, cut in strips
1 onion, sliced and separated into
  rings
Hot cooked rice

Drain pineapple, reserving juice. Add water to juice to make ½ c.; combine with tomato juice, vinegar, soy sauce, brown sugar, and bouillon in skillet. Bring to a boil. Add liver; reduce heat, cover and simmer 15 minutes.

Blend together cornstarch and water. Add to liver mixture and cook, stirring, until thickened. Stir in green pepper, onion and pineapple. Cover and simmer about 7 minutes, until vegetables are tender-crisp. Serve over rice. Makes 8 servings.

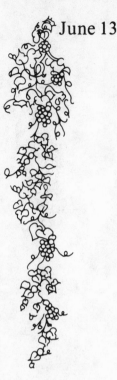

June 13

Lunch

Special Chef's Salad*

Italian Tomato Dressing*

Crusty Herb Buttered Rolls

Raspberry Gelatin with Sliced Bananas

Tea   Milk

Dinner

Baked Chicken

Boiled Potatoes with Cheese Sauce

Sautéed Zucchini Strips

Spinach Salad

Strawberry-Orange Bombe

Coffee   Milk

Strawberry-Orange Bombe

1 qt. strawberry ice cream,
  slightly softened
2 egg yolks
⅓ c. sugar
1 tblsp. grated orange peel
2 tblsp. orange juice
1 tblsp. cold water
1 egg white
2 tblsp. sugar
1 c. heavy cream, whipped
Fresh or frozen strawberries

Chill a 7-c. mold in freezer. Quickly spread softened ice cream as evenly as possible with back of spoon or spatula on inside of mold to make a shell lining about ½" thick. Return to freezer to harden.

Meanwhile, in top of double boiler beat egg yolks well. Beat in ⅓ c. sugar, orange peel and juice and water. Cook over rapidly boiling water, stirring constantly, until thickened (about 10 minutes). Cool completely.

In a small mixing bowl, beat egg white until frothy. Gradually beat in 2 tblsp. sugar; beat until stiff peaks form. Fold in orange mixture; then whipped cream. Pour into ice cream-lined mold. Freeze.

To unmold, dip into lukewarm water and turn out onto chilled plate. Return to freezer to harden. To serve, garnish with fresh or frozen strawberries. Makes 8 to 10 servings.

*See Index for recipe

Lunch

Low-Cal Clam Dip
Assorted Raw Vegetables
Whole-Wheat Melba Toast
Fresh Cherries
Tea   Milk

Dinner

Beef Stroganoff
Buttered Noodles   Julienne Green Beans
Tossed Salad
Peachy Cheese Dessert*
Iced Coffee

Low-Cal Clam Dip

1 (8-oz.) can minced clams
1½ c. cottage cheese
½ tsp. seasoned salt
2 tsp. lemon juice
1 tsp. Worcestershire sauce
1 tblsp. minced green onions
Assorted crisp vegetable dippers

In blender container combine clams with liquid, cottage cheese, seasoned salt, lemon juice and Worcestershire sauce. Cover and whirl until smooth. Stir in green onions. Cover and chill at least several hours to blend flavors. Serve with cauliflowerets and strips of carrot, celery, zucchini and/or cucumber. Makes about 2 cups.

June 15

Lunch

Hamburgers
Blue Cheese Onions
Lime Gelatin with Grapes
Assorted Cookies
Tea   Milk

Dinner

Corned Beef Hash
Grilled Tomato Halves   Steamed Broccoli
Romaine, Black Olive and Radish Salad
Date and Apricot Bars*
Coffee   Tea   Milk

Blue Cheese Onions

½ c. crumbled blue cheese (2 oz.)
¼ c. vegetable oil
2 tblsp. lemon juice
¼ tsp. salt
⅛ tsp. pepper
⅛ tsp. paprika
2 large onions, thinly sliced and
  separated into rings

In bowl mash blue cheese with oil, lemon juice, salt, pepper and paprika until blended. Add onion rings and toss. Cover and chill several hours or overnight, stirring occasionally.

Serve with broiled ground beef patties in buns, or cold beef sandwiches. Makes enough for 12 sandwiches.

*See Index for recipe

Lunch

Fresh Fruit Salad

Orange-Honey Dressing*

Sesame Bread Sticks

Chocolate Cupcakes

Tea   Milk

Dinner

Pork Chops

New Potatoes with Lemon Butter

Mixed Vegetables

Shredded Lettuce and Green Pepper Salad

Maple Walnut Ice Cream

Coffee   Milk

New Potatoes with Lemon Butter

3 lb. new potatoes (20 to 24 small)
¼ c. melted butter or regular
  margarine
½ tsp. grated lemon peel
2 tblsp. lemon juice
2 tblsp. chopped fresh chives
1 tsp. salt
Dash of pepper

Scrub potatoes and leave whole, but pare a narrow strip around center. Place in saucepan containing 1″ salted water (1 tsp. salt to 1 c. water), cover and cook until tender, 20 to 25 minutes. Drain.

Meanwhile, heat remaining ingredients in saucepan to boiling. Turn potatoes into serving dish. Stir hot lemon mixture and pour over potatoes; serve at once. Makes 8 servings.

June 17

Lunch

Eggs in Vinaigrette Sauce*

Assorted Luncheon Meats   Rolls

Pineapple Chunks

Tea   Milk

Dinner

Crab Meat Salad in Avocado Halves

Banana Bread

Lemon Sherbet with Blueberries

Tea   Milk

Banana Bread

3½ c. sifted flour
3 tsp. baking powder
1 tsp. salt
1 tsp. baking soda
2 c. mashed, ripe bananas
2 tblsp. lemon juice
¾ c. shortening
1½ c. sugar
3 eggs
¾ c. milk
½ c. chopped pecans or walnuts

Sift together flour, baking powder, salt and baking soda.

Combine bananas and lemon juice; mix well.

Cream together shortening and sugar in bowl with electric mixer at medium speed until fluffy. Add eggs and beat thoroughly until very light and fluffy. Add dry ingredients alternately with milk; fold in bananas and nuts. Beat after each addition. Pour batter into 2 greased 8½x4½x2½" loaf pans.

Bake in 350° oven 1 hour, or until cake tester or wooden pick inserted in center of loaf comes out clean. Cool in pans 10 minutes. Remove from pans and cool on racks. Wrap in foil or plastic wrap and let stand in cool place overnight before slicing, or freeze. Makes 2 loaves.

See Index for recipe

Lunch

Roast Beef and Cucumber Sandwiches

Marinated Tomatoes

Apple Turnovers

Lemon Iced Tea*

Dinner

Pan-Broiled Minute Steaks

Danish Sugar-Browned Potatoes

Minted Carrot Chunks

Escarole and Sliced Mushroom Salad

Strawberry Shortcake

Coffee   Milk

Danish Sugar-Browned Potatoes

24 small new potatoes
¼ c. butter or regular margarine
6 tblsp. sugar
2 tsp. salt

Cook scrubbed potatoes in their jackets in boiling water until tender. Drain and pare.

Melt butter in skillet; stir in sugar and cook, stirring constantly, until mixture is a light caramel color.

Add potatoes; continue cooking, shaking the potatoes to roll about until lightly browned. Sprinkle with salt during cooking. Makes 8 servings.

Lunch

Reubens
Green Pepper Strips
Cantaloupe Cubes
Walnut Pound Cake
Tea   Milk

Dinner

Chicken Supreme*
Hot Fluffy Rice   New Peas in Cream
Pineapple Sherbet in Orange Shells
Iced Coffee

Walnut Pound Cake

3 c. sifted flour
½ tsp. baking powder
½ tsp. baking soda
¾ tsp. salt
1 c. butter or regular margarine
2 c. sugar
3 eggs
2 tsp. vanilla
1 c. sour milk
½ c. finely ground walnuts
Sifted confectioners' sugar

Sift together flour, baking powder, baking soda and salt; set aside.

Cream together butter and sugar in mixing bowl until light and fluffy, using electric mixer at medium speed. Add eggs, one at a time, beating well after each addition. Blend in vanilla (total beating time: 10 minutes).

Add dry ingredients alternately with sour milk to creamed mixture, beating well after each addition, using electric mixer at low speed. Stir in walnuts. Pour batter into greased 10″ tube pan.

Bake in 350° oven 1 hour, or until cake tester inserted in center comes out clean or top springs back when lightly touched with finger. Cool in pan on rack 10 minutes. Remove from pan; cool on rack.

Sprinkle with sifted confectioners' sugar. Makes 12 servings.

*See Index for recipe

Lunch

Shrimp Salad in Tomato Cups
Cold Marinated Asparagus
Golden Sesame Braid*
Watermelon Wedges
Tea   Milk

Dinner

Golden Broiled Flounder
French Fried Potatoes
Brussels Sprouts with Water Chestnuts
Tossed Salad
Lemon Chiffon Pie
Iced Coffee

Golden Broiled Flounder

2 lb. flounder or other fish fillets,
   frozen or fresh
⅓ c. salad oil
1 tsp. salt
¼ tsp. pepper
2 egg yolks, beaten
2 tblsp. finely chopped onion
1 tblsp. dried parsley flakes
½ c. mayonnaise or salad dressing
2 egg whites, stiffly beaten

Thaw fish fillets if frozen. Cut in serving-size pieces.

Combine oil, salt and pepper.

Combine egg yolks, onion, parsley and mayonnaise; fold in egg whites.

Place fish on oiled broiler pan; brush with half of oil mixture. Broil about 3″ from source of heat 3 to 4 minutes. Turn carefully and brush with remaining oil mixture. Broil 3 to 4 minutes, or until fish flakes easily when tested with a fork. Top fish with mayonnaise mixture and broil 5″ from source of heat 1 to 3 minutes, or until golden brown. Serve immediately. Makes 6 servings.

*See Index for recipe

Breakfast

Tropical Fruit Shake

Shredded Wheat Biscuits with Honey and Milk

Buttered Raisin Toast

Coffee

Tropical Fruit Shake

1 c. orange juice
1 banana, cut in chunks
1 c. vanilla ice cream

Combine ingredients in blender container. Cover and whirl just until smooth. Makes about 2 cups.

Brunch

Cinnamon-Glazed Broiled Grapefruit Sections

Chili with Cheese Soufflé

Zingy Coleslaw*

Jellied Fruit Compote*

Coffee   Tea

Chili with Cheese Soufflé

1 lb. ground beef
½ c. chopped onion
2 tblsp. flour
1 tsp. salt
1 tsp. chili powder
⅓ c. butter or regular margarine
⅓ c. flour
1 tsp. salt
1½ c. milk
2 c. shredded process American
  cheese (8 oz.)
4 egg yolks, slightly beaten
4 egg whites, stiffly beaten

Cook beef and onion in skillet until onion is soft (do not brown). Stir in 2 tblsp. flour, 1 tsp. salt and chili powder. Place mixture in bottom of greased 2-qt. casserole.

Melt butter in saucepan. Stir in ⅓ c. flour and 1 tsp. salt. Add milk and cook, stirring constantly, until mixture comes to a boil. Add cheese and cook over low heat, stirring, until cheese melts. Blend a little of the hot mixture into egg yolks. Add to cheese mixture and blend thoroughly. Fold mixture into egg whites. Spoon lightly over chili.

Bake in 350° oven 55 to 65 minutes. Makes 6 servings.

*See Index for recipe

Breakfast

Grapefruit Juice with a Mint Sprig

Golden Sausage Boats

Cocoa   Coffee

Golden Sausage Boats

12 pork sausage links
3 tblsp. water
6 eggs
⅓ c. milk
Pinch salt
6 frankfurter buns

Place links in unheated skillet. Do not prick skins. Add 3 tblsp. water. Cook, covered, 5 minutes over low heat. Uncover; drain off liquid. Finish cooking over low heat, turning until well browned on all sides.

Meanwhile, beat together eggs, milk and salt. Dip buns in mixture. Grill on both sides until browned.

Place sausages in buns. Makes 6 servings.

Brunch

Creamed Eggs Supreme

Cold Asparagus with French Dressing

Fresh Whole Strawberries in Pineapple Halves

Coffee

Creamed Eggs Supreme

3 tblsp. butter or regular margarine
3 tblsp. flour
¾ tsp. salt
⅛ tsp. pepper
1½ c. milk
1½ c. shredded process sharp
   American cheese (6 oz.)
6 hard-cooked eggs, chopped
4 slices crisp-cooked bacon, crumbled
Toast, toasted English muffins or hot
   biscuits

Melt butter in saucepan; blend in flour, salt and pepper. Add milk, and cook, stirring constantly, until mixture comes to a boil. Add cheese and stir until melted. Stir in eggs and bacon; heat thoroughly. Serve over toast. Makes 6 servings.

*See Index for recipe

Shortcuts
& Seasonings

• To make a great inexpensive topping for puddings, frostings and even some vegetables such as squash, grate the rind from several oranges. (Navel oranges are best for grating.) Spread the rind on a sheet of foil or a cookie sheet and dry in oven at 250° for about 10 minutes.

• Dried herbs are much more concentrated than fresh ones. If a recipe calls for dried herbs and you wish to use fresh herbs, double the amount indicated in the recipe. To reverse the rule, if a recipe calls for fresh herbs, cut the amount in half if you wish to use dried herbs.

• Citrus fruits will yield more juice if you pop them into a bowl of hot water for a few minutes, or roll them in your hands before squeezing.

• To peel a tomato easily, spear with a kitchen fork and plunge into boiling water for half a minute. The skin will slice right off.

• For a quick and easy decoration, top unbaked meat loaf with crisscross strips of bacon. When loaf is baked, remove from oven and place slices of stuffed olives at the points where the bacon strips cross.

• When cooking with vinegar, always use a glass, enamel or stainless steel saucepan. Aluminum pans react to the vinegar and will produce an unpleasant metallic taste.

• To slice meat or poultry to paper-thin thickness, freeze it first for a few minutes and then cut against the grain.

• For a simple, delicious dessert, line a disposable foil pan with strips of leftover cake, spread with a layer of slightly softened ice cream, and freeze. Cut into squares and top with hot fudge, butterscotch or strawberry sauce.

June 21-
September 20

ummer

S U M M E R

Summertime—this is the season when everyone wants to head for the outdoors and relax, and that includes the cook. It's the season for grilling in the back yard or on the terrace, and for gathering together for a family reunion, picnic, or barbecue. It's also the time to think about doing much of your cooking in the cool of the morning, to rely on your skillet for many of your main dishes and to treat the family to cool, refreshing molded salads and ice cream desserts.

The menus in this section are geared to take advantage of the season's delights. They feature recipes for summer fruits and vegetables, grilled meats, fish and poultry, and they're kind to the cook by emphasizing easy meals cooked on top of the stove.

Now is the time to experiment with new ways of combining fruit juices to create refreshing, nutritious drinks. We've included several fruit refreshers in our menus, and you might like to come up with some original combinations of your own favorite flavors.

Chilled salads and frosty desserts offer boundless possibilities for family and company meals. Creamy Orange Charlotte is a cool, velvety salad that can double as a dessert and is perfect to take along on a picnic. Both the Cucumber-Cabbage Mold and Grandmother's Best Potato Salad are marvelous for entertaining at a back yard buffet. For those who want to splurge on dessert and forget the calories, we offer a refreshing Pineapple Sherbet and a mouth-watering Rainbow Parfait that combines vanilla ice cream with three sherbets.

Just about everyone has a favorite recipe for Barbecued Ribs, and we have one that we think is super. Hot mustard, lime juice and soy sauce in the marinade give a very special taste to the succulent ribs. On days when you know you don't want to turn on the oven, turn to our recipes for Chinese Pepper Steak, Summer Chicken with Peas and New Potatoes, or one of our other easy skillet main dishes.

When you're shopping for all the glorious fruits and vegetables of summer, be sure to get your money's worth.

Everyone looks forward to the first corn of summer. But as soon as the corn is picked, the sugar in the kernels begins to turn to starch, so the faster you pop your ears of corn into a pot of boiling water, the better. Look for fresh green husks and check to see that the stems aren't dry and brown. Pull the husk down an inch or so to be sure that the kernels are tender and milky, and avoid ears with dented kernels.

Select firm, plump nectarines that are well-shaped and slightly soft along the seam. They should have a bright red blush; green nectarines will never ripen. Choose peaches that are free from brown spots and ripe enough to yield to a little pressure when pressed lightly with your fingers.

Blueberries should be plump; don't buy berries in a container that is stained with juice.

Melons—and that includes all kinds, from honeydew to cantaloupe—should be heavy for their size. Ripeness is indicated by the softening of the fruit around the blossom end. If a melon is soft and mushy, don't buy it; if it sloshes when you shake it, put it back.

Buy firm, fresh, well-shaped cucumbers. Cucumbers that are streaked with yellow are too old to be tender.

You'll find all types of lettuce available—velvety Boston lettuce, early leaf lettuce and romaine. Never store lettuce next to apples, plums, pears, avocados, tomatoes or melons because they give off ethylene gas, which can spot lettuce.

After you've chosen the finest of summer's treasures, we hope you'll take advantage of the casual summer recipes and menus that follow as you enjoy the sun and good times with family and friends.

Lunch

Herbed Onion Soup*

Crusty Rolls

Tossed Salad

Riced Cherry Gelatin with Grapes

Tea   Milk

Dinner

Broiled Lamb Steaks

Peas with Sautéed Mushroom Slices

Buttered New Potatoes with Dill

Watercress and Sliced Onion Salad

Creamy Orange Charlotte

Iced Coffee

Creamy Orange Charlotte

4 medium oranges
2 (3-oz.) pkg. orange flavor gelatin
2 c. boiling water
1 c. cold water
2 c. heavy cream, whipped
Sweetened whipped cream
Orange sections

Peel oranges with a sharp knife, removing all of white membrane. Cut into sections, catching juice in bowl. Squeeze the membranes to extract juice. Reserve juice. Add water, if necessary, to make ½ c. Dice oranges; blot with paper towels.

Dissolve gelatin in boiling water in bowl. Stir in cold water and reserved ½ c. juice. Chill gelatin until thick and syrupy.

Fold gelatin into whipped cream. Cover and chill until mixture is thickened, about 10 minutes. Fold in oranges. Pour into 3-qt. serving bowl. Chill until set. Decorate with puffs of whipped cream and orange sections just before serving. Makes 12 to 16 servings.

*See Index for recipe

June 22

Lunch

*Green Soup**

Grilled Cheese and Tomato Sandwiches

Sliced Pears   Honeydew Melon Balls

Iced Tea

Dinner

<u>*Hot Frank Potato Salad*</u>

Corn on the Cob   Buttered Spinach

Endive Salad

Gingerbread with Whipped Cream

Limeade with Lemon Wedges

Hot Frank Potato Salad

½ lb. bacon
¾ c. chopped onion
3 tblsp. sugar
3 tblsp. flour
1½ tsp. salt
l tsp. celery seeds
¾ c. cider vinegar
1½ c. water
6 c. sliced, cooked potatoes
8 frankfurters, sliced
2 hard-cooked eggs, chopped
Chopped fresh parsley

Fry bacon until crisp in skillet. Remove and drain on paper towels. Crumble. Sauté onion in ⅓ c. bacon drippings until tender (do not brown). Add sugar, flour, salt and celery seeds. Stir in vinegar and water. Cook over medium heat, stirring constantly, until thick. Combine with bacon, potatoes, frankfurters and eggs. Turn potato mixture into greased 3-qt. casserole.

Bake, covered, in 350° oven 20 minutes, or until heated. Garnish with parsley. Makes 8 servings.

*See Index for recipe

Lunch

Jellied Beef Bouillon

Thinly Sliced Ham with Hot Mustard

Onion Buttermilk Biscuits

Vanilla Ice Cream Topped with Hot Maple Syrup

Tea   Milk

Dinner

Broiled Liver

French-Fried Onion Rings

Marinated Sliced Tomatoes and Cucumbers

Pie-Pan Asparagus*

Chocolate Pudding with Toasted Pecans

Coffee   Milk

Onion Buttermilk Biscuits

2 tblsp. butter, melted
2 tblsp. minced onion
1/8 tsp. onion salt
1 (8-oz.) pkg. refrigerator buttermilk
  biscuits

Combine butter, onion and salt. Flatten biscuits on ungreased baking sheet with bottom of floured custard cup. Leave rim that cup makes. Place 1 tsp. butter-onion mixture on center of each biscuit. Bake in 425° oven 8 minutes, or until biscuits are light golden brown. Makes 10 biscuits.

*See Index for recipe

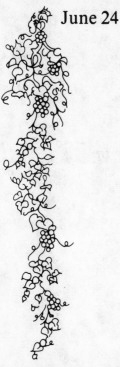

June 24

Lunch

Cold Potato Soup with Chives
Toasted Wheat Crackers
Coconut Layer Cake
<u>*Lemon Iced Tea*</u>

Dinner

Jambalaya*
Hot Fluffy Rice
Marinated Green Beans
Peach Ice Cream with Sliced Peaches
Coffee   Milk

Lemon Iced Tea

12 tea bags
1 qt. boiling water
2 qt. cold water
1 (6-oz.) can frozen lemonade
  concentrate

Steep tea in boiling water 5 minutes. Remove tea bags. Stir in remaining water and lemonade concentrate. Serve in ice-filled glasses. Makes 12 servings.

*See Index for recipe

d inspire you.

A LOVE OF THE LAND

Darrell Sifford, nationally syndicated columnist, presents intimate portraits of real people...from a tough minded, computer-age businessman farmer to hardworking farm families keenly aware of their importance in the world economy. This book leaves no doubt that the traditional values still exist. A book that every farm family and friend would be proud to read and own. 50 photographs. (Bookstore price, $11.95)

Our price, $9.95

LET PRAYER HELP YOU

Here is a practical book about the many ways prayer can help us cope with the trials and strains of modern life. Included are 23 prayer patterns for building — or rebuilding — your personal prayer life. (Bookstore price, $6.95)

Our price, $4.95

Helpful Paperbacks

FARM JOURNAL'S COUNTRY-STYLE MICROWAVE COOKBOOK

104 time-tested country favorite recipes converted to the microwave oven. Main dishes, soups and sandwiches, vegetable dishes, desserts. Soft cover. (Bookstore price, $3.50)

Our price, $2.95.

FARM JOURNAL'S EVERYDAY FAVORITE RECIPES

110 recipes...main dishes, vegetables, salads and desserts...for affordable dishes that please family members and offer variety...every day. Soft cover. (Bookstore price, $3.50)

Our price, $2.95

ORDER FORM
Mail to: Farm Journal Books, Box 1927, Philadelphia, PA 19105

how many	code	title	price each	total
____	149039	Best-Ever Cookies	$9.95	____
____	147033	Country Style Microwave Cookbook	$2.95	____
____	146035	Everyday Favorite Recipes	$2.95	____
____	711051	Let Prayer Help You	$4.95	____
____	315036	Let's Make a Patchwork Quilt	$8.95	____
____	712034	Love of the Land	$9.95	____
____	148031	Meal and Menu Planner Cookbook	$9.95	____
____	145037	Speedy Skillet Meals	$6.95	____

VISA®

____

master charge

____

Total for Books	$____
Pa. residents add 6% sales tax	____
Delivery charge	$1.00
Amount enclosed or charged	$____

(make check payable to Farm Journal)

CHARGE MY

Account # ☐☐☐☐☐☐☐☐☐☐☐☐☐☐☐☐☐☐☐☐☐

Card expires_____ Signature_____

Name_____

Address_____

City_____ State_____ ZIP_____

Lunch

Thinly Sliced Salami

Bacon-Spinach Salad

Whole-Wheat Melba Toast

Sliced Strawberries and Bananas

Tea   Milk

Dinner

Swiss Cheese Soufflé

Buttered Lima Beans

Olive Wreath Mold*

Coffee Ice Cream-Filled Cream Puffs with Powdered Sugar

Iced Tea

Bacon-Spinach Salad

4 slices bacon
1 tblsp. dry mustard
¼ c. salad oil
¼ c. vinegar
½ tsp. onion salt
1 lb. spinach, washed and
    stems removed

Pan-broil bacon until crisp. Remove and save for later use.

Measure bacon drippings. Place 3 to 4 tblsp. in skillet. Stir in mustard, oil, vinegar and onion salt; heat to boiling. Add spinach leaves and toss to coat with dressing. Serve at once in salad bowl, crumbling bacon over top. Makes 8 servings.

*See Index for recipe

June 26

Lunch

Yogurt Cucumber Soup

Egg Salad and Lettuce Sandwiches

Cantaloupe Wedges

Iced Tea

Dinner

Roast Beef Hash

Buttered Zucchini   Sliced Tomatoes

Corn Kernel Biscuits*

Vanilla Pudding and Toasted Coconut Parfaits

Iced Coffee

Yogurt Cucumber Soup

2 (8-oz.) cartons plain yogurt
1½ c. water
2 medium cucumbers, pared and
   thinly sliced
2 tblsp. chopped parsley
1 tblsp. chopped green onion
1 tsp. salt
½ tsp. dried dill weed
⅛ tsp. pepper

Blend together yogurt and water in bowl. Add remaining ingredients. Cover and chill at least 30 minutes. Makes 5 cups.

*See Index for recipe

Lunch

Hamburgers with Mushrooms
Blue Cheese Onions*
Tossed Salad
Rice Pudding with Caramel Sauce
Iced Tea

Dinner

Grilled Knockwurst
Coleslaw   Peas with Pimientos
Endive Salad
Orange Frost
Iced Coffee

Orange Frost

1 env. unflavored gelatin
½ c. cold water
1½ c. orange juice
¼ c. sugar

Sprinkle gelatin over cold water in small saucepan. Cook and stir over low heat 3 minutes, or until gelatin is dissolved. Remove from heat. Stir in orange juice and sugar. Pour into metal bowl. Chill ½ hour, or until very thick.

Beat with electric mixer until creamy and doubled in volume, about 5 minutes. Pour into 8½x4½x2½" loaf pan. Cover and freeze overnight.

Before serving, allow to stand at room temperature 5 minutes. Scoop into sherbet dishes. If desired, garnish with mandarin orange sections. Serve immediately or return to freezer until serving time, as dessert softens quickly. Makes 4 servings.

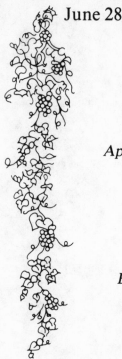

June 28

Lunch

Liverwurst   Sliced Onions

Assorted Pickles and Olives

Delicious Date Walnut Loaf*

Apple Yogurt with Brown Sugar and Cinnamon

Lemonade

Dinner

Miniature Ham Loaves

Buttered Broccoli Spears   Potato Puffs*

Romaine Salad

Yellow Cake with Chocolate Frosting

Iced Coffee au Lait

Miniature Ham Loaves

6 c. ground fully cooked ham
2 eggs, slightly beaten
1 c. soft bread crumbs
1 c. apple juice
½ c. milk
¼ c. finely chopped celery
¼ c. finely chopped onion
¼ tsp. dry mustard
⅛ tsp. pepper
Pineapple Glaze (recipe follows)

Combine ham, eggs, bread crumbs, apple juice, milk, celery, onion, mustard and pepper in large bowl. Mix lightly, but well. Shape into 8 small loaves. Place on waxed paper-lined baking sheet. Freeze loaves 2 hours, or until firm.

To bake, arrange frozen ham loaves on 15½ x 10½ x 1″ jelly roll pan. Bake in 350° oven 30 minutes. While ham loaves are baking, prepare Pineapple Glaze.

Remove ham loaves from oven; pour off pan drippings. Arrange 3 pineapple pieces on top of each loaf. Brush half of Pineapple Glaze over loaves. Reserve remaining glaze.

Bake 15 minutes more. Brush with remaining Pineapple Glaze. Bake 15 minutes more. Makes 8 servings.

Pineapple Glaze: Drain 1 (8¼-oz.) can sliced pineapple in juice, reserving juice. Cut each pineapple slice into 6 pieces; set aside. Combine 1 tblsp. brown sugar (firmly packed), 1 tblsp. cornstarch and a dash of ground cloves in small saucepan. Stir in reserved pineapple juice, 1 tblsp. lemon juice and ½ c. water. Cook over medium heat, stirring constantly, until mixture boils and thickens. Keep warm.

*See Index for recipe

Lunch

Tuna Carrot Salad*
Ham and Watercress Sandwiches
Honeydew Melon Wedges Topped with
Raspberry Gelatin Cubes
Orange Juice and Club Soda over Crushed Ice

Dinner

Grilled Turkey Legs
Grilled Corn on the Cob   Green Beans with Almonds
Sautéed Cherry Tomatoes
Parmesan Cheese Crescents
Coffee Ice Cream with Crushed Peanut Brittle
Iced Tea

Parmesan Cheese Crescents

2 c. sifted flour
3 tsp. baking powder
1 tsp. salt
½ c. shortening
¾ c. milk
1 tblsp. melted butter or
   regular margarine
2 tblsp. grated Parmesan cheese
1 tblsp. minced fresh parsley
Milk

Sift together flour, baking powder and salt into bowl. Cut in shortening with pastry blender until crumbly. Add ¾ c. milk all at once, stirring just enough with fork to make a soft dough that sticks together.

Turn onto lightly floured surface and knead gently 10 times. Roll into 13″ circle. Brush with melted butter. Sprinkle with Parmesan cheese and parsley. Cut into 12 wedges. Roll up each from wide end. Place crescents, point down, on greased baking sheet. Brush with milk.

Bake in 425° oven 25 minutes, or until golden brown. Serve warm. Makes 12.

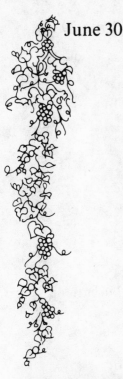

June 30

Lunch

Turkey Salad in Crusty Rolls
Dilly Cheese-Stuffed Celery*
Fresh Pineapple and Strawberries
Tea   Milk

Dinner

Grilled Hamburgers
Hot Spiced Beets
Escarole and Chicory Salad
Cherry Tarts
Coffee   Milk

Hot Spiced Beets

4 c. sliced cooked beets
2 tblsp. butter or regular margarine
1 tblsp. flour
2 tblsp. dark brown sugar
3 tblsp. vinegar
¼ c. boiling water
½ tsp. salt
¼ tsp. paprika
¼ tsp. ground cinnamon
⅛ tsp. ground nutmeg
⅛ tsp. ground cloves

Place beets in a greased 1½-qt. casserole. Melt butter in saucepan; blend in flour and sugar. Add vinegar and boiling water, and cook, stirring constantly, until bubbly. Add remaining ingredients. Pour over beets.

Cover and bake in 350° oven 25 minutes. Makes 6 servings.

*See Index for recipe

Lunch

Macaroni Salad
Thinly Sliced Roast Beef
Tomato Wedges
Sunflower Refrigerator Cookies*
Tea   Milk

Dinner

Broiled Scallops and Bacon Curls
Buttered Carrots and New Peas
Tossed Salad
Butterscotch Biscuit Swirls
Lemon Sherbet
Iced Coffee

Butterscotch Biscuit Swirls

2 c. sifted flour
5 tsp. baking powder
½ tsp. salt
¼ c. butter or regular margarine
¾ c. milk
½ c. melted butter or regular
   margarine
1 c. brown sugar, firmly packed

Sift together flour, baking powder and salt into mixing bowl. Cut in ¼ c. butter with pastry blender until crumbs form. Add milk to dry ingredients all at once, stirring just enough with fork to make a soft dough that sticks together.

Turn out onto lightly floured surface and knead gently 10 times. Roll out to 12x10″ rectangle. Brush with ½ c. melted butter. Sprinkle with brown sugar. Roll up like a jelly roll, starting at wide side. Cut in 12 slices. Place slice, cut side down, in each greased 3″ muffin-pan cup.

Bake in 400° oven 18 minutes, or until golden brown. Place a piece of aluminum foil under pan to catch drips during baking. Serve warm. Makes 12.

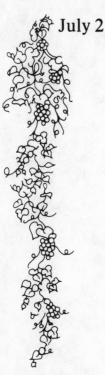

Lunch

Parmesan Garden Salad Bowl*

Pumpernickel Bread

Soft Ginger Cookies

Coffee Floats

Dinner

Assorted Sliced Cold Cuts

Low-Calorie Scalloped Potatoes

Buttered Spinach with Toasted Sesame Seeds

Sliced Zucchini

Fresh Raspberries in Cream

Iced Tea with Mint Sprigs

Low-Calorie Scalloped Potatoes

2 lb. potatoes, pared and thinly sliced
   (about 5 c.)
1 c. thinly sliced onion
2 tblsp. flour
1 tsp. salt
⅛ tsp. pepper
1 c. skim milk, scalded
1 c. chicken broth
Paprika

Arrange one third of the potatoes in a lightly greased 2-qt. casserole. Arrange one third of the onion on top of the potatoes. Combine flour, salt and pepper. Sprinkle one third of flour mixture over potatoes and onion. Repeat layers twice. Pour hot milk and chicken broth over all. Sprinkle with paprika. Cover.

Bake in 375° oven 1¼ hours. Uncover and bake 30 minutes, or until potatoes are tender. Makes 5 cups.

*See Index for recipe

Lunch

Double Dairy Salad*

Thinly Sliced Salami

Bread Sticks

Fresh Figs and Grapes

Tea   Milk

Dinner

Summer Chicken with Peas and New Potatoes

Tomatoes with Fresh Basil

Cantaloupe Chunks with Sliced Peaches

Coffee   Tea

Summer Chicken with Peas and New Potatoes

6 tblsp. butter or regular margarine
1 broiler-fryer (about 2½ lb.) cut in
   serving pieces
1 lb. small new potatoes, scrubbed,
   with a strip pared around the
   centers
Salt
Freshly ground pepper
2 tblsp. lemon juice
3 green onions with tops, thinly sliced
1 lb. fresh peas, shelled (about 1 c.),
   or 1 (10-oz.) pkg. frozen peas
¼ c. chopped fresh parsley
1 c. dairy sour cream
1 tsp. dried thyme leaves
½ tsp. salt
¼ tsp. pepper
Parsley (for garnish)

Melt butter in a large skillet. Add chicken and potatoes and brown slowly on all sides; season with salt and pepper. (Be generous with pepper.) Sprinkle chicken with lemon juice; reduce heat, cover pan and simmer 30 minutes.

Add green onions to butter in bottom of skillet; sprinkle peas and parsley over chicken and potatoes; cover again and simmer 10 minutes more, or until chicken and potatoes are tender.

Remove chicken and vegetables to serving platter; keep warm.

Remove skillet from heat. Add sour cream, thyme, ½ tsp. salt and ¼ tsp. pepper; stir to mix well and loosen pan drippings.

Pour over chicken or pass as sauce. Garnish with additional parsley; serve immediately. Makes 6 servings.

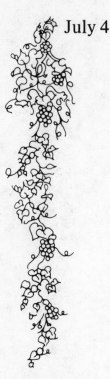

Lunch

*Creamed Eggs Supreme**
Sautéed Green Pepper Strips
Strawberry Ice Cream Sundaes
Tea   Milk

Dinner

Cold Sliced Turkey Roll
Corn on the Cob
Green Beans with Garlic Dressing
Boston Lettuce
Cherry Pie
Coffee   Milk

Green Beans with Garlic Dressing

4 c. fresh green beans (1 lb.)
½ c. water
1 tsp. salt
2 slices bacon, diced
½ c. garlic French dressing
2 tblsp. minced green onion
¼ tsp. dried oregano leaves

Cook beans, either whole or cut in 1″ lengths, in ½ c. water with 1 tsp. salt added, for 10 minutes, or until just tender-crisp.

Fry bacon until crisp; drain on paper towels. Add bacon, salad dressing, onion and oregano to beans; heat through and serve. Makes 6 servings.

See Index for recipe

Lunch

Corned Beef Sandwiches

Dill Pickles

Chewy Coconut Macaroons*

Iced Tea

Dinner

Barbecued Sweet Italian Sausages and Mushrooms

Coleslaw   Potato Salad

Sliced Tomatoes and Lettuce

Strawberries and Cream Spectacular

Coffee   Milk

Strawberries and Cream Spectacular

1 (18½-oz.) pkg. yellow cake mix
1 tblsp. grated orange rind
2 pt. strawberries, hulled
2 c. heavy cream
¼ c. sugar
1 tsp. vanilla
¾ c. red currant jelly

Prepare yellow cake mix according to package directions, adding orange rind to batter. Bake in 2 greased 9″ round cake pans as package directs. Cool well.

Chop enough strawberries to make 1 c.; reserve remaining berries.

Whip cream until it begins to thicken. Gradually beat in sugar; blend in vanilla. Beat until soft peaks form. Remove 1 c. cream; refrigerate remaining whipped cream. Fold 1 c. strawberries into 1 c. whipped cream.

Place one cake layer, top side down, on serving plate. Spread with strawberry/cream filling. Top with second cake layer, top side up.

Slice remaining strawberries. Arrange sliced strawberries on top of cake, starting at outer edge. (Place berries with point along edge of cake.) After first circle of berries is completed, continue placing berries in this manner until top is covered. Refrigerate 10 minutes.

Melt currant jelly in small saucepan over low heat, stirring constantly. Carefully spoon or brush jelly over strawberries.

Spread whipped cream on sides of cake. Using rosette tip #190, pipe rosettes between strawberry points along top edge of cake. Fill in spaces with star tip #24. Pipe border along bottom edge of cake, using tip #71. If you do not wish to decorate cake with tips, spoon remaining cream in small puffs between strawberries. Refrigerate until serving time. Makes 10 to 12 servings.

*See Index for recipe

July 6

Lunch

Cold Cream of Chicken Soup with Sour Cream and Chives

Chef's Salad

Chocolate Pecan Sponge Cake*

Iced Tea with Mint

Dinner

Poached Halibut Fillets

Buttered Carrots with Fresh Dill

Spinach Salad

Popovers

Lemon Chiffon Pie

Coffee   Tea   Milk

Popovers

3 eggs
1½ c. sifted flour
1½ c. milk
¾ tsp. salt
1½ tblsp. cooking oil

Combine eggs, flour, milk and salt in mixing bowl. Beat with electric mixer at low speed 1½ minutes. Add oil. Beat ½ minute more. Pour into 8 well-greased (6-oz.) custard cups.

Bake in 450° oven 15 minutes. Reduce heat to 350°. Bake 35 minutes.

Slit tops. Turn oven off. Let popovers stand in oven 10 minutes. Cool on rack. Wrap in aluminum foil. Freeze up to 1 month.

To serve, place frozen popovers on baking sheet. Bake in 350° oven 8 minutes, or until hot. Makes 8.

*See Index for recipe

Lunch

Grilled Ham and Cheese Sandwiches

Celery Sticks

Brownies

Pineapple Sherbet

Tea   Milk

Dinner

Miniature Cheese Loaves*

Herbed Rice   Peas with Water Chestnuts

Chicory and Endive Salad

Raspberries in Cantaloupe Wedges

Iced Coffee

Pineapple Sherbet

¾ c. sugar
⅓ c. water
1½ c. pineapple juice
1 (8¼-oz.) can crushed pineapple, drained
2 tblsp. lemon juice
1 c. light cream
2 egg whites, stiffly beaten

Combine sugar, water and pineapple juice in saucepan; cook 15 minutes. Remove from heat; add crushed pineapple and lemon juice. Cool. Pour into refrigerator tray and freeze until mushy.

Remove partially frozen mixture to chilled bowl; beat until light, gradually adding cream. Beat well. Fold in egg whites. Return to refrigerator tray and freeze until firm. Makes about 6 servings.

*See Index for recipe

July 8

Lunch

Snacker's Tomato Soup
Turkey Club Sandwiches
Assorted Sweet Pickles
Blueberries and Cream
Tea   Milk

Dinner

Polynesian-style Liver*
Broiled Tomato and Green Pepper Kabobs
Marinated Sliced Sweet Red Onions in Lettuce Cups
Coconut Cake
Tea   Milk

Snacker's Tomato Soup

1 (46-oz.) can vegetable juice cocktail
1 c. finely chopped celery
2 beef bouillon cubes
1 tsp. sugar
¼ tsp. chili powder
⅛ tsp. pepper

Combine all ingredients in saucepan. Bring to a boil. Reduce heat and simmer, covered, 20 minutes. Serve hot or chilled. Makes 1½ quarts.

See Index for recipe

Lunch

*Coney Island Hot Dogs**
Fresh Fruit Cup
Filled Vanilla Cookies
Pink Lemonade

Dinner

Broiled Meat Patties with Herbed Mushrooms

Broiled Potato Slices   *Buttered Zucchini*

Romaine and Sliced Radish Salad

Apricot Pie à la Mode

Coffee   Milk

Apricot Pie à la Mode

1 (1-lb. 13-oz.) can apricot halves, drained
1 unbaked 9″ pie shell
1 tblsp. lemon juice
½ c. flour
¾ c. sugar
¼ tsp. cinnamon
¼ tsp. nutmeg
¼ c. butter or regular margarine
1 pt. vanilla ice cream

Spread apricots in pastry-lined pan. Sprinkle with lemon juice.

Combine flour, sugar and spices. Mix with butter until crumbly. Sprinkle over apricots.

Bake in 400° oven 40 minutes. Serve warm or cold, topped with scoops of ice cream. Makes 1 (9″) pie.

July 10

Lunch

Assorted Cold Cuts

Cheese Potato Salad

Carrot Sticks

Layered Cherry and Lime Gelatin

Iced Tea

Dinner

Broiled Tenderized Chuck Steak

Sautéed Summer Squash

Minted Carrots and Peas*

Tossed Salad

Peach Pie with Peach Ice Cream

Iced Coffee Topped with Whipped Cream and Cinnamon

Cheese Potato Salad

4 to 5 medium potatoes
2 tblsp. vinegar
½ tsp. salt
¼ tsp. pepper
1 lb. Swiss cheese, cut in ¼ " cubes
3 hard-cooked eggs, chopped
1 (16-oz.) can green beans, drained
¾ c. chopped celery
⅓ c. chopped green onion
¼ c. chopped green pepper
1½ c. mayonnaise or salad dressing
2 tblsp. vinegar
2 tblsp. prepared mustard
1½ tsp. salt

Cook potatoes in jackets; let cool slightly. Pare and cube warm potatoes (should have about 4 c.); toss with 2 tblsp. vinegar, ½ tsp. salt and pepper. Cool.

Add cheese, eggs, beans, celery, onion and green pepper.

Combine mayonnaise, 2 tblsp. vinegar, mustard and 1½ tsp. salt. Gently stir into potato mixture. Cover and chill thoroughly. Makes 9 cups.

See Index for recipe

Lunch

Tuna-Cheese Buns*
Diced Apples and Chopped Walnuts in Lettuce Cups
Vanilla Milkshakes

Dinner

Barbecued Ribs
Potato Salad   *Coleslaw in Green Pepper Cups*
Black Olives   *Stuffed Olives*   *Radish Roses*
Strawberry Shortcake
Lemonade

Barbecued Ribs

6 lb. spareribs
1 tsp. salt
½ c. chopped onion
2 tblsp. butter or regular margarine
¾ c. ketchup
¾ c. pineapple juice
¼ c. lime juice
2 tblsp. brown sugar
1½ tsp. soy sauce
1 tsp. salt
1 tsp. dry mustard

Cut ribs into serving pieces. Place in large saucepan and cover with water. Add 1 tsp. salt. Simmer for 45 minutes, or until tender. Drain well.

Sauté onion in melted butter in saucepan until tender (do not brown). Stir in ketchup, pineapple juice, lime juice, brown sugar, soy sauce, 1 tsp. salt and dry mustard. Bring mixture to a boil. Remove from heat.

Grill ribs over hot coals, basting frequently with sauce, until tender and crisp. Makes 6 to 8 servings.

July 12

Lunch

Raw Cauliflowerettes, Celery Sticks and Cucumber Slices

Low-Cal Clam Dip*

Toasted Corn Muffins

Honeydew Melon

Tea   Milk

Dinner

Marinated Chuck Roast

Whipped Potatoes   Buttered Zucchini Strips

Chicory and Sliced Black Olive Salad

Jellied Fruit Compote

Coffee   Tea   Milk

Jellied Fruit Compote

2 (3-oz.) pkg. peach-flavor gelatin
2 c. boiling water
2 c. cold water
1 (13½-oz.) can pineapple chunks, drained
1 (11-oz.) can mandarin orange segments, drained
1 large grapefruit, peeled and cut in sections
20 red maraschino cherries, drained
Sweetened whipped cream
Mandarin orange segments
Red maraschino cherries

Dissolve gelatin in boiling water in bowl. Stir in cold water. Cover and chill until thick and syrupy.

Fold in pineapple chunks, mandarin orange segments, grapefruit and maraschino cherries. Pour into 2-qt. crystal serving bowl. Cover and chill until set. Decorate with whipped cream, mandarin orange segments and maraschino cherries just before serving. Makes 12 servings.

*See Index for recipe

Lunch

Cheeseburgers in Toasted Buns
Mixed Vegetable Marinade*
Pineapple Chunks with Chopped Fresh Mint
Lemonade and Orange Juice over Crushed Ice

Dinner

Sautéed Chicken Livers
Savory Green Beans   *Buttered Noodles*
Marinated Tomato Wedges
Strawberry Shortcake
Coffee   Milk

Savory Green Beans

1 lb. green beans
2 tblsp. salad oil
1 clove garlic
1 tblsp. chopped onion
1½ tsp. salt
1 tsp. dried basil leaves
½ tsp. sugar
⅛ tsp. pepper
¼ c. boiling water

Wash beans; remove tips, then cut in halves crosswise.

Heat oil in skillet. Cut garlic clove in half and add to oil along with onion; cook until soft. Remove garlic.

Add beans and remaining ingredients. Cover and cook over medium heat until tender-crisp, about 25 minutes. Add 1 tblsp. additional water if necessary. Makes 6 servings.

*See Index for recipe

July 14

Lunch

Assorted Cold Cuts and Cheeses
Sliced Tomatoes with <u>Poppy Seed Salad Dressing</u>
Coffee Floats

Dinner

Grilled Sausages
Brown Rice   Corn Fritters
Shredded Lettuce with Russian Dressing
Walnut Pound Cake*
Lemonade

Poppy Seed Salad Dressing

1 c. sugar
½ tsp. salt
1 tsp. dry mustard
1½ tsp. paprika
½ c. vinegar
1½ c. salad oil
1 tsp. grated onion
2 tblsp. poppy seeds

Mix sugar, salt, dry mustard, paprika and vinegar in 1-qt. jar.

Add oil. Cover and shake until blended.

Add onion and poppy seeds; cover and shake until well mixed. Makes 2½ cups.

See Index for recipe

Lunch

Cold Sliced Roast Beef

Spinach Salad with Hard-Cooked Egg Slices

High-Protein Muffins

Fresh Cherries

Tea   Milk

Dinner

Broiled Chicken Legs

Buttered Lima Beans with Basil   Creamed Potatoes

Curly Endive Salad

Party Angel Food Cake*

Iced Coffee

High-Protein Muffins

2½ c. 40% Bran Flakes cereal
1½ c. raisins
1¾ c. milk
1 c. stirred whole-wheat flour
1 c. soy flour
1 c. toasted wheat germ
4 tsp. baking powder
1½ tsp. ground nutmeg
¾ tsp. salt
4 eggs, slightly beaten
⅔ c. honey
⅔ c. cooking oil
¼ c. dark molasses

Combine Bran Flakes, raisins and milk in large mixing bowl.

Stir together whole-wheat flour, soy flour, wheat germ, baking powder, nutmeg and salt; set aside.

Combine eggs, honey, oil and molasses in small bowl; blend well. Add egg mixture to soaked bran flakes; mix well.

Add dry ingredients all at once to bran mixture, stirring just enough to moisten. Spoon batter into paper-lined 3″ muffin-pan cups, filling two-thirds full.

Bake in 350° oven 25 minutes, or until golden brown. Serve warm. Makes 30.

*See Index for recipe

July 16

Lunch

Chicken Salad Sandwiches

Coleslaw with Pimiento

*Slimmers' Deviled Eggs**

Nectarines

Iced Coffee

Dinner

Buttered Spaghetti with Parmesan Cheese and Oregano

Peas with Sliced Mushrooms

<u>*Frosty Tomato Cup*</u>

Hot Rolls

Honeydew Melon with Lime Wedges

Tea   Milk

Frosty Tomato Cup

3 (1-lb. 12-oz.) cans tomatoes,
  drained, or 5 medium size fresh
  tomatoes, chopped
1½ c. green pepper strips
1 medium onion, cut into rings
⅓ c. oil
2 tblsp. vinegar
1 tsp. salt
¾ tsp. dried oregano leaves
¾ tsp. dried basil leaves
¼ tsp. pepper

Combine all ingredients in bowl; mix well. Cover and chill. Makes 8 servings.

*See Index for recipe

Lunch

Cream of Mushroom Soup

Swiss Salmon Sandwiches*

Chocolate Cake with Coffee Icing

Tea   Milk

Dinner

Grilled Shoulder Lamb Chops

Grilled Roasted New Potatoes   Carrots with Mint

Shredded Lettuce Salad

Strawberry Cream Deluxe

Coffee   Milk

Strawberry Cream Deluxe

1 (1-lb.) can fruit cocktail
2 (3-oz.) pkg. strawberry flavor
  gelatin
2 c. boiling water
1 c. cold water
¼ c. lemon juice
2 env. whipped topping mix
3 c. cooked rice
2 c. sliced fresh strawberries
Sweetened whipped cream
Fresh strawberries

Drain fruit cocktail, reserving juice. Add enough water to reserved juice to make 1 c.; set aside.

Dissolve gelatin in boiling water in bowl. Stir in cold water, 1 c. reserved liquid and lemon juice. Cover and chill until thick and syrupy.

Prepare whipped topping mix according to package directions. Fold syrupy gelatin into prepared whipped topping mix. Fold in fruit cocktail, rice and strawberries. Pour into 4-qt. serving bowl. Chill 15 minutes. Stir mixture gently to disperse solids. Cover; chill until set. Decorate with sweetened whipped cream and fresh strawberries. Makes 12 servings.

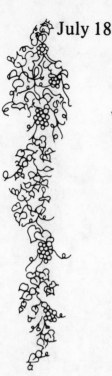

July 18

Lunch

Mexican Salad Bowl

Whole-Wheat Bread and Butter Sandwiches

Fresh Pineapple Cubes

Sugar Cookies

Tea   Milk

Dinner

Spanish-style Pork Chops*

Corn on the Cob   Grilled Potato Slices

Iceberg and Romaine Lettuce Salad

Lemon Meringue Pie

Coffee   Milk

Mexican Salad Bowl

2 qt. mixed greens
¼ c. chopped green onion
¼ c. chopped green pepper
¼ c. sliced, pitted ripe olives
2 tomatoes, cut in wedges
¼ c. shredded Cheddar cheese
1 c. coarsely crushed corn chips
Avocado Salad Dressing
   (recipe follows)

Combine greens, onion, green pepper, olives and tomatoes in salad bowl. Sprinkle with cheese, then corn chips. Top with Avocado Salad Dressing and toss lightly. Makes 6 to 8 servings.

Avocado Salad Dressing: Mash 1 avocado with 2 tblsp. lemon juice. Combine with ½ c. dairy sour cream, ¼ c. salad oil, 1 tsp. seasoned salt and ¼ tsp. chili powder. Cover and refrigerate several hours.

*See Index for recipe

Lunch

Ham and Swiss Cheese Omelets

Marinated Cherry Tomatoes

Cinnamon Jumbles*

Iced Chocolate Milk

Dinner

Veal Loaf

Broccoli with Almonds

Boiled Potatoes with Lemon Butter

Tossed Salad

Blueberry Pie

Tea   Milk

Veal Loaf

1½ lb. ground veal
¼ lb. ground lean pork
¼ tsp. garlic salt
½ c. finely chopped onion
2 c. bread cubes (4 slices)
¼ c. shredded Cheddar cheese
2 tsp. salt
½ tsp. pepper
2 eggs, beaten
¾ c. milk

Combine all ingredients in bowl; mix well. Pack into 9x5x3″ loaf pan.

Bake in 375° oven 1¼ hours. Serve hot or cold. Makes 8 servings.

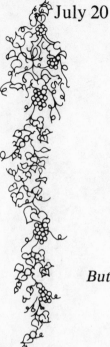

Lunch

Cold Sliced Veal Loaf

Potato Salad   Dill Pickles

Carrot Sticks

Brown-Rim Butter Cookies*

Iced Tea

Dinner

Grilled Sirloin Steak Patties

Buttered Noodles   Sautéed Shredded Zucchini

Cucumber-Cabbage Mold

Ice Cream Sundaes

Iced Coffee

Cucumber-Cabbage Mold

2 (3-oz.) pkg. lime flavor gelatin
¼ tsp. salt
3 c. boiling water
1 c. mayonnaise
1½ c. finely shredded cabbage
¾ c. chopped, pared cucumber
3 tblsp. chopped green pepper
3 tblsp. minced onion
2 tblsp. shredded carrot
½ tsp. celery seeds

Dissolve gelatin and salt in boiling water in bowl. Cover and chill until thick and syrupy.

Beat in mayonnaise with rotary beater. Then fold in cabbage, cucumber, green pepper, onion, carrot and celery seeds. Pour into lightly oiled 6-c. mold. Cover and chill until set. Makes 4 to 6 servings.

Lunch

Sliced Turkey Roll and Lettuce Sandwiches

Coleslaw with Sliced Black Olives

Coffee-Iced Brownies*

Ginger Ale and Pineapple Juice over Crushed Ice

Dinner

Beef Chow Mein

Hot Fluffy Rice   Sliced Tomatoes

Escarole and Radish Salad

Fresh Plums

Iced Coffee

Beef Chow Mein

1½ lb. chuck steak
2 tblsp. salad oil
2 beef bouillon cubes
1½ c. water
¼ c. soy sauce
½ tsp. ground ginger
1 (1-lb.) can bean sprouts
1 green pepper
1 medium onion
1 c. diagonally sliced celery
3 tblsp. cornstarch
¼ c. water
1½ c. uncooked rice
1 (3-oz.) can chow mein noodles

Cut beef in 1x½" pieces. Brown beef in hot oil in large skillet. Add bouillon cubes, 1½ c. water, soy sauce and ginger. Cover and simmer 30 to 45 minutes, until beef is tender. Add bean sprouts.

Meanwhile, cut green pepper in strips; slice onion and separate into rings. Add with celery to skillet. Continue simmering 10 minutes, until vegetables are tender-crisp.

Blend cornstarch with ¼ c. water; add to skillet. Cook, stirring constantly, until mixture is thickened and comes to a boil.

Cook rice following package directions; drain. Serve meat mixture over hot rice; sprinkle with noodles. Makes 6 servings.

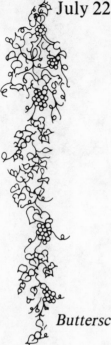

July 22

Lunch

Cheeseburgers on Toasted Buns

Cantaloupe Balls with Sliced Plums

Spicy Raisin Cupcakes*

Tea   Milk

Dinner

Roast Chicken

Roasted Potatoes

Speedy Squash au Gratin

Endive Salad

Butterscotch Pie with Whipped Cream and Chocolate Curls

Coffee   Milk

Speedy Squash au Gratin

3 medium yellow squash (2 lb.)
½ c. chopped onion (1 small)
¼ c. water
1 tsp. salt
¼ tsp. pepper
3 tblsp. butter or regular margarine
1 c. herb-seasoned croutons
½ c. grated Cheddar cheese

Wash squash; trim ends and slice ¼" thick. Place in skillet with onion, water, salt and pepper; cover. Cook, stirring once or twice, until just tender, 10 to 12 minutes. Drain. Season with 1 tblsp. butter.

Meanwhile, melt 2 tblsp. butter in small skillet. Stir in croutons, over very low heat.

Spoon squash into serving bowl. Top with the croutons and cheese. Makes 6 servings.

*See Index for recipe

Lunch

Cold Asparagus Soup

Salmon and Cucumber Sandwiches

Orange Cupcakes*

Iced Tea

Dinner

Chicken Salad

Potato Puffs

Broiled Tomatoes with Sour Cream

Chicory and Green Pepper Salad

Vanilla Ice Cream with Blueberries

Limeade

Potato Puffs

Mashed Potatoes (recipe follows)
4 strips bacon, diced, cooked and
  drained
2 tblsp. minced fresh parsley
¼ c. flour
¼ tsp. salt
2 eggs, slightly beaten
1 c. fine dry bread crumbs
½ c. cooking oil

Combine Mashed Potatoes, bacon, and parsley in bowl. Mix well. Shape into 40 (1¾″) logs, using 1½ tblsp. mixture for each.

Combine flour and salt. Roll potato puffs in flour mixture, then dip in eggs. Roll in bread crumbs. Place puffs on baking sheet. Freeze 2½ hours, or until firm.

To cook, heat oil in 12″ electric frypan to 340°. Add half of the frozen potato puffs to the hot oil. Fry, turning frequently, for 8 minutes, or until golden. Remove potato puffs; drain on paper towels. Repeat with remaining potato puffs. Makes 8 servings.

Mashed Potatoes: Cook 8 medium (2½ lb.) all-purpose potatoes, pared and quartered, with 1 tsp. salt in boiling water in Dutch oven 20 minutes, or until tender. Drain. Mash potatoes until smooth. Stir in ⅓ c. milk, ½ tsp. salt and ¹⁄₁₆ tsp. pepper. Cool at room temperature 45 minutes before shaping.

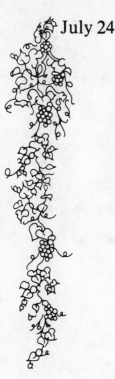

Lunch

Gazpacho
Garlic French Bread Fingers
Lemon Sherbet with Blueberries
Iced Tea

Dinner

Roast Beef
Whipped Potatoes
Broiled Mushrooms*
Romaine and Radish Salad
Spice Cake with Orange Glaze
Tea   Milk

Gazpacho

3 medium tomatoes, peeled and
   finely chopped (2 c.)
½ cucumber, pared and finely
   chopped (½ c.)
¼ c. finely chopped green pepper
2 tsp. grated onion
1 small garlic clove, minced
½ tsp. salt
⅛ tsp. pepper
2 c. tomato juice
2 tblsp. vegetable or olive oil
2 tblsp. wine vinegar
Few drops Tabasco sauce

Combine all ingredients in bowl; cover and chill thoroughly. Serve very cold for a summer soup. Makes 6 servings.

*See Index for recipe

Lunch

Spaghetti Soufflé*
Sliced Oranges and Peaches
Toasted Pound Cake Topped with Honey and Walnuts
Tea   Milk

Dinner

Broiled Liver
Steamed Spinach Topped with Hard-Cooked Egg Slices
Buttered Carrots
Fiesta Vegetable Salad
Riced Lemon Gelatin with Cream
Coffee   Tea

Fiesta Vegetable Salad

Lettuce
4 tomatoes, peeled and sliced
1 sweet onion, thinly sliced
1½ c. cooked whole green beans, or
   1 (1-lb. 1-oz.) can whole green
   beans
1 large cucumber, sliced,
   but not pared
French dressing

Line platter or chop plate with lettuce. Arrange tomatoes, onion, beans and cucumber on lettuce in separate sections.

Serve with French dressing. Makes 6 servings.

July 26

Lunch

Smothered Burgers*
Grated Carrot, Raisin and Sunflower Seed Salad
Chocolate Cupcakes Filled with Whipped Cream
Tea   Milk

Dinner

Baked Salmon Steaks
Boiled New Potatoes
Baked Tomato Halves
Coleslaw
Open-Faced Raspberry Pie
Iced Tea with Lime Juice

Baked Tomato Halves

6 tomatoes
2 tblsp. chopped onion
2 tblsp. butter
½ c. bread crumbs
2 tblsp. chopped parsley
½ tsp. salt
⅛ tsp. pepper

Cut stem end out of tomatoes. Cut tomatoes in halves and place in shallow baking pan.

Cook onion in butter until soft. Add remaining ingredients and toss. Spread mixture on top of tomato halves.

Bake in 400° oven about 25 minutes, or until lightly browned. Makes 6 servings.

See Index for recipe

Lunch

Chicken Tostadas*

Escarole Salad with Oil and Vinegar Dressing

Fresh Cherries

Iced Coffee

Dinner

Meat Loaf

Corn on the Cob   Buttered Green Beans

Hearts of Lettuce Salad

Company Dessert Bowl

Lemonade

Company Dessert Bowl

2 (3-oz.) pkg. lemon flavor gelatin
2 c. boiling water
2 c. cold water
1 (13½-oz.) can pineapple chunks
1 c. miniature marshmallows
2 medium bananas, diced
½ c. sugar
1½ tblsp. flour
Pinch of salt
1 egg, beaten
1 c. heavy cream, whipped
Toasted slivered almonds

Dissolve gelatin in boiling water in bowl. Stir in cold water. Cover and chill until thick and syrupy.

Drain pineapple chunks, reserving 1 c. juice.

Fold pineapple, marshmallows and bananas into gelatin. Pour into 2-qt. crystal serving bowl. Cover and chill until top is almost set.

Meanwhile, combine sugar, flour and salt in small saucepan. Gradually stir in reserved juice. Cook over medium heat, stirring constantly, until mixture is thickened. Stir some of the hot mixture into egg; mix well. Add egg to remaining hot mixture, blending well. Cook over low heat, 1 minute, stirring constantly. Remove from heat. Cool completely.

Fold whipped cream into cooked custard. Spread over gelatin. Top with almonds. Cover and chill until serving time. Makes 12 servings.

*See Index for recipe

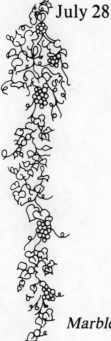

July 28

Lunch

Tuna Bisque*

Meat Loaf and Lettuce Sandwiches

Poached Pears and Dried Apricots

Tea   Milk

Dinner

Broiled Ham Slices

Potato Salad with Hard-Cooked Eggs

Cucumbers with Celery

Sliced Tomatoes and Onions Vinaigrette

Marble Cake with Whipped Cream and Chocolate Curls

Iced Tea with Mint Leaves

Cucumbers with Celery

4 large cucumbers, pared
    (about 2½ lb.)
1 c. diagonally sliced celery
1 (10½-oz.) can condensed chicken
    broth
1 tsp. lemon juice
1 tblsp. cornstarch
2 tblsp. water
2 tblsp. butter or regular margarine
¼ tsp. dried basil leaves
2 tblsp. diced pimientos

Slice cucumbers in half lengthwise; remove seeds. Cut into 1″ pieces. Combine cucumbers, celery, chicken broth and lemon juice in saucepan. Cover and bring to a boil. Cook over low heat for 10 minutes, or until vegetables are tender.

Combine cornstarch and water. Slowly stir into vegetable mixture. Add butter, basil and pimientos. Heat well. Makes 6 to 8 servings.

See Index for recipe

Lunch

*Easy Nachos**

Tossed Salad

Carrot Strips

Broiled Bananas Topped with Brown Sugar

Coffee   Milk

Dinner

Grilled Lamb Shoulder Steaks

Baked Potato Quarters   Cold Sliced Beets

Zingy Coleslaw

Butter Pecan Ice Cream with Toasted Chopped Pecans

Tea   Milk

Zingy Coleslaw

2 c. cider vinegar
2 c. sugar
1½ tsp. mustard seeds
1½ tsp. celery seeds
1 tsp. salt
½ tsp. ground turmeric
20 c. shredded cabbage
3 c. chopped onion
2 (4-oz.) jars pimientos, drained
   and chopped

Combine vinegar, sugar, mustard seeds, celery seeds, salt and turmeric in 2-qt. saucepan. Cook over medium heat, stirring occasionally, until mixture boils. Cool to room temperature.

Combine cabbage, onion and pimientos in very large bowl. Pour vinegar mixture over cabbage mixture, tossing to coat. Cover and chill salad overnight. Makes 25 (½ c.) servings.

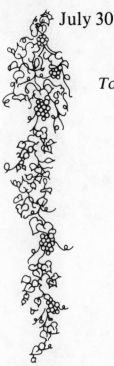

July 30

Lunch

Tomato Juice Spiked with Worcestershire Sauce

Vegetable-Egg Combo*

Crusty Rolls

Orange Sherbet with Mandarin Oranges

Tea   Milk

Dinner

Broiled Scallops

Fresh Spinach   Buttered Carrot Strips

Boston Lettuce Salad

Blueberry Chess Pie

Iced Coffee

Blueberry Chess Pie

1½ c. sugar
½ c. butter or regular margarine
⅛ tsp. salt
3 eggs
2 tblsp. flour
2 tblsp. cornstarch
1 tblsp. vinegar
1½ tsp. vanilla
1 pt. fresh blueberries
1 unbaked 9″ pie shell

Cream together sugar, butter and salt in large mixing bowl until light and fluffy. Beat in eggs, one at a time, beating well after each addition. Add flour, cornstarch, vinegar and vanilla; beat until smooth. Stir in blueberries. Pour into pie shell.

Bake in 400° oven 15 minutes. Reduce temperature to 300°. Bake 35 minutes or until firm in center. Cool on rack. Makes 6 to 8 servings.

*See Index for recipe

Lunch

*Garden Tomato Juice**
Fish Sticks on Toasted Buns
Assorted Sweet Pickles
Lime Gelatin with Custard Sauce
Tea   Milk

Dinner

Chinese Chicken with Vegetables
Parslied Rice   Spiced Crabapples
Watercress Salad
Plums Topped with Vanilla Yogurt and Orange Rind
Coffee   Milk

Chinese Chicken with Vegetables

2 whole chicken breasts, split,
   skinned and boned (about 12 oz.
   each)
3 tblsp. cooking oil
1 lb. fresh mushrooms, sliced
2 medium onions, sliced and
   separated into rings
1 c. diagonally sliced (¼″) celery
2 cloves garlic, minced
¾ tsp. ground ginger
½ c. water
¼ c. soy sauce
2 (6-oz.) pkg. frozen pea pods,
   partially thawed
2 tblsp. cornstarch
2 tblsp. water
Hot cooked rice
½ c. chopped walnuts

Freeze chicken 20 minutes to make cutting easier.

Cut and measure all ingredients before starting to cook.

Cut chicken breasts crosswise into 2x¼″ strips.

Cook chicken in hot oil in 12″ skillet over high heat 5 minutes, stirring constantly. Add mushrooms, onion, celery, garlic, ginger, ½ c. water and soy sauce. Cook until mixture comes to a boil. Reduce heat to low. Cover and simmer 5 minutes. Increase heat to medium. Stir in pea pods. Return to boil. Cover; cook 3 minutes more.

Dissolve cornstarch in 2 tblsp. water; stir into chicken mixture. Cook and stir until mixture thickens and boils, about 2 minutes. Serve over hot cooked rice. Garnish with chopped walnuts. Makes 6 servings.

August 1

Lunch

Cold Borscht

Salami and Muenster Cheese Sandwiches

Peachy Cheese Dessert

Iced Tea

Dinner

Quiche

Buttered Zucchini   Potato Sticks

Special Corn Meal Muffins*

Cantaloupe with Vanilla Ice Cream

Coffee   Milk

Peachy Cheese Dessert

1 c. large-curd creamed cottage
  cheese
1 (8-oz.) carton peach flavor yogurt

Combine cottage cheese and yogurt in bowl. Cover and chill at least 30 minutes. Makes 2 cups or 4 servings.

*See Index for recipe

Lunch

Skillet Salmon Chowder*
Cream Cheese and Olive Sandwiches
Sliced Nectarines   Gingersnaps
Tea   Milk

Dinner

Corned Beef Hash with Poached Eggs
Oven-Roasted Corn
Spinach Salad
Watermelon and Cantaloupe Kabobs
Ginger Ale Floats

Oven-Roasted Corn

12 ears sweet corn, including husks
Savory Butter (recipe follows)

Pull back husks on freshly picked sweet corn, leaving husks fastened to the stem end. Remove silk.

Spread kernels generously with Savory Butter. Pull husks around corn and tie a string snugly around ear, close to open end.

Lay corn ears in a large roasting pan. Bake in 350° oven 40 minutes. Remove strings; remove husks, if you wish, and serve. Makes 12 ears.

Savory Butter: Combine ¾ c. soft butter or margarine with 2½ tsp. salt. Season with 1½ tsp. dried oregano leaves and ½ tsp. garlic salt.

August 3

Lunch

Green Bean Soup*

Crusty Rolls

Frosted Lemon Cupcakes

Iced Tea

Dinner

Grilled Hamburgers with Herbed Tomato Sauce

Grilled Green Pepper and Onion Kabobs

Endive and Parsley Salad

Glazed Peach Pie

Coffee   Milk

Glazed Peach Pie

6 c. sliced pared peaches (6 large)
1 c. sugar
3 tblsp. cornstarch
¼ tsp. ground cinnamon
½ c. orange juice
1 baked 9″ pie shell
Whipped cream or whipped dessert
  topping

Mash enough sliced peaches to measure 1 c. Reserve remaining sliced peaches.

Combine sugar, cornstarch and cinnamon in saucepan. Stir in orange juice and mashed peaches. Cook over medium heat, stirring constantly, until mixture comes to a boil. Boil, stirring, 1 minute.

Spread half the glaze over bottom and sides of baked pie shell. Fill with reserved sliced peaches. Pour remaining glaze over fruit; spread to completely cover peaches. Cover and chill at least 3 hours. Serve topped with whipped cream. Makes 8 servings.

See Index for recipe

Lunch

Assorted Cold Cuts
Pineapple Muffins*
Vanilla Pudding with Sliced Bananas
Iced Tea

Dinner

Grilled Cheddar Cheese-Stuffed Frankfurters
Golden Carrots Supreme   *New Potatoes*
Chicory and Sliced Radish Salad
Honeydew Melon with Lemon Sherbet
Tea   *Milk*

Golden Carrots Supreme

¼ c. butter or regular margarine
¾ c. chicken broth
2 tsp. salt
⅛ tsp. pepper
2 tsp. sugar
5 c. diagonally sliced (¼") carrots
2 tsp. lemon juice
¼ c. chopped parsley

Add butter to boiling chicken broth in saucepan. Stir in salt, pepper, sugar and carrots. Simmer, covered, until carrots are tender-crisp, about 10 minutes.

Stir in lemon juice and parsley. Makes 6 servings.

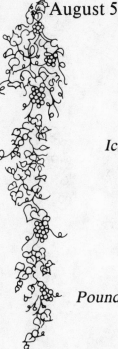

August 5

Lunch

Bologna and Pickle Relish Sandwiches

Marinated Cucumber Salad

Chocolate Cookies

Iced Coffee Topped with Coffee Ice Cream

Dinner

Gingered Chicken with Grapes*

Herbed Rice   Buttered Green Beans

Tossed Salad

Pound Cake with Blackberries and Whipped Cream

Coffee   Milk

Marinated Cucumber Salad

2 large cucumbers, pared and sliced
1 medium onion, sliced
½ c. cider vinegar
¼ c. salad oil
2 tblsp. brown sugar, firmly packed
½ tsp. seasoned salt
¼ tsp. celery seeds
⅛ tsp. pepper

Combine cucumbers and onion in a bowl.

Mix together vinegar, oil, brown sugar, seasoned salt, celery seeds and pepper in jar. Cover and shake until blended. Pour over cucumber mixture. Cover and chill several hours or overnight. Makes 4 to 6 servings.

*See Index for recipe

Summer

Refreshing summer salads, just right
for a picnic: Zingy Coleslaw (p. 145);
Sour Cream Potato Salad (p. 170) and
Kidney Bean Salad (p. 174).

Pretty party desserts in a bowl. From
top: Strawberry Cream Deluxe (p. 133);
Company Dessert Bowl (p. 143);
Jellied Fruit Compote (p. 128).

Build a dinner around Miniature Ham Loaves (p. 114), glazed with pineapple. Round out the meal with Potato Puffs (p. 139), Popovers (p. 122) and dessert.

For a really spectacular homemade dessert, try Rainbow Parfaits (p. 164): tangy sherbets and country vanilla ice cream layered together in frosty swirls.

Lunch

Mediterranean Salad
Corn Bread
Orange Gelatin Cubes with Blueberries
Tea   Milk

Dinner

Curried Shrimp on Rice Tossed with Chutney
Marinated Tomato Slices with Black Olives
Herbed Batter Bread*
Baked Custard Topped with Melted Brown Sugar
Iced Tea

Mediterranean Salad

2 small zucchini, thinly sliced
1 cucumber, pared and thinly sliced
1 tomato, chopped
1 c. shredded cabbage
¼ c. chopped green onion
¼ c. chopped parsley
1½ tsp. salt
½ c. plain yogurt
1 tblsp. lemon juice
¼ tsp. dried dill weed

Combine vegetables in bowl. Stir in salt. Cover and chill 1 hour; drain. Combine remaining ingredients. Stir into vegetables. Cover and chill at least 2 hours, or up to 24 hours. Makes 8 servings.

*See Index for recipe

Lunch

Scandinavian Egg Salad

Celery Sticks   Radishes

Gingerbread à la Mode

Chocolate Milk

Dinner

London Broil

Roasted Corn   Roasted Potatoes

Lettuce Wedges with Oil and Vinegar Dressing

Raspberry Parfait Pie*

Coffee   Milk

Scandinavian Egg Salad

8 hard-cooked eggs, chopped
1½ c. chopped celery
½ c. chopped dill pickle
¼ c. chopped onion
¼ c. drained capers
1 (2-oz.) can anchovy fillets, drained
    and chopped
½ c. mayonnaise or salad dressing
¼ tsp. dried dill weed
¼ tsp. salt
⅛ tsp. pepper

Combine all ingredients in bowl. Cover and chill. Use within 2 days. Serve on rye bread or toast. Makes 1 quart.

*See Index for recipe

Lunch

Cheddar Cheese Snack Bread*
Sliced Salami and Green Pepper Rings
White Cake with Mocha Icing
Iced Tea

Dinner

Cold Sliced London Broil
Corn-Tomato Skillet
Spinach and Endive Salad
Sliced Pears with Rum-Flavored Custard Sauce
Lemonade and Cranberry Juice

Corn-Tomato Skillet

1 green pepper, chopped
½ c. chopped onion
2 tblsp. butter or regular margarine
1 tsp. salt
1 tsp. sugar
⅛ tsp. pepper
4 tomatoes, peeled and sliced
2 c. corn, cut from cob

Cook green pepper and onion in butter in skillet until soft. Add remaining ingredients and cook until tomatoes and corn are tender, about 10 to 15 minutes. Makes 6 servings.

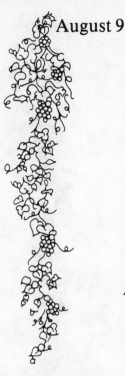

August 9

Lunch

Sloppy Joes on Toasted Buns

Carrot Curls   *Watermelon Pickles*

Coconut Squares*

Strawberry Floats

Dinner

Grilled Lamb Chops with Fresh Mint

Grandmother's Best Potato Salad

Buttered Peas with Small White Onions

Deep-Dish Cherry Pie

Iced Coffee

Grandmother's Best Potato Salad

1½ tblsp. sugar
1 tblsp. flour
1¼ tsp. salt
¼ tsp. celery seeds
⅛ tsp. pepper
1 tblsp. butter or regular margarine
1 tsp. prepared mustard
¾ c. milk
½ c. cider vinegar
2 eggs, separated
4 c. diced, cooked potatoes (about
   2 lb.)
½ c. sliced celery
2 tblsp. chopped onion
2 tblsp. sliced pimiento-stuffed olives

Combine sugar, flour, salt, celery seeds and pepper in small saucepan. Stir in butter, mustard, milk, vinegar and beaten egg yolks. Cook, stirring constantly, until mixture thickens. Cool slightly.

Beat egg whites until stiff. Fold into cooled mixture.

Combine potatoes, celery, onion and olives in a large bowl. Pour dressing over vegetables; toss gently. Cover and chill until serving time. Makes 4 to 6 servings.

*See Index for recipe

Lunch

Tomato Cheeseburgers*

Potato Chips   Black Olives

Fresh Cherries   Soft Molasses Cookies

Limeade

Dinner

Charcoal-Broiled Chicken

Summer Squash and Zucchini

Spinach Salad

Peaches in Cream

Iced Tea

Peaches in Cream

2 (3-oz.) pkg. peach flavor gelatin
2 c. boiling water
1 pt. vanilla ice cream
⅓ c. orange juice
2 c. chopped pared peaches
2 medium bananas, diced

Dissolve gelatin in boiling water in bowl. Immediately stir in ice cream and orange juice, stirring until ice cream is melted. Cover and chill until thick and syrupy.

Fold in peaches and bananas. Pour into lightly oiled 6-c. ring mold. Cover and chill until set. Makes 8 to 10 servings.

Lunch

Sliced Chicken Sandwiches with <u>Mock Russian Dressing</u>
Coleslaw
Chocolate-Frosted Brownies
Coffee   Milk

Dinner

Mustard Ham Loaf*
Buttered Noodles with Almonds   Green Beans
Escarole Salad with Oil and Vinegar Dressing
Grapes with Sour Cream and Brown Sugar
Iced Coffee Topped with Coffee Ice Cream and Nutmeg

Mock Russian Dressing

1 c. mayonnaise or salad dressing
1 (8-oz.) carton plain yogurt
1 (8-oz.) can tomato sauce
¼ c. finely chopped onion
¼ c. finely chopped celery
¼ c. finely chopped green pepper

Combine all ingredients in bowl; blend well. Cover and chill at least 2 hours. Makes 3 cups dressing.

*See Index for recipe

Lunch

Cold Cream of Chicken Soup Dusted with Chopped Chives

Fresh Apricots and Camembert Cheese

Wheat Crackers

Orange Cupcakes*

Iced Coffee

Dinner

Broiled Sausage Patties

Ratatouille   *Corn Niblets*

Chicory with Lettuce Salad

Hot Fudge Sundaes

Tea   Milk

Ratatouille

2 medium onions, sliced
2 cloves garlic, chopped
¼ c. olive oil
2 small zucchini, cut in ½" slices
3 tomatoes, peeled and diced
1 small eggplant, pared and cut in
  1" cubes
1 large green pepper, cut in strips
2 tblsp. chopped parsley
2 tsp. salt
½ tsp. dried basil leaves
⅛ tsp. pepper

Cook onions and garlic in hot olive oil in bottom of Dutch oven. Add remaining ingredients. Cover and cook 15 minutes. Uncover and continue cooking until vegetables are tender and juice is thickened. Stir occasionally. Makes 8 servings.

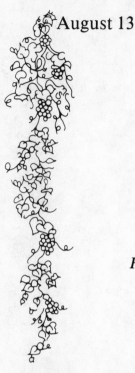

August 13

Lunch

Sliced Ham
Pickled Cucumbers with Dill
Bread Sticks
Watermelon Wedges
Iced Coffee

Dinner

Fresh Fruit Salad   Cottage Cheese
Sunflower Wheat Muffins*
Apple Pie à la Mode
Tea   Milk

Pickled Cucumbers with Dill

½ c. vinegar
¼ c. sugar
2 tblsp. water
½ tsp. salt
⅛ tsp. pepper
2 medium cucumbers
2 tblsp. chopped fresh dill

Combine vinegar, sugar, water, salt and pepper in saucepan. Bring to a boil. Remove from heat. Cool.

Remove strips of peel lengthwise from cucumbers, leaving alternate strips of peel intact. Cut cucumbers in thin slices and place in bowl. Add vinegar mixture. Sprinkle with dill. Toss gently. Cover and chill 2 to 3 hours. Makes 6 servings.

See Index for recipe

Lunch

Cantaloupe Cubes and Honeydew Balls in Lettuce Cups
Orange-Honey Dressing
Corn Muffins with Apple Jelly
Vanilla-Filled Cookies
Lemonade with Orange Sherbet

Dinner

Grilled Ground Beef Patties with Blue Cheese Dressing
Broiled Zucchini Halves
Potato Sticks
Tossed Salad
Lemon Sponge Pie*
Coffee   Milk

Orange-Honey Dressing

¼ tsp. paprika
½ tsp. dry mustard
1 tsp. salt
½ tsp. celery salt
½ c. honey
3 tblsp. lemon juice
2 tblsp. cider vinegar
3 tblsp. frozen orange juice
  concentrate, thawed
1 c. salad oil

Combine dry ingredients in 1-qt. mixer bowl. Add honey, lemon juice, vinegar and orange juice concentrate; blend well. Beating constantly, slowly add oil; beat 5 minutes longer at medium speed. (Or blend all ingredients in blender for 20 seconds at high speed.) Cover and chill. Shake before serving. Makes 1 pint.

*See Index for recipe

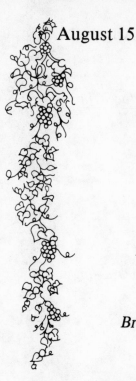

August 15

Lunch

Tomato Bouillon*
Egg Salad Sandwiches
Gingersnaps
Tea   Milk

Dinner

Broiled Scallop and Shrimp Kabobs
<u>*Golden Corn Fry*</u>
Sliced Tomatoes with Basil
Broiled Peach Halves with Brown Sugar
Iced Coffee with Cinnamon Sticks

Golden Corn Fry

2 tblsp. butter or regular margarine
3 c. corn, cut from cob
½ c. light cream
2 tblsp. chopped chives
1 clove garlic, minced
½ tsp. salt
⅛ tsp. pepper
¼ c. grated Parmesan cheese

Melt butter in skillet. Add remaining ingredients, except cheese. Cover and simmer until corn is tender, 10 to 15 minutes. Stir in grated Parmesan cheese. Makes 6 servings.

*See Index for recipe

Lunch

Roast Beef Sandwiches

Celery Sticks   Green Pepper Strips

Minted Fruit Cup*

Limeade and Club Soda

Dinner

Barbecued Lamb Shoulder Chops

Buttered Broccoli   Glazed Onions

Fruit and Rice Salad

Shortbread

Iced Coffee

Fruit and Rice Salad

2 c. cooked rice
1 (20-oz.) can crushed pineapple,
   drained
2 c. miniature marshmallows
½ c. sugar
3 medium apples, cored and cubed
½ c. sliced red maraschino cherries
1 c. heavy cream, whipped

Combine cooked rice, pineapple, marshmallows and sugar in bowl; toss gently to mix. Cover and chill at least 3 hours.

Fold in apples and cherries. Then fold in whipped cream. Cover and chill 1 more hour. Makes 18 (½-c.) servings.

August 17

Lunch

Special Chef's Salad*
Hot Garlic Bread
Baked Custard
Tea   Milk

Dinner

Roast Chicken
Whipped Potatoes   Julienne Green Beans
Orange and Radish Salad
Rainbow Parfaits
Iced Tea

Rainbow Parfaits

6 eggs
1 c. sugar
2 c. milk
2 tsp. vanilla
½ tsp. salt
2 c. heavy cream, whipped
1 pt. orange sherbet
1 pt. raspberry sherbet
1 pt. lime sherbet
Maraschino cherries (optional)

Beat eggs in bowl until thick and lemon colored.

Add sugar, milk, vanilla and salt; blend well. Fold into whipped cream. Pour into 2 cold refrigerator trays. Freeze until partially set.

Break into chunks in large, chilled bowl. Beat until light and fluffy, not melted.

Return to trays; freeze until firm.

To serve, spoon alternate layers of ice cream and sherbets into parfait glasses to form swirled effect. If you wish, garnish each parfait with a maraschino cherry. Makes 10 servings.

See Index for recipe

Lunch

Lemon-Spiked Tomato Juice

Cheese and Chive Omelets

Broiled Tomato Halves

Whole-Wheat Toast

Streusel Pear Pie*

Tea   Milk

Dinner

Chicken-Fried Rice

Buttered Fresh Spinach   Sautéed Spiced Crabapples

Escarole and Sliced Mushroom Salad

Watermelon

Iced Coffee

Chicken-Fried Rice

4 tblsp. cooking oil
3 eggs
1 c. chopped onion
½ c. chopped green pepper
2 cloves garlic, minced
2 c. cubed, cooked chicken (½ ")
2 tblsp. soy sauce
3 c. cold cooked rice
¼ c. sliced green onions

Heat 2 tblsp. of the oil in 12″ skillet over medium heat. Beat eggs slightly with rotary beater. Add eggs to skillet and cook 2 minutes, stirring frequently, or until set. Remove eggs from skillet and set aside.

Add remaining oil to skillet. Sauté onion, green pepper and garlic in oil 5 minutes, or until tender.

Stir in chicken, soy sauce and rice. Cover and reduce heat to low. Cook 5 minutes, stirring occasionally, or until heated. Cut egg into small pieces and stir into rice. Sprinkle with green onions. Makes 6 servings.

*See Index for recipe

August 19

Lunch

Jellied Consommé with Lime Wedges

Luncheon Meat-Cheese Sandwiches*

Fresh Plums and Nectarines

Vanilla Cookies

Iced Tea

Dinner

Cube Steaks with Sliced Mushrooms and Onions

Julienne Carrots   Broiled Tomato Wedges

Jellied Cucumber Mold with Dill Dressing

Baked Apples with Cinnamon and Cream

Iced Coffee

Jellied Cucumber Mold with Dill Dressing

2 c. shredded, pared cucumber and
   juice
1¼ tsp. salt
1 tsp. sugar
⅛ tsp. pepper
2 env. unflavored gelatin
½ c. cold water
2 c. dairy sour cream
2 tblsp. lemon juice
3 tblsp. chopped pimiento
3 tblsp. minced green onions
1 tblsp. minced fresh dill
Dill Dressing (recipe follows)

Combine cucumber and juice, salt, sugar and pepper in bowl; set aside.

Soften gelatin in cold water in small saucepan 5 minutes. Place over low heat; heat until gelatin is dissolved. Remove from heat.

Combine sour cream, lemon juice, pimiento, green onions and dill in bowl; mix well. Stir in cucumber mixture and gelatin. Pour into lightly oiled 5-c. mold. Cover; chill until set.

Unmold and serve with Dill Dressing. Makes 6 to 8 servings.

Dill Dressing: Combine ½ c. dairy sour cream, ½ c. mayonnaise; 2 tblsp. milk, 2 tblsp. minced fresh dill and ¼ tsp. salt; blend well. Cover and chill until serving time.

*See Index for recipe

Lunch

Cottage Cheese-Stuffed Apricot Halves

Cold Sliced Turkey

Banana-Strawberry Pudding*

Tea   Milk

Dinner

Corn Scramble

Endive, Radish and Onion Salad

Crusty Rolls

Peach Shortcake

Iced Tea

Corn Scramble

12 slices bacon, diced
2 c. corn, cut from cob
½ c. milk
12 eggs, slightly beaten
1½ tsp. salt
½ tsp. pepper
½ c. grated Cheddar cheese

Fry bacon in 10″ skillet until crisp. Remove bacon; drain on paper towels. Drain off fat from skillet and reserve. Return 3 tblsp. fat to skillet. Add corn and cook 8 to 10 minutes, or until golden brown. Stir in milk; simmer 2 or 3 minutes.

Add eggs, salt and pepper. Cook and stir until set. Serve topped with bacon and cheese. Makes 8 servings.

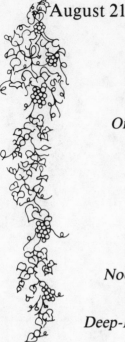

August 21

Lunch

Marinated Sausage Sandwiches
Spinach Salad
Orange Yogurt with Grated Orange Rind
Thin Vanilla Wafers
Tea   Milk

Dinner

Pan-Fried Liver and Onions
Noodles Parmesan*   Buttered Zucchini
Tossed Salad
Deep-Dish Plum Pie with Cinnamon Hard Sauce
Coffee   Milk

Marinated Sausage Sandwiches

½ c. vegetable oil
⅓ c. vinegar
1 tblsp. chopped parsley
½ tsp. salt
½ tsp. dried basil
¼ tsp. pepper
1½ lb. Polish sausage, cooked and
   cut in ¼″ slices
3 peeled tomatoes, thinly sliced
½ medium onion, sliced and
   separated in rings
12 slices Italian or rye bread

Combine oil, vinegar, parsley, salt, basil and pepper in 12x8x2″ (2-qt.) glass baking dish. Add sliced sausage, tomatoes and onion. Toss gently to coat sausage and vegetables. Cover and refrigerate at least 4 hours, stirring occasionally.

Drain marinade from sausage mixture. Arrange sausage mixture on bread slices and serve open-face style. Makes 12 sandwiches.

*See Index for recipe

Lunch

Tuna Salad with Hard-Cooked Egg Slices

Bread and Butter Finger Sandwiches

Vegetable Confetti Mold*

Eclairs

Tea   Milk

Dinner

Pork Kabobs

Broiled Eggplant

Tomato and Lettuce Salad

Watermelon Chunks in Lemonade

Cinnamon-Spiked Iced Coffee

Pork Kabobs

1 c. finely chopped onion
¼ c. cooking oil
1 c. ketchup
¼ c. brown sugar, firmly packed
¼ c. lemon juice
1 tsp. salt
¼ tsp. pepper
1½ lb. pork, cut in 1½" cubes
3 green peppers, cut in large pieces
½ lb. fresh mushrooms, sliced
3 medium tomatoes, quartered

Sauté onion in hot oil in saucepan until tender (do not brown). Stir in ketchup, brown sugar, lemon juice, salt and pepper. Simmer, uncovered, for 5 minutes. Cool slightly.

Pour sauce over pork cubes in a bowl. Cover. Refrigerate for 1 hour.

Place marinated pork cubes on broiler pan. Broil 7" from source of heat for 6 minutes. Turn and brush with sauce. Broil for 6 more minutes.

Meanwhile, simmer green pepper with water in small saucepan until tender.

Thread meat, green pepper, mushrooms and tomatoes on skewers. Brush with sauce. Broil for 5 to 6 minutes. Brush with sauce and broil for 5 more minutes, or until meat is well browned. Makes 6 servings.

Lunch

Broiled Hamburgers with Bacon on Toasted Buns

Romaine and Sliced Onion Salad

Individual Schaum Tortes*

Iced Coffee

Dinner

Sliced Bologna

Sour Cream Potato Salad

Green Pepper Strips

Riced Cherry Gelatin with Pineapple Cubes

Cinnamon-Spiced Iced Tea

Sour Cream Potato Salad

2½ lb. new potatoes
½ tsp. salt
½ c. bottled Italian salad dressing
4 hard-cooked eggs
¾ c. thinly sliced celery
⅔ c. sliced green onions
1½ c. mayonnaise
½ c. dairy sour cream
1½ tsp. prepared mustard
¾ tsp. salt
½ tsp. prepared horseradish
¼ tsp. celery seeds
⅛ tsp. pepper
⅔ c. chopped, pared cucumber
1 tblsp. sliced green onion tops

Cook potatoes in 1″ boiling water with ½ tsp. salt in Dutch oven 30 minutes, or until tender. Drain; cool 10 minutes. Pare potatoes and slice into bowl. Pour Italian dressing over potatoes. Cover and chill 2 hours.

Remove egg yolks from egg whites; set aside. Chop egg whites. Toss egg whites, celery and green onions with potatoes. Press egg yolks through sieve. Reserve 2 tblsp. egg yolk. Mix together remaining egg yolks, mayonnaise, sour cream, mustard, salt, horseradish, celery seeds and pepper in bowl. Pour mayonnaise mixture over potatoes. Toss lightly. Cover and chill at least 2 hours.

Before serving, toss cucumbers with potato salad. Garnish with remaining sieved egg yolk and green onion tops. Makes 16 (½-c.) servings.

See Index for recipe

Lunch

Sliced Egg and Pickle Sandwiches
Potato Chips
Blueberry Sicles
Pineapple Juice Spritzer

Dinner

Spaghetti and Meatballs
Arizona Green Salad*
Toasted French Bread
Cantaloupe Halves Filled with Grapes
Iced Coffee

Blueberry Sicles

2 c. fresh blueberries or 1 (9-oz.) carton frozen blueberries
1 (8-oz.) carton blueberry yogurt

Combine blueberries and yogurt in blender. Cover and whirl until smooth. Pour into 6 (3½-oz.) paper drinking cups. Partially freeze; insert wooden sticks. Freeze firm. To eat, remove paper cup. Makes 6.

August 25

Lunch

Peanut Butter and Chopped Bacon Sandwiches

Carrot and Celery Curls

Brown-Rim Butter Cookies*

. Chocolate Milkshakes

Dinner

Baked Ham

Sautéed Summer Squash   Buttered Peas

Lettuce and Radish Salad

Double Lime Supreme

Tea   Milk

Double Lime Supreme

1 (3-oz.) pkg. lime flavor gelatin
¼ tsp. salt
3 eggs, separated
½ c. lime juice
½ tsp. grated lime rind
⅓ c. water
¼ tsp. cream of tartar
⅓ c. sugar
1 c. heavy cream, whipped
Sweetened whipped cream
Toasted coconut

Combine gelatin, salt, egg yolks, lime juice, lime rind and water in small saucepan; mix well. Cook over medium heat, stirring constantly, until mixture comes to a boil. Remove from heat. Pour into bowl. Cover and chill until thick and syrupy.

Beat egg whites until foamy. Add cream of tartar. Gradually add sugar, beating until stiff glossy peaks form. Fold gelatin mixture into egg whites and then fold in whipped cream. Pour into 1½-qt. serving bowl. Cover and chill until set. Decorate with puffs of whipped cream and sprinkle with coconut just before serving. Makes 12 servings.

See Index for recipe

Lunch

Black Bean Soup
Midwestern Turkey-Cheese Sandwiches*
Raspberry Yogurt
Tea   Milk

Dinner

Swiss Steak
Parslied Rice   Buttered Lima Beans
Pickled Beets
Deep-Dish Plum Pie
Iced Coffee

Deep-Dish Plum Pie

1 c. sugar
¼ c. flour
¼ tsp. ground cinnamon
2½ lb. prune plums, halved and
 pitted
2 tblsp. butter or regular margarine
Patty shell for 1-crust 9″ pie
Milk
1 tsp. sugar

Combine 1 c. sugar, flour and cinnamon. Stir into plums. Turn into 8″ square pan. Dot with butter.

Roll patty shell into a 9″ square. Place over plums. Turn edges under and seal to edge of pan. Cut steam vents. Brush top with milk.

Bake in 425° oven 45 to 50 minutes, or until golden brown. Sprinkle top with 1 tsp. sugar. Serve warm or cold. Makes 6 servings.

August 27

Lunch

Sloppy Joes on Toasted French Bread
Tossed Salad
Glazed Peach Pie*
Root Beer Floats

Dinner

Barbecued Chicken Wings
Kidney Bean Salad
Cherry Tomatoes and Cucumber Strips
Tapioca Pudding   Lemon Cookies
Coffee   Milk

Kidney Bean Salad

5 (15-oz.) cans red kidney beans,
   drained
1 c. chopped onion
½ c. chopped celery
⅓ c. sweet pickle relish
½ c. cider vinegar
½ c. sugar
1 egg, slightly beaten
2 tsp. dry mustard

Combine kidney beans, onion, celery, and pickle relish in bowl.

Combine vinegar, sugar, egg and mustard in small saucepan. Cook over low heat, stirring constantly, 7 minutes, or until mixture thickens.

Pour vinegar mixture over vegetables, tossing gently to coat. Cover and chill in refrigerator at least 6 hours. Makes 16 (½-c.) servings.

*See Index for recipe

Lunch

Cold Sliced Ham

Spinach Salad

Bread Sticks

Poppy Seed Coffee Cake*

Tea   Milk

Dinner

Fish Piquant

Baby Carrots with Chives   New Potatoes

Coleslaw

Honeydew Melon Wedges

Iced Tea

Fish Piquant

2 lb. frozen fish fillets (haddock, flounder or perch)
½ c. French dressing
2 tblsp. butter or regular margarine
1 small onion, chopped

Thaw fish as directed on package.
Dip pieces in French dressing.

Heat butter in skillet. Add fish; sprinkle onion over top.

Cook over medium heat 7 to 8 minutes on each side, turning once. Makes 6 servings.

Lunch

Grilled Bacon and Cheese Sandwiches

Watermelon Pickles

Apricot Snowdrifts*

Vanilla Milkshakes

Dinner

Chinese Pepper Steak

Grilled Whole Small Zucchini

Sautéed Cherry Tomatoes and Onions

Sliced Oranges and Bananas

Iced Tea

Chinese Pepper Steak

1 lb. beef chuck, cut in 3x1″ strips
1 tsp. salt
¼ c. cooking oil
2 tblsp. soy sauce
1 clove garlic, minced
½ c. water
1 c. green pepper strips
1 c. sliced onion
½ c. sliced celery
2 tomatoes, cut in 8 wedges
1 tblsp. cornstarch
1 c. water
Hot cooked rice

Season meat with salt. Brown meat in hot oil in large skillet. Add soy sauce, garlic and ½ c. water. Bring to a boil; reduce heat. Cover. Simmer for 45 minutes, or until tender.

Add green pepper, onion and celery. Cover. Simmer for 10 minutes. Add tomatoes.

Combine cornstarch and 1 c. water. Slowly stir into mixture. Bring to a boil; boil for 1 minute. Serve on rice. Makes 6 servings.

*See Index for recipe

Lunch

Cold Sliced Salami and Sliced Cucumbers

Toasted Corn Muffins

Almond Rice Pudding*

Tea   Milk

Dinner

Lobster Salad

Peas with Pimientos   Tomato Wedges

<u>*Luscious Blueberry Cake*</u>

Iced Coffee

Luscious Blueberry Cake

3 c. sifted flour
2 tsp. baking powder
½ tsp. salt
1 c. shortening
1½ c. sugar
4 eggs, separated
2 tsp. vanilla
⅔ c. milk
½ c. sugar
3 c. blueberries, fresh, frozen or
    canned and drained
1 tblsp. flour
Confectioners' sugar

Sift together 3 c. flour, baking powder and salt.

Cream together shortening and 1½ c. sugar in bowl until light and fluffy. Beat in egg yolks and vanilla.

Add dry ingredients alternately with milk to creamed mixture, beating well after each addition.

Beat egg whites until stiff. Gradually beat in ½ c. sugar. Fold into batter. Combine blueberries and 1 tblsp. flour; fold into batter. Pour batter into greased 13x9x2″ cake pan.

Bake in 350° oven 50 minutes, or until cake tests done. Cool in pan on rack. Sprinkle with confectioners' sugar. Makes 16 servings.

August 31

Lunch

Jellied Beef Consommé

Sliced Egg and Anchovy Salad

Italian Tomato Dressing

Bread Sticks

Fresh Plums   Gingersnaps

Tea   Milk

Dinner

Grilled Lamb and Onion Kabobs

Basque Potatoes*

Buttered Carrots

Chicory and Green Pepper Salad

Watermelon Wedges

Iced Coffee

Italian Tomato Dressing

½ c. salad oil
⅓ c. cider vinegar
1 (8-oz.) can tomato sauce
½ tsp. salt
2 tblsp. sugar
1 tsp. dry mustard
1 tsp. paprika
½ tsp. dried oregano leaves
2 tsp. Worcestershire sauce
½ clove garlic, finely chopped
2 tsp. finely chopped onion
1 tblsp. finely chopped celery
2 tblsp. salad dressing

Combine all ingredients in 1-qt. mixing bowl. Beat at medium speed 2 minutes. (Or blend in blender for 15 seconds on high speed.) Cover and chill. Makes 1 pint.

*See Index for recipe

# September 1

Lunch

Cold Tomato Juice

Swiss Cheese and Salami

Mile-High Biscuits*

Raspberry Gelatin Cubes and Vanilla Yogurt

Iced Coffee

Dinner

Golden Broiled Chicken

Corn on the Cob

Sautéed Zucchini Strips

Tossed Salad

Peach Shortcake

Iced Tea

Golden Broiled Chicken

1 c. cider vinegar
¾ c. cooking oil
4½ tsp. salt
1 tblsp. poultry seasoning
½ tsp. white pepper
1 egg, beaten
½ c. sliced onion
2 (3-lb.) broiler-fryers, quartered

Combine vinegar, oil, salt, poultry seasoning, pepper, egg and onion in 2-qt. saucepan. Stirring constantly, bring mixture to a boil. Pour over chicken and let stand at room temperature for 1 hour.

Place chicken skin side down on broiler pan. Place pan in broiler, 7" to 9" from heat. Broil for 30 minutes, basting frequently with marinade. Turn chicken over; baste. Broil 15 minutes more, or until chicken is tender and golden. Makes 8 servings.

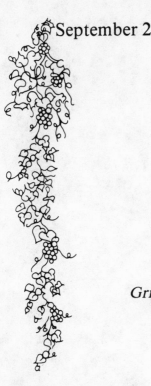

September 2

Lunch

Corned Beef Sandwiches

Carrot and Celery Curls

Nectarines

Oliebollen*

Iced Tea

Dinner

Grilled Sirloin Steak

Grilled Potatoes   Brussels Sprouts

Watercress Salad

Luscious Lime Pie

Iced Coffee

Luscious Lime Pie

1⅓ c. graham cracker crumbs
¼ c. sugar
¼ c. melted butter or regular
  margarine
1 env. unflavored gelatin
¾ c. cold water
1 (14-oz.) can sweetened condensed
  milk
½ c. fresh lime juice
1 tsp. grated lime rind
10 drops green food coloring
4 drops yellow food coloring

Combine graham cracker crumbs, sugar and butter in bowl; mix well. Press crumb mixture into 9″ pie plate.

Bake in 375° oven 7 minutes, or until golden brown. Cool on rack.

Soften gelatin in cold water in small saucepan. Stir over low heat until gelatin is dissolved.

Combine gelatin, sweetened condensed milk, lime juice, lime rind, green and yellow food coloring in bowl; mix well. Pour into graham cracker crust. Cover and chill until set. Makes 6 to 8 servings.

See Index for recipe

Lunch

Grilled Muenster Cheese and Oregano Sandwiches
Raw Vegetable Strips
Custard-Filled Cream Puffs
Super Cyder Float*

Dinner

Veal Patties

Whipped Potatoes   *Buttered Green Beans*
Marinated Tomato Wedges
Blackberry Pie with Cinnamon Whipped Cream
Iced Coffee

Veal Patties

1½ lb. ground veal
½ c. melted fat (chicken fat if
  available)
½ tsp. lemon juice
Salt
Pepper
1 egg, beaten
2 tblsp. water
1 c. cracker crumbs

Combine veal, fat, lemon juice, salt and pepper. Shape into 6 patties.

Mix egg with water.

Dip patties in egg mixture and then into cracker crumbs. Brown on both sides in hot fat. Cook about 15 minutes. Makes 6 servings.

September 4

Lunch

Chicken Noodle Soup
Tuna Club Sandwiches
Butterscotch Pudding with Toasted Almonds
Iced Chocolate Milk

Dinner

Broiled Cube Steaks with Mushrooms
Minted Carrots and Peas*
Marinated Cucumbers and Onions
Honeydew Melon with Lemon Sherbet
Coffee   Milk

Tuna Club Sandwiches

2 cucumbers, pared and thinly sliced
2 tblsp. salt
2 tblsp. vinegar
2 tblsp. salad oil
⅛ tsp. pepper
⅛ tsp. dried dill weed
2 (7-oz.) cans tuna, drained and
  flaked
1 c. chopped celery
½ c. chopped parsley
½ c. mayonnaise or salad dressing
18 slices toast
Butter or regular margarine
6 hard-cooked eggs, sliced

Combine cucumbers and salt. Set aside in strainer to drain 1 hour; rinse with cold water. Place drained cucumbers in bowl. Stir in vinegar, oil, pepper and dill weed. Marinate at least 30 minutes.

Combine tuna, celery, parsley and mayonnaise in bowl.

Spread 6 slices toast with butter. Spread each with ½ c. tuna mixture. Top each with a toast slice, then with egg and drained cucumber slices.

Butter remaining 6 toast slices; place over cucumber slices, buttered side down. Cut sandwiches diagonally in halves. Hold layers together with wooden pick. Makes 6 servings.

Lunch

Guacamole Burgers
Carrot Curls   Radishes
Melon Balls in Orange Juice
Iced Tea

Dinner

Barbecued Lamb Kabobs
New Potatoes with Lemon Butter*
Buttered Zucchini Strips
Tomato and Chicory Salad
Lemon Meringue Pie
Tea   Milk

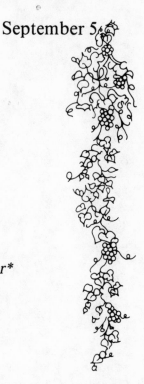

Guacamole Burgers

1 medium avocado
1 tblsp. lemon juice
1 tblsp. finely chopped onion
½ tsp. salt
¼ tsp. bottled hot pepper sauce
1½ lb. ground beef
Salt
Pepper
6 hamburger buns, split and toasted
6 slices tomato
1 c. shredded lettuce

Mash avocado in small bowl. Stir in lemon juice, onion, ½ tsp. salt and hot pepper sauce.

Form ground beef into 6 patties. Pan-broil on both sides or broil in oven. Sprinkle with salt and pepper to taste. Place each patty on bun half. Top with tomato slice, avocado mixture, lettuce and bun top. Makes 6 servings.

*See Index for recipe

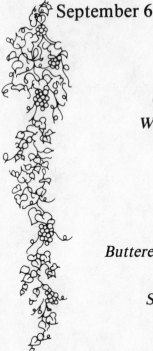

Lunch

Cottage Cheese Sandwiches

Celery and Green Pepper Strips

Watermelon Cubes and Blueberries

Iced Coffee

Dinner

Grated Vegetable Meat Loaf*

Buttered Noodles   Broiled Tomato Halves

Romaine and Radish Salad

Sliced Fresh Apricots and Grapes

Coffee   Milk

Cottage Cheese Sandwiches

1½ c. small-curd creamed cottage cheese (12 oz.)
½ c. shredded carrots
¼ c. finely chopped celery
2 tblsp. chopped green onion
¼ tsp. salt
¼ tsp. dried dill weed
6 slices buttered whole-wheat toast
Thin tomato slices (optional)

Combine cottage cheese, carrots, celery, onion, salt and dill weed. Cover and store in refrigerator at least 30 minutes before using. Chilled mixture will keep a couple of days.

When ready to make sandwich, lay tomato slice, if desired, on toast slice. Top with ⅓ c. cottage cheese mixture. Makes 6 open-face sandwiches.

*See Index for recipe

Lunch

Grilled Salami Sandwiches

Watermelon Pickles

Blackberries and Diced Peaches

Lemon Slices

Ginger Ale and Vanilla Ice Cream Floats

Dinner

Beef Chuck Roast Supreme*

Roasted Potato Wedges   Buttered Lima Beans

Boston Lettuce Salad

Banana Cream Pie

Coffee   Milk

Lemon Slices

2 c. sifted flour
½ c. sifted confectioners' sugar
1 c. butter or regular margarine
4 eggs
2 c. sugar
½ tsp. salt
⅓ c. lemon juice
1 tsp. grated lemon rind
¼ c. unsifted flour
2 tsp. confectioners' sugar
Confectioners' sugar

Combine 2 c. flour and ½ c. confectioners' sugar in a bowl. Cut in butter until mixture is crumbly. Press mixture into ungreased 13x9x2" baking pan.

Bake in 350° oven 25 minutes, or until golden.

Beat eggs until thick and lemon-colored. Slowly beat in sugar, salt, lemon juice and lemon rind. Combine ¼ c. flour and 2 tsp. confectioners' sugar. Stir into egg mixture. Pour over baked crust. Return to oven and bake 25 minutes, or until brown.

Cool in pan on rack. Cut into 2x1" bars. Roll bars in confectioners' sugar. Makes about 4 dozen.

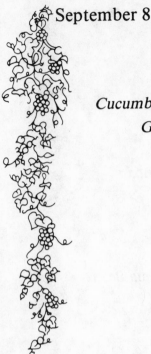

September 8

Lunch

Cream of Potato Soup*

Cucumber, Tomato and Watercress Sandwiches

Green Grapes, Dates and Apricots

Pound Cake Fingers

Iced Tea

Dinner

Cheese Soufflé

Sweet-Sour Green Beans

Endive and Sliced Onion Salad

Apple Streudel

Iced Coffee

Sweet-Sour Green Beans

3 lb. green beans
3 onions, thinly sliced and separated
   into rings
1⅓ c. vinegar
1⅔ c. sugar
⅔ c. water
3 tblsp. salad oil
1½ tsp. salt
½ tsp. pepper

Cut off tips of beans; leave whole. Cook in boiling salted water until tender. Drain.

Combine beans and onion rings in a large bowl. Stir together remaining ingredients. Pour over beans. Cover and refrigerate at least 24 hours, stirring occasionally. Makes about 3½ quarts (14 cups).

*See Index for recipe

Lunch

Liverwurst and Onion Sandwiches

Lettuce Wedges with <u>Creamy Thousand Island Dressing</u>

Brownies

Iced Tea

Dinner

Chicken Breasts Cordon Bleu*

Broiled Mushroom Caps   Buttered Carrot Strips

Watercress and Avocado Salad

Banana Ice Cream with Sliced Bananas

Iced Coffee

Creamy Thousand Island Dressing

½ c. salad dressing
½ c. chili sauce
1 tsp. Worcestershire sauce
Dash of Tabasco sauce
½ tsp. salt
¼ tsp. paprika
2 tblsp. chopped celery
2 tblsp. pickle relish
2 tblsp. chopped pimiento-stuffed
  olives
1 tsp. minced onion
1 hard-cooked egg, chopped
½ c. dairy sour cream

Combine salad dressing, chili sauce, Worcestershire, Tabasco, salt and paprika in 1-qt. bowl. Stir in celery, relish, olives, onion and egg; mix well. Fold in sour cream. Cover and chill. Makes 1 pint.

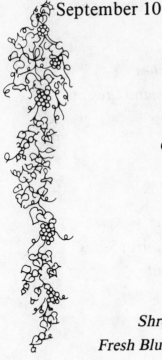

Lunch

Meat Loaf Sandwiches

Eggs in Vinaigrette Sauce

Carrot Curls

Chocolate-Frosted Cupcakes

Coffee   Milk

Dinner

Cold Sliced Chuck Roast

Buttered Diced Beets

Corn 'n' Celery Sauté*

Shredded Lettuce and Radish Salad

Fresh Blueberry and Vanilla Ice Cream Parfaits

Iced Tea

Eggs in Vinaigrette Sauce

3 tblsp. salad oil
1½ tblsp. vinegar
2 tsp. pickle relish
2 tsp. chopped parsley
2 tsp. finely chopped onion
½ tsp. garlic salt
⅛ tsp. pepper
6 hard-cooked eggs, peeled and
  halved

Combine salad oil, vinegar, pickle relish, parsley, onion, garlic salt and pepper. Cover and chill at least 1 hour. Shake well to mix. Spoon over hard-cooked egg halves. Makes 6 servings.

Lunch

Beef Bouillon on the Rocks with Lime Slices

Salmon Mousse with Marinated Cucumbers*

Cantaloupe Wedges

Raisin Cookies

Tea   Milk

Dinner

Sweet-and-Sour Pork Chops

Hot Fluffy Rice   Buttered Spinach

Lettuce Wedges with Grated Carrot Salad

Rice Pudding with Whipped Cream and Nutmeg

Coffee   Milk

Sweet-and-Sour Pork Chops

6 pork chops
Salt and pepper
1 (4-oz.) can mushrooms
2 medium onions, sliced
½ c. chopped green pepper
2 tblsp. vinegar
2 tblsp. soy sauce
2 tblsp. molasses
2 tsp. cornstarch
2 tblsp. water

Sprinkle pork chops with salt and pepper. Brown on both sides in a large skillet.

Drain mushrooms, reserving liquid. Add enough water to liquid to make 1 c. Arrange onions, green pepper and mushrooms on top of chops. Combine vinegar, soy sauce, molasses and reserved liquids; pour over vegetables. Bring to a boil; reduce heat and simmer, covered, for 1 hour, or until tender.

Remove chops. Combine cornstarch with water. Gradually add to boiling liquid, stirring constantly. Boil 1 minute. Serve over chops. Makes 6 servings.

Lunch

Sliced Egg and Chopped Green Pepper Sandwiches
Radishes   Celery Sticks
Frosted Cranberry Squares*
Limeade and Apricot Nectar

Dinner

Buttermilk Stroganoff
Buttered Summer Squash   Broccoli Spears
Escarole and Iceberg Lettuce Salad
Angel Food Cake with Crushed Strawberries
Iced Tea

Buttermilk Stroganoff

1 lb. ground beef
1 c. chopped onion
6 oz. noodles
1¾ c. buttermilk
¼ c. flour
¾ tsp. salt
⅛ tsp. pepper
¼ c. ketchup
2 tsp. Worcestershire sauce
1 (4-oz.) can chopped mushrooms
1 c. shredded process cheese spread
    (Velveeta, 4 oz.)

Cook ground beef and onion in skillet until beef is browned.

Meanwhile, cook noodles as package directs; drain.

Blend part of buttermilk into flour to make a smooth paste, then stir in remaining buttermilk. Add salt, pepper, ketchup, Worcestershire sauce and mushrooms.

Combine beef mixture, noodles and sauce. Spoon into 2-qt. casserole. Bake in 350° oven 30 minutes. Remove from oven and sprinkle with cheese. Return to oven about 3 minutes, long enough to melt cheese. Makes 6 servings.

*See Index for recipe

Lunch

*Famous Clam Chowder**

Wheat Crackers   *Cheddar Cheese Strips*

Vanilla Yogurt with Brown Sugar and Cinnamon

Tea   *Milk*

Dinner

Grilled Knockwurst

Coleslaw in Green Pepper Cups

Patio-Baked Beans

Custard Pie with Sliced Peaches

Iced Coffee

Patio-Baked Beans

5 strips bacon
½ c. chopped onion
⅓ c. brown sugar, firmly packed
1 tblsp. vinegar
¼ c. water
1 tsp. dry mustard
1 tsp. instant coffee powder
2 (1-lb. 12-oz.) cans pork and beans
  in tomato sauce

Fry bacon until almost crisp in 10″ skillet. Remove and drain on paper towels. Cut into 1″ pieces.

Sauté onion in 2 tblsp. bacon fat until tender (do not brown). Add brown sugar, vinegar, water, mustard, coffee powder, pork and beans and bacon. Bring to a boil. Turn into 2-qt. casserole.

Bake in 350° oven 1 hour. Makes 8 servings.

*See Index for recipe

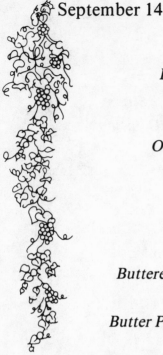

Lunch

Hot Corned Beef Sandwiches

Watermelon Pickles

Tomato Aspic

Oatmeal Refrigerator Cookies*

Iced Tea

Dinner

Veal in Sour Cream

Buttered Noodles   Whole Green Beans

Tossed Salad

Butter Pecan Ice Cream with Caramel Sauce

Coffee   Tea

Veal in Sour Cream

1½ lb. cubed veal steaks, cut in
  serving-size pieces
2 tblsp. butter or regular margarine
1 (10-oz.) can mushroom gravy
½ c. water
½ c. dairy sour cream
Parsley

Cook veal in hot butter in skillet over medium heat about 5 minutes on each side, or until tender. Lift to warm platter and keep warm.

Pour butter from skillet. Add gravy and water to skillet. Cook, stirring constantly, until mixture comes to a boil.

Remove from heat; stir in sour cream. Pour over veal. Garnish with parsley. Makes 6 servings.

*See Index for recipe

Lunch

Hot Dog Curls

Potato Salad   Black Olives

Chocolate Milkshakes

Dinner

Teriyaki Steak*

Mixed Vegetables   Broiled Eggplant Slices

Romaine Salad with Lemon Juice and Oil

Compote of Kumquats and Pineapple Chunks

Iced Tea

Hot Dog Curls

½ c. chopped onion
½ c. chopped green pepper
½ c. chopped celery
1 tblsp. butter or regular margarine
1 lb. frankfurters, sliced lengthwise
1 tblsp. flour
1 (8-oz.) can tomato sauce
½ c. water
6 frankfurter buns or rolls, toasted

Sauté onion, green pepper and celery in butter in skillet until tender (do not brown).

Add frankfurters and fry until they curl up and are deep red in color. Stir in flour and cook until slightly brown. Add tomato sauce and water. Cover and simmer for 10 minutes.

Serve spooned over frankfurter buns. Makes 6 servings.

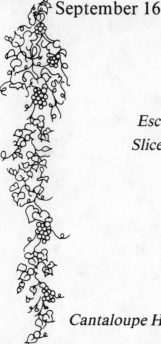

September 16

Lunch

Mexican Cheeseburgers

Refried Beans

Escarole and Sliced Avocado Salad

Sliced Oranges with Powdered Sugar

Tea   Milk

Dinner

Broiled Lamb Steaks

Creamed Potatoes

Herbed Spinach*

Cantaloupe Halves Filled with Grapes and Blackberries

Iced Tea

Mexican Cheeseburgers

1 lb. ground beef
½ c. chopped onion
½ c. chopped green pepper
1 (8-oz.) can tomato sauce
1 tsp. salt
½ tsp. chili powder
¼ tsp. cumin
8 slices process American cheese
8 tortillas

In skillet, cook ground beef with onion and green pepper until meat is browned. Add tomato sauce, salt, chili powder and cumin. Cook and stir until meat absorbs most of sauce. Use immediately or cool, cover and refrigerate.

Reheat beef mixture when ready to serve. For each cheeseburger, place a slice of cheese on a tortilla. Top with hot beef mixture and roll up. Makes 8 servings.

*See Index for recipe

Lunch

Tuna Carrot Salad*
Cream Cheese and Chopped Parsley Sandwiches
Watermelon Wedges
Lemonade

Dinner

Chicken Supreme
Corn on the Cob   Sautéed Sliced Zucchini
Lettuce Wedges with Oil and Vinegar Dressing
Warm Spice Cake Topped with Softened Vanilla Ice Cream
Iced Coffee

Chicken Supreme

1 c. soft bread crumbs
½ c. grated Parmesan cheese
4 whole chicken breasts, split
  (about 12 oz. each)
1 c. butter or regular margarine,
  melted

Combine bread crumbs and Parmesan cheese. Dip chicken breasts in butter, then roll in crumb mixture. Arrange chicken breasts in 15½x10½x1″ jelly roll pan. Pour remaining butter over chicken.

Bake in 350° oven 30 minutes. Baste with pan drippings. Bake 30 minutes more, or until chicken is tender. Makes 8 servings.

September 18

Lunch

Cheese and Chive Omelets

<u>*Skillet Corn Bread*</u>

Sliced Tomatoes with Basil

Chocolate Cake

Iced Tea

Dinner

Grilled Halibut Steaks*

Grilled Potato Slices   Buttered Beets

Chicory and Grapefruit Salad

Coffee Ice Cream Topped with Toasted Almonds

Iced Coffee

Skillet Corn Bread

½ lb. bacon
1 c. sifted flour
1 c. yellow corn meal
3 tblsp. sugar
3 tsp. baking powder
1 tsp. baking soda
1 tsp. salt
2 eggs
1 c. buttermilk

Fry bacon in 10″ heavy skillet with heat-proof handle until crisp. Remove bacon and drain on paper towels. Crumble bacon. Reserve ¼ c. bacon drippings. Do not wash skillet.

Sift together flour, corn meal, sugar, baking powder, baking soda and salt into a mixing bowl.

Combine eggs, buttermilk and ¼ c. bacon drippings in another bowl. Beat with rotary beater until well blended. Add to dry ingredients. Stir just until moistened. Stir in crumbled bacon. Pour batter into same skillet.

Bake in 425° oven 20 minutes, or until cake tester or wooden pick inserted in center comes out clean. Cut in wedges. Serve warm. Makes 10 servings.

    *See Index for recipe

Lunch

Ham and Tomato Sandwiches
Double Dairy Salad*
Blueberry Tarts
Iced Coffee

Dinner

Spaghetti with Meat Sauce
Garlic French Bread
Escarole and Sliced Orange Salad
Watermelon Wedges
Peanut Butter Cookies
Coffee   Milk

Peanut Butter Cookies

2½ c. sifted flour
2 tsp. baking soda
1 c. butter or regular margarine
1 c. peanut butter
1 c. sugar
1 c. brown sugar, packed
2 eggs
2 tsp. vanilla
Flour

Sift together 2½ c. flour and baking soda; set aside.

Cream together butter, peanut butter, sugar and brown sugar in bowl until light and fluffy, using electric mixer at medium speed. Add eggs, one at a time, beating well after each addition. Blend in vanilla.

Gradually stir dry ingredients into creamed mixture, blending well. Shape dough into 1″ balls. Place balls, about 2″ apart, on greased baking sheets. Flatten each with a floured fork, making a crisscross pattern.

Bake in 350° oven 10 to 12 minutes, or until golden brown. Remove from baking sheets; cool on racks. Makes about 8½ dozen.

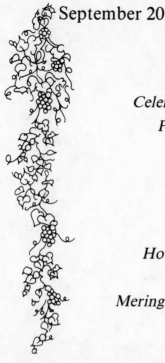

September 20

Lunch

Barbecued Beef Buns
Celery Strips   Green Pepper Rings
Fresh Blackberries and Cream
Tea   Milk

Dinner

Party Crab Bake*
Hot Fluffy Rice   Buttered Peas
Cucumber Salad
Meringue Shells Filled with Sliced Peaches
Iced Coffee

Barbecued Beef Buns

1½ lb. ground beef
1 c. chopped onion
1½ c. ketchup
1 c. water
¼ c. sugar
¼ c. Worcestershire sauce
2 tblsp. cider vinegar
2 tblsp. lemon juice
4 tsp. prepared mustard
2 tsp. salt
¼ tsp. pepper
⅛ tsp. cayenne pepper
12 hamburger buns or rolls

Brown ground beef in large skillet until meat turns color. Add onion and cook until meat is well browned.

Add ketchup, water, sugar, Worcestershire sauce, vinegar, lemon juice, mustard, salt, pepper and cayenne pepper. Bring mixture to a boil; reduce heat and simmer for 30 minutes, stirring occasionally. Skim off excess fat.

Spoon over hamburger buns. Makes about 4 cups or 12 servings.

*See Index for recipe

Breakfast

Honeydew Melon with Lime

Blintzes with Pineapple Sauce

Sausage Links

Coffee   Milk

Pineapple Sauce

3 tblsp. butter or regular margarine
1 (8¼-oz.) can crushed pineapple
2 tblsp. brown sugar
⅛ tsp. nutmeg

Melt butter in small saucepan. Add undrained crushed pineapple, brown sugar and nutmeg. Heat about 5 minutes, or until sauce cooks down a little. Makes about 1 cup.

Brunch

Cranberry and Orange Juice Topped with Lemon Sherbet

Potato-Bacon Omelet

Broiled Tomato Halves

Brioches   Lime Marmalade

Coffee   Milk

Potato-Bacon Omelet

6 slices bacon
1 c. diced, pared potatoes
2 tblsp. chopped onion
¼ tsp. salt
2 tblsp. chopped fresh parsley
1 tblsp. chopped pimientos
1 tblsp. cooking oil
8 eggs, well beaten
1 tblsp. water
½ tsp. salt
⅛ tsp. pepper

Fry bacon until crisp in skillet. Remove; drain on paper towels. Crumble. Reserve 2 tblsp. bacon fat. Add potatoes, onion and ¼ tsp. salt to bacon fat; cook until potatoes are tender and golden. Stir in parsley, bacon and pimientos; set aside.

Heat oil in 10″ skillet over medium heat. In bowl, beat together eggs, water, ½ tsp. salt and pepper. Stir in potato mixture; pour into skillet. Lift cooked edges so uncooked portion flows underneath. Cook until mixture is set, but top is creamy. Fold in half. Makes 4 servings.

Breakfast

Chilled Apple Juice

Golden Crispies Cereal with Fresh Blueberries

Cinnamon Buns

Coffee   Milk

Golden Crispies Cereal

4 c. rolled oats
2 c. raw wheat germ
1 c. hulled sunflower or sesame seeds
1 c. chopped walnuts
½ c. flaked coconut
¾ c. brown sugar, firmly packed
¾ c. cooking oil
⅓ c. water
2 tblsp. vanilla

Combine all ingredients and mix well. Spread in 15½x10½x1″ jelly roll pan. Bake in 350° oven 1 hour, stirring frequently. Cool and store in tightly covered container. Makes about 10 cups.

Brunch

Garden Tomato Juice

Chicken Crepes

Honeydew Melon Slices, Blueberries and Apricot Compote

Iced Tea with Clove-Studded Lemon Slices

Garden Tomato Juice

12 medium tomatoes, peeled, cored and chopped (about 4 lb.)
1 (8″) celery branch
4 sprigs parsley
1 slice onion
½ bay leaf
½ c. water
1½ tsp. salt
½ tsp. sugar
¼ tsp. paprika

Combine tomatoes, celery, parsley, onion, bay leaf and water in Dutch oven. Bring to a boil. Reduce heat and simmer, covered, 20 minutes. Press through sieve. Add salt, sugar and paprika. Cover and chill thoroughly. Makes about 5½ cups.

Shortcuts
& Seasonings

• Make a tangy topping for ice cream, pancakes or waffles by stirring together equal parts of orange marmalade and melted butter with a dash of lemon juice.

• Here's a refreshing summer cooler: Combine lemon juice, orange juice, and grapefruit juice in a 1-2-3 proportion. Add sugar to taste and serve over ice cubes.

• For a quick dessert, roll a scoop of ice cream in cookie crumbs, and serve with hot fudge or fresh fruit sauce. Try vanilla ice cream rolled in chocolate cookie crumbs and serve with whipped cream topped with toasted coconut; or peach ice cream rolled in gingersnap crumbs topped with fresh sliced peaches; or coffee ice cream rolled in graham cracker crumbs topped with hot butterscotch sauce.

• Use your small electric appliances whenever possible to keep the kitchen cool and save time and energy. A toaster-oven heats up more quickly than a large oven and is great for baking small casseroles. When using the electric skillet, place it wherever your kitchen is the breeziest.

• For a pretty garnish, dip tiny bunches of green grapes into lemon juice and sprinkle generously with granulated sugar. Use to garnish a dish of sherbet or a pretty fruit salad platter.

• To make a low-calorie banana split, cut a peeled banana in half lengthwise. Top with crushed pineapple, sliced strawberries and yogurt.

• To dress up hamburgers, combine ⅓ c. crumbled blue cheese with ⅔ c. dairy sour cream and 1 tblsp. thinly sliced green onions. Place a green pepper ring on each hamburger and fill center with cheese mixture. Top with extra-finely sliced green onions, if desired.

Shortcuts & Seasonings

• To make a great cold soup in seconds from leftover vegetable salads, just whirl the salad in the blender with tomato juice until smooth. Cover, chill until frosty cold, and serve.

• For a quick mayonnaise that's a little different, fold 2 c. finely chopped cucumbers into 2½ c. mayonnaise. Season to taste with salt and pepper, and add a dash of curry powder if you plan to serve it with a cold fish salad. Tastes great on chicken and ham salad, too.

• Be kind to your salad bowl and it will last for years. Never soak a wooden bowl in water. After each use, rinse it quickly with lukewarm water, wipe dry with a clean towel and store in a dry place. Eventually, the garlic and other flavorings from salads will season your salad bowl.

• Salads will taste twice as refreshing if the individual plates or bowls are pre-chilled in the refrigerator.

• Try this unique decoration for vanilla or rice pudding: Pour flavored gelatin in a flat pan to a depth of ½″ to 1″ and let set. Cut gelatin into the shape of animals or flowers, and arrange on top of pudding.

• Before measuring syrup, jelly, molasses, honey or any other sticky substance, grease your measuring cup.

• Beat softened butter until light and fluffy to make it last longer. Add chopped fresh dill for fish or chives or thyme for steak for a quick and delicious topping.

September 21–
December 20

Autumn

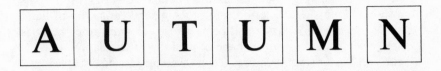

AUTUMN

Autumn begins with the warm glow of summer, but the air soon sharpens and fills with swirling leaves. Children head back to school, football games are in full swing, and everyone looks forward to heartier meals. This is the time to fill your home with the aroma of rich stews and fresh-baked bread, and to treat yourself to a batch of homemade cookies.

Roadside stands and supermarket bins are piled high with the autumn harvest of fruits and vegetables. Acorn and Butternut squash, pumpkins, sweet potatoes and cauliflower are abundant, and you'll also find lots of broccoli, cabbage, Brussels sprouts, artichokes, turnips, rutabagas and eggplant as well as crisp apples, pears and grapes. All of these colorful fruits and vegetables are featured in the menus that follow, along with robust meat-and-vegetable recipes and rib-sticking casseroles.

When you're in the mood to bake yeast bread, there's a luscious recipe for every occasion. Sour Cream Cinnamon Rolls taste great at breakfast, lunch or dinner. The tender, crumbed Cheddar Cheese Snack Bread and the handsome Golden Sesame Braid are marvelous for sandwiches or to serve along with steaming hot soup. When friends drop in for coffee, serve buttery crumb-topped Streusel Kuchen, or tuck a few slices into lunch boxes for an extra-special surprise. And for days when you only have time to make a quick bread, we offer Graham Muffins, Orange-Date Muffins and velvety-textured Luscious Pumpkin Bread.

To provide a warm welcome home on a brisk evening, there's a wide choice of nutritious soups from the files of farm and ranch women. Try ham-laced Green Bean Soup, an heirloom recipe from Mennonite cooks in Kansas, or stir up a big pot of Pennsylvania Dutch Chicken Corn Soup. Espanola Valley Soup, a favorite with one Iowa family, is a make-your-own-topping soup based on vegetables and pork that lets everyone use their creativity.

Main-dish casseroles are especially important to farm cooks during the busy harvest season, and here you'll find recipes for Ham and Sweet Potato Casserole, Beef Florentine Casserole and Macaroni-Sausage Casserole—all good candidates for freeze-ahead meal planning.

For dessert, some of the seasonal choices include Lace-Crusted Apples with a crackling-crisp crust, a butter pecan-based Frozen Pumpkin Pie and a beautiful Pecan Meringue Pie. On a cold fall night, your family will appreciate tart Crisp Cranberry Crumble or a plate of Molasses-Ginger Cookies.

When you shop for fall produce, look for the best quality fruits and vegetables. Apples come in many varieties: Choose Greening and Rome Beauties for applesauce, pies and cobblers. Buy Baldwins, Gravensteins, McIntosh and Northern Spies both for cooking and eating out-of-hand. Delicious apples aren't as tart and firm-textured as some other varieties, so they're best for eating out-of-hand or used raw in salads.

Pears, too, offer several choices, all good either cooked or served fresh from the tree. There's the yellow, buttery Bartlett and the thick-skinned green Anjou, juicy and smooth-textured with a rich spicy flavor. The Comice also is green-skinned, often with a red blush, and has a fine-grained texture and a slightly spicy flavor. The Bosc, distinguished by its long tapering neck, is a rich golden russet color and at its peak of ripeness is tender, buttery and sugar-sweet.

With such a variety of autumn's bounty from which to choose, you can create colorful, nutritious meals each day throughout the season.

Lunch

Broiled Chicken Liver and Mushroom Kabobs

Parslied Rice   Cauliflower with Cheese Sauce

Romaine and Sliced Radish Salad

Peach Melba

Lemon Iced Tea*

Dinner

Baked Lamb Chops with Herbed Dressing

Broiled Tomato Halves   Buttered Lima Beans

Lace-Crusted Apples

Coffee   Milk

Lace-Crusted Apples

5 tart cooking apples
3 tblsp. raisins
1 tblsp. lemon juice
Water
1½ tsp. grated lemon rind
1 tblsp. lemon juice
½ tsp. ground cinnamon
1½ c. brown sugar, firmly packed
½ c. finely chopped walnuts
½ c. melted butter or regular
   margarine
Vanilla ice cream

Pare and core apples. Cut into ½" thick lengthwise slices. Place in saucepan with raisins, lemon juice and water to cover halfway. Cover, bring to a boil, simmer until tender, about 5 minutes. Drain well. Turn into a 10" oven glassware pie plate.

Sprinkle with lemon rind, lemon juice and cinnamon. Combine brown sugar, walnuts and melted butter. Sprinkle over fruits.

Broil about 6" from heat until sugar is melted and golden brown. Cool slightly. Tap crust to break, and top with ice cream. Makes 6 servings.

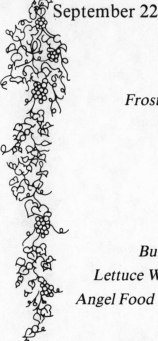

September 22

Lunch

Cucumber-Egg Salad

Frosty Tomato Cup*   Bread Sticks

Chocolate Cupcakes

Tea   Milk

Dinner

Spaghetti Soufflé

Buttered Carrots   Minted Peas

Lettuce Wedges with Tarragon French Dressing

Angel Food Cake Topped with Crushed Strawberries

Coffee   Milk

Spaghetti Soufflé

2 c. soft bread crumbs
½ c. melted butter or regular
    margarine
6 eggs, separated
2 c. drained, cooked spaghetti (about
    5 oz. uncooked, broken in 2"
    lengths)
2 tblsp. chopped fresh parsley
2 tblsp. chopped pimientos
2 tblsp. chopped green pepper
2 tblsp. chopped onion
1½ tsp. salt
2 c. milk
Mushroom Sauce (recipe follows)

Combine bread crumbs and butter in mixing bowl. Stir in egg yolks and all other ingredients except egg whites and Mushroom Sauce.

Beat egg whites until stiff but not dry. Fold into spaghetti mixture.

Pour into 2-qt. casserole or soufflé dish. Bake in 350° oven 1 hour, or until set in center. Serve with Mushroom Sauce. Serves 6 to 8.

Mushroom Sauce: Sauté 1 (4-oz.) can drained mushroom stems and pieces in 3 tblsp. butter. Stir in 2 tblsp. flour, ¼ tsp. salt and ⅛ tsp. pepper. Gradually add 1 c. milk, stirring until smooth. Cook over medium heat, stirring until of medium thickness. Makes 1¼ cups.

*See Index for recipe

Lunch

Clam Chowder

Luscious Pumpkin Bread

Plums with Camembert Cheese and Roasted Walnut Halves

Iced Coffee

Dinner

Roasted Turkey Legs

Cheese-Stuffed Baked Potatoes   *Buttered Sliced Beets*

Overnight Tossed Salad*

Cherry Cobbler

Coffee   *Milk*

Luscious Pumpkin Bread

3½ c. sifted flour
2 tsp. baking soda
2 tsp. salt
1 tsp. baking powder
1 tsp. ground cinnamon
1 tsp. ground nutmeg
1 tsp. ground allspice
½ tsp. ground cloves
3 c. sugar
1 c. cooking oil
4 eggs
1 (1-lb.) can pumpkin (2 c.)
⅔ c. water

Sift together flour, baking soda, salt, baking powder, cinnamon, nutmeg, allspice and cloves in bowl.

In a larger bowl, beat together sugar, oil and eggs until light and fluffy. Add pumpkin; blend well.

Add dry ingredients alternately to pumpkin mixture with water, beating well after each addition. Pour batter into 2 greased 9x5x3″ loaf pans.

Bake in 350° oven 1 hour, or until bread tests done. Remove from pans. Cool on racks. Makes 2 loaves.

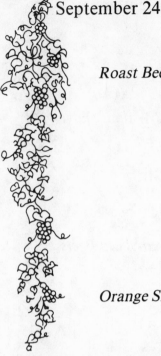

September 24

Lunch

Roast Beef and Shredded Lettuce in Pita Bread
Potato Salad
Spicy Raisin Cupcakes
Coffee   Milk

Dinner

Turkey à la King
Baked Acorn Squash
Savory Green Beans*
Orange Sherbet and Vanilla Ice Cream Parfaits
Iced Coffee

Spicy Raisin Cupcakes

1 lb. raisins
2 c. water
2⅓ c. sifted flour
2 tsp. baking soda
2 tsp. ground nutmeg
2 tsp. ground cinnamon
¼ tsp. salt
1½ c. sugar
1 c. butter or regular margarine
2 eggs
1 c. chopped walnuts

Combine raisins and water in a small saucepan. Bring to a boil, reduce heat and simmer for 10 minutes. Drain and reserve cooking liquid. If necessary, add water to make 1 c.

Sift together flour, baking soda, nutmeg, cinnamon and salt in bowl.

Cream together sugar and butter in large bowl until light and fluffy. Add eggs, one at a time, beating well after each addition.

Add dry ingredients alternately with cooking liquid, beating well after each addition. Stir in raisins and walnuts. Pour batter into paper-lined 2½" muffin-pan cups, filling two-thirds full.

Bake in 375° oven 20 to 25 minutes, or until done. Remove from pans. Cool on racks. Makes 3 dozen.

*See Index for recipe

Lunch

Yogurt Cucumber Soup*
Sliced Bologna and Coleslaw Sandwiches
Poached Pears
Tea   Milk

Dinner

Broiled Pork Steaks with Onions
Broccoli with Toasted Almonds
Tomatoes with Bread Stuffing
Lettuce, Radish and Onion Salad
Bread Pudding with Hot Maple Syrup
Coffee   Milk

Tomatoes with Bread Stuffing

8 tomatoes
1 c. chopped onion
½ c. chopped celery with leaves
¼ c. butter or regular margarine
1 tblsp. dried parsley flakes
½ tsp. dried basil leaves
¼ tsp. instant minced garlic
1 tsp. salt
⅛ tsp. pepper
5 c. bread cubes

Cut slice off top of each tomato. Scoop out center and save. Turn tomatoes upside down to drain.

Cook onion and celery in butter until soft in 2-qt. saucepan. Chop tomato centers; add to onion mixture with parsley, basil, garlic, salt and pepper. Cook until mixture thickens, about 15 minutes. Stir occasionally.

Add bread cubes. Place tomato shells in muffin-pan cups. Fill with bread stuffing. Bake in 350° oven 30 minutes. Makes 8 servings.

---

*See Index for recipe

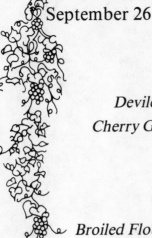

September 26

Lunch

Espanola Valley Soup
Deviled Ham Sandwiches with Mustard
Cherry Gelatin Cubes with Crushed Pineapple
Iced Tea

Dinner

Broiled Flounder Fillets with Toasted Sesame Seeds
Broiled Potato Slices   Corn with Pimientos
Chicory and Sliced Orange Salad
Walnut Pound Cake*
Iced Coffee

Espanola Valley Soup

3 lb. fresh pork hocks
3 qt. water
1 (1-lb.) can tomatoes, cut up
2 c. chopped onion
1 clove garlic, minced
5 tsp. salt
1 tblsp. chili powder
2 (1-lb.) cans whole-kernel corn
   or hominy
1 (10-oz.) pkg. frozen lima beans
Chopped fresh parsley
Assorted toppings: shredded carrots,
   chopped lettuce, sliced radishes,
   sliced green onions, avocado cubes
   and shredded Monterey Jack or
   Muenster cheese

Combine pork hocks, water, tomatoes, onion, garlic, salt and chili powder in 8-qt. kettle. Cover and bring mixture to a boil. Reduce heat and simmer 1½ hours, or until pork is tender. Remove pork. Cut up meat and return to broth; discard fat and bones. Cool broth. Cover and chill.

Skim off fat from broth. Add corn and lima beans to broth in kettle. Bring to a boil. Reduce heat and simmer 15 minutes, or until beans are tender.

Garnish bowls of soup with parsley. Pass several bowls of the assorted toppings to spoon on soup. Makes about 4 quarts or 12 servings.

*See Index for recipe

Lunch

Tomato Soup

Cream Cheese and Grated Carrot Sandwiches

Cinnamon Jumbles*

Coffee   Milk

Dinner

Green Pepper Casserole

Garlic Bread

Endive and Cucumber Salad

Lime Sherbet

Iced Tea

Green Pepper Casserole

1 c. uncooked regular rice
2 tblsp. melted butter or regular
  margarine
3 green peppers, cut in strips
3 chicken bouillon cubes
2 c. boiling water
1 lb. ground beef
1 c. chopped onion
1 c. chopped celery
1 clove garlic, minced
1 (15-oz.) can tomato sauce
1 tsp. dried oregano leaves, crushed
1 tsp. salt
¼ tsp. pepper
1½ c. shredded Cheddar cheese
  (6 oz.)

Cook rice in butter in skillet until lightly toasted, stirring frequently. Spread in greased 13x9x2″ baking pan. Arrange green pepper on top.

Dissolve bouillon cubes in boiling water; pour over rice mixture. Cover with foil and bake in 375° oven 20 minutes.

Meanwhile, cook ground beef, onion, celery and garlic in same skillet until meat is browned. Stir in tomato sauce, oregano, salt and pepper. Cover; simmer 5 minutes. Pour over peppers and rice. Cover and continue baking 15 minutes. Remove cover, sprinkle with cheese and bake, uncovered, 5 minutes. Makes 6 servings.

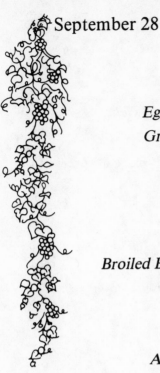

September 28

Lunch

*Tuna Bisque**

Egg Salad and Bacon Sandwiches

Green Grapes and Sliced Peaches

Oatmeal Cookies

Iced Coffee

Dinner

Broiled Beef Patties with Sautéed Mushrooms

Buttered Peas

Eggplant Parmesan

Tossed Salad

Apple Pie with Cheddar Cheese

Coffee   Milk

Eggplant Parmesan

1 large eggplant (1½ lb.)
2 eggs, beaten
2 tblsp. water
¾ c. dry bread crumbs
¾ c. cooking oil
½ c. grated Parmesan cheese
1 tsp. dried oregano leaves
1 tsp. dried basil leaves
½ tsp. salt
½ lb. mozzarella cheese, sliced
3 (8-oz.) cans tomato sauce

Pare eggplant; cut in ¼" slices. Dip slices in mixture of beaten eggs and water, then in bread crumbs. Brown on both sides in hot oil in 10" skillet, removing slices as they brown.

Combine Parmesan cheese, oregano, basil and salt. Place ⅓ of eggplant in greased 2-qt. casserole; sprinkle with ⅓ of Parmesan cheese mixture. Top with ⅓ of mozzarella cheese slices and 1 can tomato sauce. Repeat layers twice.

Bake in 350° oven about 30 minutes, or until sauce is bubbly. Makes 6 servings.

*See Index for recipe

Lunch

Beef Bouillon

Special Chef's Salad

Pumpernickel Bread with Herbed Butter

Fruit Cocktail

Iced Tea

Dinner

Broiled Veal Chops with Lemon Slices

Buttered Noodles with Poppy Seeds

Sautéed Zucchini Strips

Escarole, Sliced Radish and Onion Salad

Creamy Cheesecake*

Coffee   Tea

Special Chef's Salad

2 c. bite-size pieces lettuce
2 c. bite-size pieces spinach
½ c. chopped green pepper
½ c. shredded carrot
½ c. halved cucumber slices
½ lb. ham, cut in strips (1 c.)
1 (3-oz.) pkg. cream cheese, cubed
2 hard-cooked eggs, chopped
1 small onion, sliced
Oil and Vinegar Dressing (recipe
  follows)

Combine lettuce, spinach, green pepper, carrot, cucumber, ham, cream cheese, eggs and onion in a large bowl.

Prepare Oil and Vinegar Dressing. Pour over salad ingredients. Toss gently. Makes 4 to 6 servings.

Oil and Vinegar Dressing: Combine ½ c. salad oil, ¼ c. vinegar, 1 tblsp. ketchup, ¾ tsp. sugar, ¾ tsp. salt, ½ tsp. garlic salt and ⅛ tsp. pepper in jar. Cover tightly and shake well.

*See Index for recipe

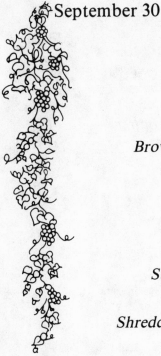

Lunch

Gazpacho*
Thinly Sliced Roast Beef
Whole-Wheat Melba Toast
Brown Sugar-Glazed Baked Custard
Lemonade

Dinner

Baked Chicken
Succotash Dusted with Nutmeg
Baked Onions
Shredded Carrot, Raisin and Apple Salad
Chocolate Layer Cake
Coffee   Tea

Baked Onions

8 medium white onions
Salt
½ c. dark corn syrup
¼ c. melted butter or regular
   margarine
2 tsp. lemon juice

Peel onions. Place in a buttered 12x8x2″ (2-qt.) glass baking dish. Sprinkle with salt. Combine corn syrup, butter and lemon juice in small saucepan. Heat to boiling. Baste onions with syrup mixture.

Bake in 325° oven 1½ hours, basting often with syrup mixture, until onions are tender. Makes 8 servings.

See Index for recipe

Lunch

Mexican Salad Bowl*

Toasted Corn Muffins

Tapioca Pudding Layered with Cranberry Sauce

Tea   Milk

Dinner

Ham and Sweet Potato Casserole

Buttered Brussels Sprouts

Chicory and Sliced Radish Salad

Apricot Cobbler with Grated Lemon Rind

Coffee   Milk

Ham and Sweet Potato Casserole

1½ tblsp. cornstarch
1½ c. apple juice
¼ c. golden raisins
2 tblsp. brown sugar
1 tblsp. lemon juice
1 tsp. prepared mustard
⅛ tsp. pepper
2 lb. cooked ham, cut in slices
2 (1-lb. 7-oz.) cans sweet potatoes or yams, drained
3 tblsp. melted butter or regular margarine
1 c. crushed corn flakes
Butter or regular margarine

Combine cornstarch and apple juice in small saucepan; mix well. Add raisins. Cook over medium heat, stirring constantly, until thickened. Add brown sugar, lemon juice, mustard and pepper; stir until smooth.

Arrange ham slices in 13x9x2″ glass baking dish. Pour sauce over ham.

Mash sweet potatoes in bowl, using fork. Add 3 tblsp. melted butter; mix until smooth. Spread half of potato mixture over ham. Top with corn flakes. Spread remaining potato mixture on top. Dot with butter.

Bake in 350° oven 30 minutes, or until hot. Makes 6 to 8 servings.

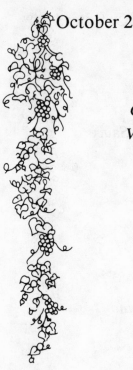

October 2

Lunch

Luncheon Meat-Cheese Sandwiches
Celery Sticks   Watermelon Pickles
Vanilla Yogurt with Mandarin Oranges
Cocoa

Dinner

Broiled Scallops with Lime Wedges
Boiled Potatoes with Cheese Sauce
Buttered Diced Beets
Romaine and Black Olive Salad
Pineapple Sherbet*
Tea   Milk

Luncheon Meat-Cheese Sandwiches

8 hot dog buns, split
Butter or regular margarine
6 slices salami
6 slices chopped ham luncheon meat
  or sliced cooked ham
1 (6-oz.) pkg. sliced mozzarella cheese

Butter bun halves completely to edges. Cut salami and luncheon meat slices in thirds, cheese slices in fourths crosswise. Place 2 pieces of each between bun halves. Wrap sandwiches individually in aluminum foil. Freeze.

To serve, place frozen, wrapped sandwiches in unheated oven. Turn oven to 425° and bake 30 minutes. Or, let wrapped sandwiches thaw in refrigerator and eat cold. Makes 8 sandwiches.

*See Index for recipe

Lunch

Chicken Corn Soup
Sliced Egg and Cucumber Sandwiches
Sliced Bananas and Canned Plums
Tea   Milk

Dinner

Broiled Lamb and Green Pepper Kabobs
Sautéed Cherry Tomatoes
Baked Potato Sticks*
Sliced Avocado and Grapefruit Sections on Escarole
Eclairs
Espresso

Chicken Corn Soup

3 strips bacon
2 tblsp. chopped onion
1 chicken bouillon cube
¼ c. boiling water
1 (10½-oz.) can condensed cream of
   chicken soup
1 (1-lb.) can cream-style corn
2 c. milk
¼ tsp. salt
¼ tsp. thyme
½ tsp. celery salt
⅛ tsp. sage
Chopped parsley

Fry bacon until crisp in heavy 2-qt. saucepan. Drain on paper towels; crumble. Set aside.

Sauté onion in drippings until tender. Dissolve bouillon cube in water; add with remaining ingredients, except parsley, to onion. Bring to boiling point over low heat. Sprinkle with parsley. Makes 6 servings.

*See Index for recipe

October 4

Lunch

Minestrone
Bacon-Spinach Salad*
Poached Pears and Dried Apricots
Tea   Milk

Dinner

Ground Beef Roll
Whipped Turnips   Peas and Water Chestnuts
Lettuce Wedges with Roquefort Dressing
Blueberry Turnovers with Hard Sauce
Coffee   Milk

Ground Beef Roll

1 c. finely chopped celery
¾ c. chopped onion
¼ c. melted butter or regular
    margarine
1 (4-oz.) can sliced mushrooms
3 c. soft bread cubes (¼")
2 tsp. poultry seasoning
2 lb. ground beef
½ c. soft bread crumbs
2 tblsp. chopped fresh parsley
1 tsp. salt
¼ tsp. pepper
2 eggs, slightly beaten
Onion Gravy (recipe follows)

Sauté celery and ½ c. of the onion in melted butter in small skillet until tender (do not brown).

Drain mushrooms; reserve ⅓ c. liquid. Combine bread cubes, poultry seasoning, sautéed vegetables, mushrooms and ⅓ c. reserved liquid in bowl. Mix lightly, but well. Set aside.

Combine ground beef, bread crumbs, ¼ c. of the onion, parsley, salt, pepper and eggs. Mix lightly, but well. Pat into 9" square on heavy-duty foil; top with stuffing. Roll up like jelly roll, using foil to shape. Wrap in foil. Place seam side down on rack in shallow roasting pan.

Bake in 375° oven 1 hour. Open foil. Bake 15 more minutes, or until loaf is nicely browned. Serve with Onion Gravy. Makes 6 to 8 servings.

Onion Gravy: Sauté 1 medium onion (thinly sliced) in 4 tblsp. melted butter in 2-qt. saucepan until tender (do not brown). Stir in 4 tblsp. flour. Gradually stir in 1 (13¾-oz.) can beef broth. Add ¼ tsp. Worcestershire sauce, ½ tsp. browning for gravy and dash of pepper. Cook over medium heat, stirring constantly, until mixture comes to a boil.

*See Index for recipe

Lunch

Cream of Asparagus Soup

Parmesan Garden Salad Bowl

Toasted Bagels

Butterscotch Pudding Topped with Crushed Peanut Brittle

Tea   Milk

Dinner

Linguini with White Clam Sauce

Broiled Mushrooms*

Escarole and Sliced Cucumber Salad

Orange Sherbet and Crushed Strawberry Parfaits

Coffee   Milk

Parmesan Garden Salad Bowl

3 small zucchini, sliced
1 small head cauliflower, broken in
  small buds
2 tomatoes, cut in wedges
½ c. vegetable oil
⅓ c. vinegar
¼ c. grated Parmesan cheese
2 tblsp. chopped fresh parsley
1½ tsp. garlic salt
¼ tsp. pepper
¼ tsp. dried oregano leaves, crushed

Combine zucchini, cauliflower and tomatoes in large salad bowl.

Combine remaining ingredients in jar with screw-top lid. Shake vigorously. Pour over vegetables; toss gently. Cover and refrigerate several hours or overnight. Makes 8 servings.

*See Index for recipe

October 6

Lunch

Tuna-Cheese Buns*

Black Olives   Green Pepper Strips

Fresh Figs

Tea   Milk

Dinner

Knockwurst with Sauerkraut

Whipped Potatoes

Hot Applesauce

Chicory and Sliced Radish Salad

Caramel Bread Pudding

Coffee   Milk

Caramel Bread Pudding

2 tblsp. butter or regular margarine
1 c. light brown sugar, firmly packed
6 slices white bread, cut in ½ " cubes
6 eggs
½ c. light brown sugar, firmly
   packed
2 c. milk
⅛ tsp. salt
1 tsp. vanilla

Generously butter the inside of double boiler top. Place 1 c. brown sugar in bottom and then a layer of bread cubes. (Do not mix.)

Beat eggs well with rotary beater. Gradually beat in ½ c. brown sugar, milk, salt and vanilla. Pour over bread cubes. (Do not stir.) Place over simmering water. Cover and cook 1 hour 30 minutes. Serve hot. Makes 6 to 8 servings.

* See Index for recipe

Lunch

Sausage Quiche

Marinated Cucumbers and Onions

Coffee-Iced Brownies*

Coffee   Milk

Dinner

Braised Swiss Steak with Gravy

Buttered Noodles

Herbed Spinach

Lettuce Wedges with Russian Dressing

Cherry Gelatin Cubes with Green Grapes

Coffee   Tea   Milk

Herbed Spinach

3 slices bacon, cut in slivers
2 medium onions, thinly sliced
2 lb. washed spinach
½ c. coarsely chopped fresh parsley
½ tsp. dried rosemary leaves, or a 1″ tip of fresh rosemary, broken in bits
1 tsp. salt
¼ tsp. pepper
2 tblsp. wine vinegar or lemon juice

Cook bacon bits in large skillet until barely crisp; remove with slotted spoon and place on paper towels.

Remove all but 1 tblsp. drippings; add onions, spinach, parsley and seasonings. Cover; cook over medium heat a few minutes (not more than 10), until wilted, stirring once or twice.

Add vinegar; sprinkle with bacon bits and serve. Makes 6 servings.

October 8

Lunch

Lima Bean Chowder
Toasted Whole-Wheat Crackers
Walnut-Stuffed Prunes
Gingerbread with Whipped Cream
Tea   Milk

Dinner

Broiled Lamb Patties
Baked Sweet Potatoes   Steamed Cauliflower
Spiced Cranberry Mold*
Cold Lemon Soufflé
Coffee   Milk

Lima Bean Chowder

2 tblsp. butter or regular margarine
2 c. chopped onions (2 medium)
½ chopped green pepper (1 small)
1 (10-oz.) pkg. frozen lima beans
1 c. cubed potatoes (1 medium)
3 c. water
2 tsp. salt
¼ tsp. pepper
1 c. shredded cabbage
1 (1-lb.) can whole-kernel corn
1 (14½-oz.) can evaporated milk
1 (4-oz.) pkg. process American
   cheese, grated

Melt butter in 3-qt. saucepan. Add onions and green pepper; sauté until tender. Add lima beans, potatoes, water and seasonings; bring to a boil and simmer 5 minutes. Add cabbage and corn; simmer until vegetables are tender, about 10 minutes.

Add remaining ingredients; cook, stirring frequently, until heated thoroughly and cheese is melted. Makes 6 servings.

*See Index for recipe

Lunch

Tomato Cheeseburgers
Tangy Slaw*
Poached Pears Topped with Candied Ginger
Lemonade

Dinner

Oven-Fried Oysters*

French Fried Potatoes   Buttered Sliced Beets

Endive and Watercress Salad

Custard Pie

Tea   Milk

Tomato Cheeseburgers

1½ lb. lean ground beef
1 small onion, chopped
2 tblsp. salad oil
1½ tsp. salt
¼ tsp. pepper
1 (1-lb.) can tomatoes, cut up
½ lb. sharp Cheddar cheese, chopped
Hamburger buns

Brown beef and onion in hot salad oil. Pour excess fat from skillet. Season beef with salt and pepper; add tomatoes. Cook 15 to 20 minutes, or until mixture has absorbed most of the juice. Add cheese; cook about 5 minutes.

Serve on heated soft buns. Makes about 8 servings.

October 10

Lunch

Cream Cheese and Chopped Raisin Sandwiches

<u>Waldorf Variation Salad</u>

Brown Sugar Cookies

Tea   Milk

Dinner

Crispy Baked Chicken*

Baked Potatoes Topped with Chives   Buttered Broccoli

Spinach Salad with Toasted Sesame Seeds

Mincemeat Tarts

Coffee   Milk

Waldorf Variation Salad

4 oranges, peeled and cut into
  sections
4 red apples, cut into wedges
1 c. sliced celery
1 (13½-oz.) can pineapple chunks,
  drained
1 (6-oz.) can frozen lemonade,
  slightly thawed

Combine all ingredients in large bowl. Toss well. Cover and chill thoroughly. Makes about 8 servings.

*See Index for recipe

October 11

Lunch

Sliced Roast Beef and Bean Sprouts in Pita Bread

Slimmers' Deviled Eggs*

Raspberry Sherbet

Tea   Milk

Dinner

Chicken à la King in Patty Shells

Peas with Pimientos   Buttered Carrots

Tossed Salad

Walnut Applesauce Cake

Coffee   Milk

Walnut Applesauce Cake

2 c. sifted flour
1 tsp. baking soda
1 tsp. baking powder
1 tsp. ground cinnamon
1 tsp. ground nutmeg
½ tsp. ground cloves
½ tsp. salt
½ c. shortening
1 c. sugar
1 egg
1 c. applesauce
1 tsp. vanilla
¾ c. raisins
1 c. chopped walnuts

Sift together flour, baking soda, baking powder, cinnamon, nutmeg, cloves and salt; set aside.

Cream together shortening and sugar in bowl until light and fluffy. Add egg, applesauce and vanilla; blend well.

Gradually blend in dry ingredients. Stir in raisins and walnuts. Pour batter into greased 9x5x3″ loaf pan.

Bake in 350° oven 55 minutes, or until cake tests done. Cool for 10 minutes. Remove from pan. Cool on rack. Makes 8 to 10 servings.

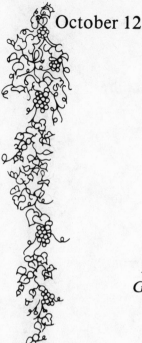

October 12

Lunch

Cream of Asparagus Soup

Mediterranean Salad*

Whole-Wheat Melba Toast

Riced Orange Gelatin

Tea   Milk

Dinner

Baked Pork Chops with Dressing

Green Beans with Toasted Almonds

Escarole and Beet Salad

Coconut Cream Pudding

Coffee   Milk

Baked Pork Chops with Dressing

6 pork chops, ¾" thick
¼ tsp. salt
⅛ tsp. pepper
1 tblsp. cooking oil
½ c. chopped onion
¼ c. butter or regular margarine
4½ c. bread cubes (½")
½ tsp. poultry seasoning
¼ tsp. celery salt
¼ c. water
3 medium potatoes, pared and
    quartered
Cooking oil
1 (10½-oz.) can condensed cream of
    mushroom soup
½ c. water

Season pork chops with salt and pepper. Brown in 1 tblsp. hot oil in skillet. Remove from skillet. Place in 13x9x2" (3-qt.) glass baking dish.

Sauté onion in melted butter in 10" skillet until tender (do not brown). Combine onion with bread cubes, poultry seasoning, celery salt and ¼ c. water. Mix lightly. Shape dressing in mounds on top of chops.

Coat potatoes with oil; place around chops.

Combine soup and ½ c. water. Pour over chops and potatoes.

Bake in 350° oven 1 hour, or until meat is tender. Makes 6 servings.

*See Index for recipe

Lunch

Tuna Club Sandwiches

Celery Sticks   Black Olives

Minted Fruit Cup*

Cocoa

Dinner

Broiled Liver with Mushrooms

Corn Niblets   Cauliflower Casserole

Avocado and Grapefruit Salad

Baked Apples

Coffee   Milk

Cauliflower Casserole

1 medium cauliflower
3 tblsp. butter or regular margarine
3 tblsp. flour
1½ c. milk
1 tsp. salt
⅛ tsp. pepper
1 tsp. dried parsley flakes
3 hard-cooked eggs, thinly sliced
½ c. cracker crumbs
2 tblsp. melted butter or regular margarine

Separate cauliflower into flowerets. Cook in boiling salted water until tender. Drain and set aside.

Meanwhile, melt 3 tblsp. butter in saucepan. Stir in flour; add milk and cook, stirring constantly, until mixture bubbles and is thickened. Remove from heat and stir in salt, pepper and parsley.

Combine cauliflower, eggs and sauce. Spoon into 1½-qt. casserole. Toss crumbs with 2 tblsp. butter. Sprinkle over top.

Bake in 350° oven 25 minutes. Makes 6 servings.

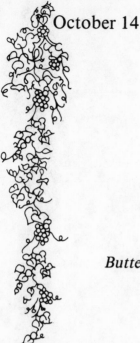

October 14

Lunch

Black Bean Soup
Thinly Sliced Boiled Ham
Cheese Muffins*
Vanilla Milk Shakes

Dinner

Pot Roast with Gravy
Buttered Noodles   Braised Red Cabbage
Olive Wreath Mold
Cherry Pie
Coffee   Milk

Olive Wreath Mold

1 (3-oz.) pkg. lime flavor gelatin
1 c. boiling water
⅔ c. cold water
2 tblsp. lemon juice
1 c. heavy cream, whipped
⅓ c. sliced pimiento-stuffed olives
½ c. shredded American cheese
1 (8½-oz.) can crushed pineapple, drained
1 tblsp. chopped pimiento
½ c. finely chopped celery
½ c. chopped walnuts
½ tsp. salt
24 slices of pimiento-stuffed olives

Dissolve gelatin in boiling water in bowl. Add cold water and lemon juice. Cover and chill until thick and syrupy. Fold in whipped cream. Add ⅓ c. sliced olives, cheese, pineapple, pimiento, celery, walnuts and salt. Blend well.

Arrange 24 olive slices in a circle around bottom of oiled 9″ ring mold. Pour mixture into mold. Cover; chill until set. Makes 6 to 8 servings.

*See Index for recipe

Lunch

Green Pepper Omelets

Sautéed Cherry Tomatoes

Orange Cupcakes*

Tea   Milk

Dinner

Oven-Fried Fish

French Fried Potatoes   Buttered Lima Beans

Spinach Salad

Butterscotch Sundaes with Toasted Pecans

Coffee   Tea   Milk

Oven-Fried Fish

½ c. butter or regular margarine
2 lb. fish fillets, fresh or frozen and
   thawed
1 egg, beaten
1 c. cracker crumbs
1 tsp. seasoned salt
¼ tsp. pepper

Melt butter in 15½x10½x1″ jelly roll pan in 375° oven.

Meanwhile, dip fish fillets in egg, then in mixture of cracker crumbs, seasoned with salt and pepper. Place each fillet in jelly roll pan, turning to coat with butter.

Bake in 375° oven 20 to 25 minutes, or until a light golden brown. Makes 6 to 8 servings.

October 16

Lunch

Chicken Soup

Frankfurters on Toasted Buns

<u>*Sauerkraut Salad*</u>

Root Beer Floats

Dinner

Corned Beef Hash

Basque Potatoes*   *Julienne Green Beans*

Endive and Marinated Artichoke Salad

Baked Custard with Crushed Strawberries

Coffee   Tea

Sauerkraut Salad

1¼ c. sugar
1¼ c. water
½ c. vinegar
½ c. salad oil
1 (27-oz.) can sauerkraut, drained, rinsed and snipped
1 c. chopped celery
½ c. coarsely grated carrots
½ c. chopped green pepper
½ c. chopped onion
2 tblsp. diced pimientos

Combine sugar, water, vinegar and oil in small saucepan; mix well. Bring to a boil, stirring occasionally. Remove from heat. Cool thoroughly.

Combine sauerkraut, celery, carrots, green pepper, onion and pimientos. Pour dressing over vegetables; toss gently. Cover and chill several hours or overnight. Makes 6 servings.

*See Index for recipe

Lunch

*Swiss Salmon Sandwiches**
Coleslaw
Soft Molasses Cookies
Cocoa

Dinner

Braised Lamb Shoulder
Baked Acorn Squash   Honey-Glazed Onions
Lettuce, Cucumber and Minced Chive Salad
Streusel Pear Pie
Coffee   Milk

Streusel Pear Pie

½ c. sugar
1½ tblsp. quick-cooking tapioca
½ tsp. ground cinnamon
⅛ tsp. ground mace
2 tblsp. lemon juice
6 c. sliced pared pears
½ c. butter or regular margarine
1 c. sifted flour
1 c. brown sugar, firmly packed
1 unbaked 9″ pie shell

Combine sugar, tapioca, cinnamon and mace in bowl. Stir in lemon juice and pears. Let stand 15 minutes.

Meanwhile, cut butter into mixture of flour and brown sugar, using pastry blender, until crumbly.

Turn pear mixture into pie shell. Sprinkle crumb mixture evenly over top. Bake in 375° oven 45 to 50 minutes, or until golden brown. Makes 6 to 8 servings.

October 18

Lunch

Cream of Potato Soup
Salami and Lettuce Sandwiches
Fruit Cocktail with Sour Cream and Brown Sugar
Tea   Milk

Dinner

Broiled Knockwurst with Hot Mustard
Baked Kidney Beans*
Escarole, Sliced Radish and Onion Salad
Vanilla Ice Cream and Lemon Sherbet Parfaits
Coffee   Milk

Cream of Potato Soup

6 c. sliced potatoes (5 large)
½ c. sliced carrots
6 slices bacon
1 c. chopped onion
1 c. sliced celery
1½ tsp. salt
¼ tsp. pepper
2 c. milk
2 c. light cream
Finely shredded Cheddar cheese
Parsley sprigs

Cook potatoes and carrots in boiling water until tender. Drain.

Sauté bacon until crisp in skillet. Drain on paper towels. Crumble. Sauté onion and celery in 2 tblsp. of the bacon fat until tender (do not brown).

Combine potatoes, carrots, bacon, onion mixture, salt, pepper, milk and cream. Simmer for 30 minutes. (Do not boil.) Garnish with shredded Cheddar cheese and parsley. Makes about 2 quarts.

*See Index for recipe

Lunch

Pepper Pot Soup
Tuna-Carrot Salad*
Toasted Corn Muffins
Super Cyder Float*

Dinner

Orange-Glazed Ham Steaks
Baked Sweet Potatoes
Brussels Sprouts with Lemon Butter
Tossed Salad
Chocolate Pecan Sponge Cake
Coffee   Milk

Chocolate Pecan Sponge Cake

1 (6-oz.) pkg. semisweet chocolate
  pieces
1¼ c. water
2 tsp. instant coffee powder
1¾ c. sifted flour
1½ tsp. baking soda
1 tsp. salt
6 eggs
1 tsp. vanilla
1½ c. sugar
½ c. finely chopped pecans
Confectioners' Sugar Glaze (recipe
  follows)

Combine chocolate pieces, water and coffee powder in top of double boiler. Place over hot water and heat until chocolate melts. Remove from heat. Cool to room temperature.

Sift together flour, baking soda and salt; set aside.

Beat eggs and vanilla in large mixing bowl until foamy, using electric mixer at high speed. Gradually add sugar, beating until very thick and lemon colored, about 5 minutes.

Add dry ingredients alternately with cooled chocolate mixture, beating well after each addition. Stir in pecans. Pour batter into well-greased 10″ fluted tube pan or tube pan.

Bake in 350° oven 1 hour, or until cake tests done. Cool in pan on rack 10 minutes. Remove from pan; cool on rack. Drizzle with Confectioners' Sugar Glaze. Makes 12 servings.

Confectioners' Sugar Glaze: Combine 1 c. sifted confectioners' sugar, 4 tsp. water and ½ tsp. vanilla in bowl. Beat with spoon until smooth.

October 20

Lunch

Chili-Topped Hamburgers on Toasted Buns

Blue Cheese Onions*

Green Pepper Strips

Lemon and Raspberry Gelatin Cubes

Tea   Milk

Dinner

Broiled Fish Fillets

Cheesed Mashed Potatoes

Green Beans with French-Fried Onion Rings

Chicory and Cherry Tomato Salad

Banana Cream Pie

Coffee   Milk

Cheesed Mashed Potatoes

4 c. hot, seasoned mashed potatoes or
   prepared instant mashed potatoes
1 c. dairy sour cream
⅓ c. chopped green onions
4 oz. sharp Cheddar cheese, cut in
   ¼″ cubes

Combine potatoes, sour cream, green onions and cheese in bowl; mix well. Turn mixture into greased 1½-qt. casserole.

Bake in 350° oven 25 minutes, or until heated. Makes 8 servings.

* See Index for recipe

Lunch

Grilled Muenster Cheese and Bacon Sandwiches
Mixed Vegetable Marinade
Oatmeal Cookies
Cinnamon-Spiced Cocoa

Dinner

Sautéed Chicken Livers

Broiled Mushroom Caps   Minted Carrots and Peas*

Lettuce Wedges with Russian Dressing

Pumpkin Pie

Coffee   Milk

Mixed Vegetable Marinade

1 medium cauliflower, cut up
4 medium carrots, pared and cut
　in 2″ strips
1 (1-lb.) can wax beans, drained
1 (1-lb.) can whole green beans,
　drained
1 c. sliced celery
1 medium onion, sliced
1 (8-oz.) bottle regular Italian
　salad dressing
12 medium pitted ripe olives

Cook cauliflower and carrots in boiling salted water in Dutch oven 5 minutes, or until tender-crisp. Drain. Plunge into iced water; drain well.

Combine cooled vegetables, wax beans, green beans, celery, onion, salad dressing and olives in bowl. Toss gently to mix. Cover; refrigerate overnight. Salad can be stored up to 5 days. Makes 10 servings.

October 22

Lunch

*Famous Clam Chowder**

Roast Beef Sandwiches

Pineapple Chunks in Orange Juice

Coffee   Tea

Dinner

Spanish-style Pork Chops

Parslied Rice   Buttered Asparagus Spears

Romaine Salad

Apple Cobbler with Cream

Tea   Milk

Spanish-style Pork Chops

6 pork chops, ¾ " thick
1 tsp. salt
⅛ tsp. pepper
1 tblsp. cooking oil
1 (1-lb.) can tomatoes, cut up
½ c. chopped onion
½ c. chopped green pepper
½ c. chopped celery
¼ c. uncooked regular rice
2 tsp. dried parsley flakes
½ bay leaf
½ c. water

Season pork chops with salt and pepper. Brown chops in hot oil in large skillet. Add tomatoes, onion, green pepper, celery, rice, parsley flakes, bay leaf and water. Bring to a boil; reduce heat. Cover. Simmer for 45 minutes, or until meat is tender. Makes 6 servings.

*See Index for recipe

Lunch

Green Pepper and Onion Omelets

Light Puffy Rolls with Currant Jelly

Tapioca Pudding with Sliced Peaches

Tea   Milk

Dinner

Lamb Stew with Dumplings

Hearts of Lettuce with Roquefort Dressing

Raspberry-Vanilla Cloud*

Coffee   Tea   Milk

Light Puffy Rolls

3 pkg. active dry yeast
2 c. lukewarm water
½ c. sugar
¼ c. cooking oil
1¼ tsp. salt
1 egg
7 c. sifted flour

Sprinkle yeast on lukewarm water in bowl; stir to dissolve.

Add sugar, oil, salt and egg; blend well. Let stand 5 minutes. Add 2 c. flour. Beat with electric mixer at medium speed until smooth, about 2 minutes, scraping bowl occasionally. Or beat with spoon until smooth.

Gradually add enough flour to make a soft dough that leaves the sides of the bowl. Turn out on floured surface and knead until smooth and satiny, about 8 minutes.

Place dough in greased bowl; turn over to grease top.

Cover and let rise in warm place until doubled, about 1½ hours.

Divide dough into quarters. Cut each quarter into 18 equal pieces. Roll each piece into a small ball and place two balls in each greased 3″ muffin-pan cup. Let rise until doubled, about 45 minutes.

Bake in 350° oven 20 minutes, or until brown. Remove from pans; cool on racks. Makes 36 rolls.

Lunch

Green Soup*
Liverwurst and Sliced Egg Sandwiches
Stuffed Olives   Celery Curls
Coconut Cookies
Tea   Milk

Dinner

Grated Vegetable Meat Loaf
Sautéed Cherry Tomatoes   Buttered Spinach
Coffee Ice Cream with Chocolate Sauce
Coffee   Milk

Grated Vegetable Meat Loaf

2 lb. ground beef
1 c. grated potato
½ c. grated carrots
½ c. chopped onion
¼ c. chopped green pepper
2 tblsp. diced pimientos
2 tsp. salt
1 tsp. dried savory leaves
½ tsp. ground nutmeg
¼ tsp. pepper
2 eggs, slightly beaten
¼ c. water

Combine all ingredients in bowl. Mix lightly, but well. Press mixture into greased 9x5x3″ loaf pan.

Bake in 350° oven 1 hour, or until done. Makes 6 to 8 servings.

*See Index for recipe

Lunch

Beef Bouillon

Sliced Chicken and Bean Sprouts in Pita Bread

Date and Apricot Bars

Tea   Milk

Dinner

Broiled Sausage Patties

Sautéed Zucchini Strips   Corn Custard Pudding*

Tossed Salad

Orange Layer Cake

Coffee   Milk

Date and Apricot Bars

1½ c. dried apricots
2 c. water
1 c. cut-up dates
½ c. sugar
1 tsp. grated lemon rind
½ c. chopped pecans
$\frac{1}{16}$ tsp. salt
2 c. sifted flour
2 c. quick-cooking oats
1 c. brown sugar, firmly packed
¾ c. melted butter or regular
   margarine
1 tsp. baking soda
1 tsp. vanilla

Cook apricots in water until tender. Drain; reserve 3 tblsp. cooking liquid. Combine cooked apricots, dates, sugar and reserved liquid in saucepan. Simmer 3 minutes. Stir in lemon rind, pecans and salt. Cool well.

Combine flour, oats, brown sugar, butter, baking soda and vanilla; mix well. Press half of mixture in greased 13x9x2" baking pan. Spread with cooled filling. Top with remaining crumb mixture.

Bake in 375° oven 35 minutes. Cool in pan on rack. Cut in 3x1" bars. Makes about 3 dozen.

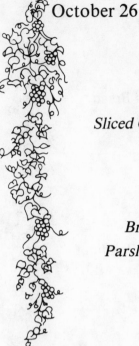

October 26

Lunch

Pasta and Bean Soup*

Toasted Garlic Bread

Sliced Oranges, Grapes and Pears in Lemonade

Coffee   Tea

Dinner

Brown Sugar-Glazed Canadian Bacon

Parslied Boiled Potatoes with Lemon Butter

Skillet Cabbage

Apple-Coconut Turnovers

Coffee   Milk

Skillet Cabbage

2 tblsp. cooking oil
3 c. chopped cabbage
1 c. chopped celery
¾ c. chopped green pepper
½ c. chopped onion
2 c. chopped seeded tomatoes
1 tsp. sugar
¾ tsp. salt
¼ tsp. pepper

Heat oil in 10″ skillet. Add cabbage, celery, green pepper, onion, tomatoes, sugar, salt and pepper; mix well. Cover; cook over medium heat 10 minutes, or until cabbage is tender but still crisp. Makes 6 servings.

* See Index for recipe

Lunch

Mugs of Hot Basil-Spiced Tomato Juice
Sliced Canadian Bacon and Muenster Cheese
Orange Date Muffins
Sliced Bananas and Pineapple Chunks
Tea   Milk

Dinner

Braised Turkey Legs
Baked Sweet Potatoes   Buttered Broccoli
Country-style Beet Salad*
Brownies à la Mode
Coffee   Milk

Orange Date Muffins

2 c. sifted flour
½ c. sugar
2½ tsp. baking powder
½ tsp. salt
½ c. chopped dates
1½ tsp. grated orange rind
1 egg, beaten
¾ c. milk
¼ c. melted butter or regular
  margarine

Sift together flour, sugar, baking powder and salt into bowl. Add dates and orange rind; stir to coat with flour mixture.

Combine egg, milk and butter. Add to dry ingredients, stirring just enough to moisten. Spoon batter into greased 2½" muffin-pan cups, filling two-thirds full.

Bake in 400° oven 20 minutes, or until done. Makes 16.

*See Index for recipe

October 28

Lunch

Tuna Club Sandwiches

Cottage Cheese and Chopped Chives

Old-Fashioned Filled Cookies*

Cocoa

Dinner

Turkey Curry with Rice

Buttered Green Beans

Endive and Kumquat Salad

Cream Puffs

Coffee   Tea   Milk

Turkey Curry with Rice

1 c. sliced onion
¼ c. sliced carrots
¼ c. sliced celery
1 apple, pared, cored and sliced
1 clove garlic, minced
¼ c. butter or regular margarine
⅓ c. flour
2½ tsp. curry powder
¼ tsp. ground ginger
¼ tsp. ground mace
¼ tsp. pepper
2 c. chicken broth
1 (4-oz.) can mushrooms
3 c. cubed cooked turkey
2 c. dairy sour cream
Hot fluffy rice
Condiments: Chopped onion, raisins,
    chopped green pepper, chopped
    tomato, chopped hard-cooked
    eggs, chopped peanuts, coconut
    and chutney

Sauté onion, carrots, celery, apple and garlic in melted butter in 12″ skillet.

Slowly blend in flour, curry powder, ginger, mace and pepper. Gradually add chicken broth and undrained mushrooms. Cook over medium heat, stirring constantly, until it comes to a boil. Simmer 5 minutes.

Stir in turkey. Heat well. Stir in sour cream; heat 2 more minutes. Serve with rice. Pass a selection of condiments. Makes 6 servings.

* See Index for recipe

Lunch

Beef Bouillon

Peanut Butter, Raisin and Grated Carrot Sandwiches

Chunky Cider Applesauce à la Mode

Tea   Milk

Dinner

Broiled Ground Beef Patties Topped with Blue Cheese

Polka Dot Carrots*   Braised Leeks

Coleslaw

Butterscotch Meringue Pie

Coffee   Milk

Chunky Cider Applesauce

9 c. pared, sliced apples
½ c. apple cider
1 tblsp. lemon juice
½ c. sugar
⅛ tsp. salt
½ tsp. ground nutmeg

Combine apples, cider and lemon juice in 3-qt. saucepan. Bring to boil over medium heat. Simmer until apples are tender, for about 20 minutes.

Add sugar, salt and nutmeg; cook for 1 minute longer. Break up apples into chunks. Makes about 1 quart.

*See Index for recipe

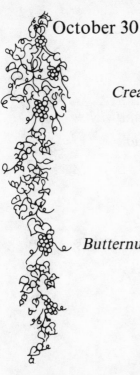

October 30

Lunch

Cream Cheese and Dried Beef Sandwiches

*Ratatouille**

Coffee Milk Shakes

Dinner

Braised Lamb Shoulder

Butternut Squash with Chives   *Brussels Sprouts*

Tossed Salad

Whole-Wheat Protein Bread

Riced Peach Gelatin

Coffee   Tea   Milk

Whole-Wheat Protein Bread

2½ c. milk
3 tblsp. sugar
1 tblsp. salt
2 tblsp. butter or regular margarine
3 c. all-purpose flour
2 pkg. active dry yeast
⅔ c. nonfat dry milk
⅓ c. stirred soy flour
¼ c. wheat germ
3 to 3½ c. stirred whole-wheat flour

Heat milk, sugar, salt and butter in a saucepan until warm, stirring to melt butter.

In large mixer bowl, combine all-purpose flour and yeast. Add warm milk mixture and beat at low speed ½ minute, scraping sides and bottom of bowl constantly. Beat at high speed 3 minutes, scraping bowl occasionally.

By hand, stir in dry milk, soy flour, wheat germ and enough whole-wheat flour to make a moderately soft dough. Turn out on lightly floured surface and knead until smooth and elastic, about 7 minutes.

Place in greased bowl, turning to grease sides. Cover; let rise in warm place until doubled, 1 to 1½ hours.

Punch down. Divide dough in half, cover and let rest 10 minutes. Shape each half into a loaf and place in 2 greased 8½x4½x2½" loaf pans. Cover and let rise in warm place until doubled, 40 to 45 minutes.

Bake in 375° oven until golden brown, about 35 minutes. Remove from pans; cool on racks. Makes 2 loaves.

See Index for recipe

Lunch

Vegetable Soup

Camembert Cheese   Green Grapes in Orange Shells

*Whole-Wheat Protein Bread**

Orange-Glazed Chocolate Cookies

Apple Cider

Dinner

Lamb Hash

Brown Sugar-Glazed Carrots   Buttered Lima Beans

*Cauliflower Salad Bowl**

Pumpkin Spice Cake

Coffee   Milk

Pumpkin Spice Cake

1 (18½-oz.) pkg. spice cake mix
1 (1-lb.) can pumpkin
2 tsp. baking soda
2 eggs
⅓ c. water
Cream Cheese Frosting
(recipe follows)

Combine cake mix, pumpkin, baking soda, eggs and water in large mixer bowl. Beat as directed on cake-mix package. Spread in 2 greased and floured 9″ round layer cake pans.

Bake in 350° oven 25 to 30 minutes. Let cool 10 minutes, then turn out of pans. Cool.

Spread Cream Cheese Frosting between layers, then frost sides and top of cake. Makes 12 servings.

Cream Cheese Frosting: Cream together ½ c. butter or regular margarine, 1 (8-oz.) pkg. cream cheese and 1 tsp. vanilla until light and fluffy. Gradually add 1-lb. pkg. sifted confectioners' sugar, beating well after each addition. If mixture is too thick to spread, add a small amount of milk.

*See Index for recipe

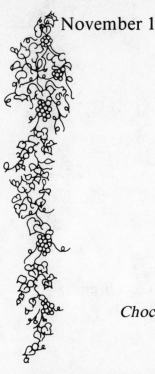

November 1

Lunch

Maine Corn Chowder*

Crackers   Sliced Salami

Cinnamon Doughnuts

Tea   Milk

Dinner

American-style Enchiladas

Buttered Sliced Beets

Romaine Salad

Chocolate Pudding with Toasted Coconut

Coffee   Milk

American-style Enchiladas

6 eggs, well beaten
3 c. milk
2 c. sifted flour
¾ tsp. salt
1 lb. ground beef
1 lb. bulk pork sausage
1 c. chopped onion
½ c. chopped green pepper
2 cloves garlic, minced
1⅔ tblsp. chili powder
1 tsp. salt
1 (10-oz.) pkg. frozen spinach,
  cooked, drained and chopped
1 (29-oz.) jar or 2 (15-oz.) cans
  meatless spaghetti sauce
1 (8-oz.) can tomato sauce
1 c. water
1 tblsp. chili powder
2 c. shredded Cheddar cheese

Combine eggs and milk. Add flour and ¾ tsp. salt; beat until smooth. Pour about ¼ c. batter into hot greased 7″ skillet, tilting skillet so batter covers surface. Turn pancakes when surface looks dry. Makes 30.

Brown ground beef and sausage in large skillet. Pour off all but 1 tblsp. fat. Add onion, green pepper, garlic, 1⅔ tblsp. chili powder and 1 tsp. salt. Simmer for 10 minutes. Add spinach; mix well. Let cool.

Combine spaghetti sauce, tomato sauce, water and 1 tblsp. chili powder; set aside.

Spoon ¼ c. meat mixture across center of each pancake. Fold sides over ½″. Roll up each pancake. Place in two 13x9x2″ (3-qt.) glass baking dishes. Pour half of sauce over rolled pancakes in each baking dish. Top each with half of shredded cheese.

Bake in 325° oven 30 minutes. Makes 15 servings.

*See Index for recipe

Autumn

When the apple crop comes in, it's a sure sign that fall is here—and time for cider! Super Cyder Float (p. 256) tastes like apple pie á la mode in a glass.

A hearty soup makes the meal in late fall and winter. Serve Chicken Vegetable Soup (p. 348) with lots of sour cream, chopped scallions or fresh dill.

A company dish that's really special is
American-style Enchiladas (p. 248). A
real timesaver, you can freeze them
ahead and reheat just before serving.

Extra turkey from the holiday bird becomes a main dish with an interna-
tional flavor: Turkey Curry with Rice
(p. 244) with assorted condiments.

Lunch

Cottage Cheese-Stuffed Tomatoes

Thinly Sliced Boiled Ham

Whole-Wheat Raisin Bread*

Poached Pears

Coffee   Tea   Milk

Dinner

Baked Fish Sticks

French Fried Potatoes   Asparagus with Lemon Butter

Escarole and Sliced Cucumber Salad

Lemon Sponge Pie

Coffee   Milk

Lemon Sponge Pie

2 c. sugar
1 tblsp. flour
1 tblsp. corn meal
4 eggs
¼ c. milk
¼ c. melted butter or regular
   margarine
¼ c. lemon juice
2 tblsp. grated lemon rind
1 unbaked 9″ pie shell

Combine sugar, flour and corn meal in bowl. Add eggs, milk, butter, lemon juice and lemon rind. Beat with rotary beater until smooth and well blended. Pour into pie shell.

Bake in 350° oven 40 minutes, or until golden brown. Cool on rack. Makes 6 to 8 servings.

*See Index for recipe

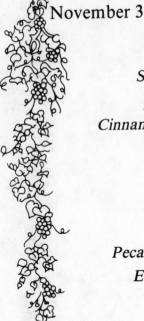

November 3

Lunch

Sliced Egg and Bacon Sandwiches
Spinach-Mushroom Vinaigrette
Cinnamon-Dusted Sliced Bananas and Cream
Tea   Milk

Dinner

Broiled Veal Chops
Pecan Sweet Potatoes*   *Buttered Peas*
Endive and Sliced Grapefruit Salad
Jelly Roll
Coffee   Milk

Spinach-Mushroom Vinaigrette

2 lb. fresh spinach
½ lb. fresh mushrooms, sliced
¼ c. minced fresh parsley
¾ c. salad oil
¼ c. lemon juice
1 clove garlic, minced
¾ tsp. salt
¼ tsp. sugar
Dash of pepper

Wash spinach and drain well. Stem spinach. Tear into bite-size pieces and place in salad bowl. Add mushrooms and parsley. Toss lightly. Combine oil, lemon juice, garlic, salt, sugar and pepper in jar. Cover and shake well. Pour dressing over spinach mixture. Toss gently and serve immediately. Makes 8 servings.

*See Index for recipe

Lunch

Hearty Split Pea Soup*
Cream Cheese and Chopped Olive Sandwiches
Soft Molasses Cookies
Tea   Milk

Dinner

Macaroni-Sausage Casserole
Stewed Tomatoes   Buttered Brussels Sprouts
Tangy Slaw*
Spiced Prunes in Apple Juice
Coffee   Milk

Macaroni-Sausage Casserole

1 (8-oz.) pkg. elbow macaroni
1 lb. bulk pork sausage
½ c. chopped onion
½ c. green pepper strips
3 tblsp. flour
½ tsp. salt
2 c. milk
2 c. shredded Cheddar cheese

Cook macaroni in 3 qt. boiling salted water for 7 to 8 minutes; drain well. Set aside.

Brown sausage in saucepan; remove and reserve ½ of sausage. Sauté onion and green pepper with remaining sausage in 2 tblsp. of fat. Stir in flour and salt. Slowly add milk. Cook over medium heat, stirring, until thick. Stir in 1½ c. cheese.

Combine macaroni and sauce; turn into greased 2-qt. casserole. Top with ½ c. cheese and reserved sausage. Bake in 400° oven 25 minutes, or until golden. Makes 6 servings.

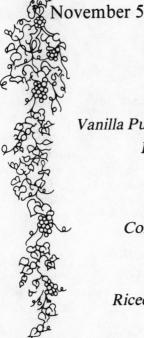

November 5

Lunch

Caesar Salad
Honey Oatmeal Bread
Vanilla Pudding Layered with Crushed Strawberries
Hot Cider with Cinnamon Sticks

Dinner

Corned Beef Hash with Poached Eggs
Corn Niblets and Peas
Arizona Green Salad*
Riced Orange Gelatin with Custard Sauce
Coffee   Milk

Honey Oatmeal Bread

1 c. quick-cooking oats
¼ c. butter or regular margarine
⅓ c. honey
1 tblsp. salt
2 c. boiling water
2 pkg. active dry yeast
1 c. lukewarm water
8 c. sifted flour
Melted butter or regular margarine

Combine oats, ¼ c. butter, honey and salt in large mixing bowl. Stir in 2 c. boiling water. Cool to lukewarm.

Sprinkle yeast on 1 c. lukewarm water; stir to dissolve. Add yeast and 2 c. flour to oat mixture. Beat with electric mixer at medium speed until smooth, for about 2 minutes, scraping bowl occasionally. Or beat with spoon until batter is smooth.

Gradually add enough remaining flour, a little at a time, to make a soft dough that leaves the sides of the bowl. Turn onto lightly floured surface and knead until smooth and satiny, for about 8 to 10 minutes.

Place in lightly greased bowl; turn dough over to grease top. Cover and let rise in warm place until doubled, for about 1 to 1½ hours.

Divide dough in thirds. Shape into loaves and place in 3 greased 9x5x3″ loaf pans. Let rise until doubled.

Bake in 400° oven 10 minutes. Reduce heat to 350°; bake 30 to 35 minutes, or until bread tests done. Remove from pans. Brush with melted butter. Cool on racks. Makes 3 loaves.

*See Index for recipe

Lunch

Tomato Bouillon
Corned Beef and Coleslaw on Toasted Buns
Green Pepper Strips
Canned Plums with Sour Cream and Orange Curls
Tea   Milk

Dinner

Baked Chicken Breasts with Almond Sauce*
Hot Fluffy Rice   Buttered Spinach
Lettuce Wedges with French Dressing
Lime Sherbet
Coffee   Milk

Tomato Bouillon

1 (16- to 17-oz.) can tomato juice
1 (10½-oz.) can condensed beef
  broth
¼ tsp. seasoned salt

Combine all the ingredients and heat. Serve piping hot with crisp crackers. Makes 6 servings.

November 7

Lunch

Welsh Rarebit on Toasted English Muffins

Tossed Salad

Apricot Snowdrifts*

Coffee   Tea   Milk

Dinner

Baked Pork Chops

Fried Apple Rings   Green Beans with Mushrooms

Romaine, Black Olive and Radish Salad

Deep-Dish Cherry Pie

Coffee   Milk

Fried Apple Rings

3 large firm apples
3 tblsp. butter or regular margarine
2 tblsp. brown sugar, firmly packed
Ground cinnamon
Ground nutmeg

Core apples, but do not pare. Cut apples in ½" slices.

Melt butter in large heavy skillet. Add apple slices; sprinkle with brown sugar, cinnamon and nutmeg. Cook over medium heat, turning apple rings until they are golden brown and tender. Makes 8 servings.

*See Index for recipe

Lunch

Vegetable Soup

Tuna Fish and Chopped Apple Sandwiches

Almond Rice Pudding*

Tea   Milk

Dinner

Roast Beef

Roasted Potatoes   Carrot Patties

Endive and Sliced Grapefruit Salad

Strawberry-Frosted Spice Cake

Coffee   Milk

Carrot Patties

1½ c. grated raw carrots
3 tblsp. grated onion
3 c. bread crumbs
¾ tsp. baking powder
2 eggs, beaten
¼ c. milk
½ tsp. salt
⅛ tsp. pepper
3 tblsp. butter or bacon fat

Combine carrots, onion, bread crumbs, baking powder, eggs, milk, salt and pepper in bowl. Mix well and form into patties similar to potato cakes, about 3″ in diameter (there should be 12).

Heat butter in a skillet; brown patties lightly on both sides. Makes 6 servings.

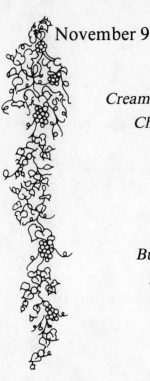

November 9

Lunch

Cream of Celery Soup with Minced Scallions
Chopped Chicken Liver Sandwiches
<u>*Super Cyder Float*</u>

Dinner

Roast Beef Hash
Buttered Broccoli   Corn Fritters
Ruby Cranberry Crunch Salad*
Vanilla Ice Cream Topped with
Crushed Peppermint Candies
Coffee   Tea   Milk

Super Cyder Float

1 qt. chilled apple cider
1 pt. vanilla ice cream
Ground nutmeg

Pour 1 c. cider into four old-fash-ioned root beer mugs or tall glasses. Top each with a scoop of ice cream. Sprinkle with nutmeg. Makes 4.

*See Index for recipe

Lunch

Sliced Ham   Sliced Tomatoes

Dilly Cheese-Stuffed Celery*

Cherry Gelatin Cubes with Crushed Pineapple

Tea   Milk

Dinner

Baked Veal Cutlet with Eggplant

Buttered Spaghetti

Buttered Lima Beans

Brownies

Coffee   Milk

Baked Veal Cutlet with Eggplant

1½ lb. veal cutlets
1 tsp. salt
¼ c. cooking oil
½ c. chopped onion
½ c. chopped green pepper
1 clove garlic, minced
1 (1-lb.) can tomatoes, cut up
½ tsp. salt
½ tsp. dried oregano leaves
¼ tsp. pepper
1 medium eggplant, pared and sliced
½ c. grated Parmesan cheese
½ lb. mozzarella cheese, sliced

Season veal cutlets with 1 tsp. salt. Brown in hot oil in skillet. Remove from skillet. Add onion, green pepper and garlic; sauté until tender (do not brown). Add tomatoes, ½ tsp. salt, oregano and pepper. Bring to a boil.

Place a layer of eggplant in 12x8x2″ (2-qt.) glass baking dish. Top with sauce and then meat. Repeat layers. Sprinkle with Parmesan cheese. Cover with aluminum foil.

Bake in 350° oven 50 minutes. Uncover. Top with mozzarella cheese. Bake for 10 more minutes. Makes 6 servings.

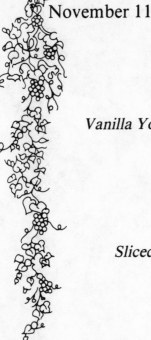

November 11

Lunch

Green Pea Soup
Coney Island Hot Dogs*
Vanilla Yogurt with Brown Sugar and Cinnamon
Tea   Milk

Dinner

Baked Turkey Legs
Sliced Turnips Cooked in Beef Bouillon
Mushroom Bread Stuffing
Lemon Meringue Pie
Espresso

Mushroom Bread Stuffing

1 c. chopped onion
1 (4-oz.) can sliced mushrooms,
  drained
¼ c. butter or regular margarine
12 c. soft bread cubes (¾″)
¼ c. minced fresh parsley
1 tsp. rubbed sage
¼ tsp. pepper
¼ c. melted butter or regular
  margarine
1 (10½-oz.) can condensed cream of
  mushroom soup
1 tblsp. milk

Sauté onion and mushrooms in ¼ c. melted butter in skillet until tender (do not brown). Toss together bread cubes, parsley, sage, pepper, ¼ c. melted butter and sautéed vegetables. Stir soup and add to mixture.

Place in greased 2-qt. casserole and sprinkle with milk. Bake in 350° oven 35 minutes, or until brown. Makes 6 to 8 servings.

See Index for recipe

Lunch

Turkey and Cucumber Sandwiches
Eggs in Vinaigrette Sauce*
Coffee-Glazed Marble Cake
Tea   Milk

Dinner

Sausages and Potatoes
Buttered Sliced Brussels Sprouts
Lettuce Wedges with Tarragon Dressing
Brown Sugar-Topped Baked Bananas
Coffee   Milk

Sausages and Potatoes

2 lb. small pork sausage links
2 c. water
2 bay leaves
10 whole allspice
1½ tsp. salt
¼ tsp. pepper
2 lb. medium potatoes,
   pared and quartered
2 tblsp. chopped fresh parsley

Place pork sausages, water, bay leaves, allspice, salt and pepper in Dutch oven. Bring to a boil. Reduce heat and simmer 20 minutes.

Add potatoes. Cover and simmer 20 minutes, or until potatoes are tender. Sprinkle with parsley. Makes 6 to 8 servings.

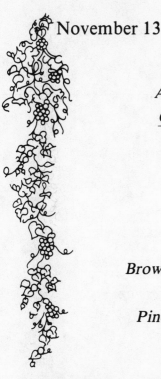

November 13

Lunch

Apple, Pear and Walnut Salad

Cheddar Cheese Snack Bread

Baked Custard with Honey

Cocoa

Dinner

Roast Duckling

Brown Rice   Braised Red Cabbage*

Escarole and Onion Salad

Pineapple Cubes Rolled in Coconut

Coffee   Milk

Cheddar Cheese Snack Bread

¾ c. milk
2 tblsp. sugar
2 tblsp. shortening
1 tsp. salt
1 pkg. active dry yeast
¼ c. lukewarm water
1 egg
2½ c. sifted flour
½ lb. Cheddar cheese,
　shredded (about 2 c.)
5 tblsp. milk
¾ tsp. grated onion
¼ tsp. salt
Paprika

Scald ¾ c. milk in saucepan. Stir in sugar, shortening and 1 tsp. salt. Pour into mixer bowl. Cool to lukewarm.

Sprinkle yeast on lukewarm water; stir to dissolve. Add yeast, egg and 1 c. flour to milk mixture. Beat with electric mixer at medium speed until smooth, for about 2 minutes, scraping bowl occasionally. Or beat with spoon until batter is smooth.

Gradually add remaining flour, a little at a time. (Dough will be sticky.) Turn onto lightly floured surface and knead for 3 minutes.

Place in lightly greased bowl; turn dough over to grease top. Cover and let rise in warm place until doubled, for about 1 to 1½ hours.

Press dough into greased 13x9x2″ baking pan. Let rise until doubled. Combine cheese, 5 tblsp. milk, onion and ¼ tsp. salt. Spread evenly over dough. Sprinkle with paprika.

Bake in 375° oven 35 minutes, or until top is golden. Cut in squares and serve warm. Makes 18 squares.

    *See Index for recipe

Lunch

Smothered Burgers*
Coleslaw   Radishes
Ginger Ale Floats

Dinner

Cheese Soufflé

Buttered Corn Niblets   Buttered Peas

Avocado and Tomato Salad

Frozen Pumpkin Pie

Coffee   Milk

Frozen Pumpkin Pie

Baked 9″ Crumb Crust
  (recipe follows)
1 pt. butter pecan ice cream, softened
1 c. canned or cooked mashed
  pumpkin
1 c. sugar
½ tsp. salt
½ tsp. ground cinnamon
¼ tsp. ground ginger
¼ tsp. ground nutmeg
½ tsp. vanilla
1½ c. miniature marshmallows
1 c. heavy cream, whipped

Spoon ice cream into cool pie shell; spread in even layer. Freeze.

Mix pumpkin, sugar, salt, spices and vanilla. Fold in marshmallows and whipped cream.

Pour into Crumb Crust on top of ice cream. Cover with foil and freeze several hours or overnight. Let thaw at room temperature 5 minutes before cutting. Makes 6 to 8 servings.

Crumb Crust: Mix 1½ c. graham cracker crumbs, 3 tblsp. sugar and ⅓ c. melted butter or regular margarine. Press mixture firmly and evenly into a 9″ pie pan. Bake in 350° oven 10 minutes. Cool before filling.

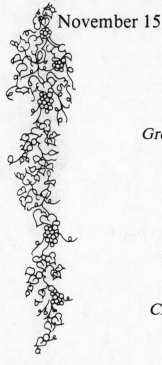

November 15

Lunch

Bean Soup

Easy Nachos

Green Grapes, Dates and Apricots

Tea   Milk

Dinner

English Fish and Chips*

Buttered Beets

Curly Endive Salad

Cream Puffs with Vanilla Glaze

Coffee   Milk

Easy Nachos

24 taco-flavored tortilla chips
½ c. canned bean dip
½ c. shredded Cheddar cheese (2 oz.)

Place tortilla chips on broiler pan. Top each chip with 1 tsp. bean dip, then with cheese. Broil 4″ from heat until cheese melts, 1 to 3 minutes. Makes 24.

See Index for recipe

Lunch

Grated Raw Carrot and Sliced Black Olive Sandwiches

Potato Salad in Green Pepper Cups

Oatmeal Refrigerator Cookies

Tea   Milk

Dinner

Roast Loin of Pork*

Buttered Lima Beans   Whipped Butternut Squash

Hearts of Lettuce with Roquefort Dressing

Honey-Drizzled Broiled Grapefruit

Tea   Milk

Oatmeal Refrigerator Cookies

1 c. butter or regular margarine
1 c. sifted confectioners' sugar
2 tsp. vanilla
1¼ c. sifted flour
½ tsp. salt
1 c. quick-cooking oats
⅓ c. chocolate jimmies

Cream together butter and confectioners' sugar in bowl until light and fluffy. Beat in vanilla.

Sift together flour and salt. Gradually stir into creamed mixture. Stir in oats. Shape dough into roll, about 2″ in diameter. Roll in chocolate jimmies. Chill for 1 hour.

Cut roll into ¼″ thick slices. Place 2″ apart on greased baking sheets.

Bake in 325° oven 15 minutes, or until golden brown. Remove from baking sheets. Cool on racks. Makes about 3 dozen.

*See Index for recipe

November 17

Lunch

Mexican Tomato-Corn Soup*

Salami and Sliced Cucumber Sandwiches

Cinnamon-Dusted Sliced Pears and Bananas

Coffee   Tea   Milk

Dinner

Chicken Livers and Mushrooms en Brochette

Sautéed Cherry Tomatoes   Snap Beans with Cheese

Chicory and Cauliflower Salad

Riced Lemon and Lime Gelatin Parfaits

Coffee   Milk

Snap Beans with Cheese

4 c. green beans, cut in 1″ pieces,
   (1 lb.)
½ c. chopped onion (1 small)
2 slices bacon, diced
¼ c. milk
½ c. shredded process American
   cheese
½ tsp. salt
⅛ tsp. pepper

Cook beans with onion and bacon in boiling salted water until tender. Drain, reserving liquid. Add ¼ c. bean liquid, milk, cheese, salt and pepper to beans. Stir until cheese melts. Makes 6 servings.

* See Index for recipe

Lunch

Molded Corned Beef Ring*

Graham Muffins

Almond-Stuffed Baked Apples

Cocoa

Dinner

Pork Curry*

Rice with Chutney   Steamed Spinach

Orange Sherbet Topped with Chopped Crystallized Ginger

Coffee   Milk

Graham Muffins

1½ c. graham cracker crumbs
2 tsp. baking powder
⅓ c. melted butter or regular
    margarine
¼ c. dark corn syrup
1 egg, beaten
½ c. milk
½ c. chopped pecans
1 tblsp. flour

Combine graham cracker crumbs and baking powder in bowl. Combine butter, corn syrup, egg and milk. Add to graham cracker mixture, stirring just enough to moisten. Stir in combined pecans and flour. Spoon batter into greased 3″ muffin-pan cups, filling two-thirds full.

Bake in 375° oven 20 minutes, or until done. Makes 12.

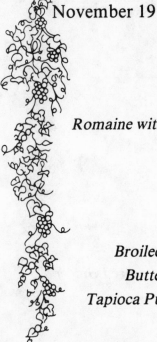

November 19

Lunch

Meatball and Lentil Soup*

Toasted Sourdough Rolls

Romaine with Oil, Vinegar and Toasted Sesame Seeds

Blueberry Turnovers

Tea   Milk

Dinner

Broiled Lamb Patties with Herbed Butter

Buttered Peas   Swedish Rutabagas

Tapioca Pudding and Crushed Pineapple Parfaits

Coffee   Milk

Swedish Rutabagas

2 medium rutabagas, pared,
  quartered and sliced ¼" thick
2 tblsp. brown sugar, firmly packed
½ tsp. ground ginger
½ tsp. salt
⅛ tsp. pepper
2 tblsp. butter or regular margarine

Cook rutabagas in boiling salted water; drain.

Meanwhile, combine brown sugar, ginger, salt and pepper; mix thoroughly. Add with butter to rutabagas. Stir gently over low heat until sugar melts, 2 to 3 minutes. Makes 6 servings.

*See Index for recipe

Lunch

Mushroom-Chive Omelets

Buttered Green Beans   Bread Sticks

Molasses-Ginger Cookies

Cocoa with Nutmeg-Dusted Marshmallows

Dinner

Stir-Fried Chicken and Snow Peas

Butter-Crumb Potatoes*

Tossed Salad

Lemon-Filled Coconut Layer Cake

Coffee   Milk

Molasses-Ginger Cookies

½ c. shortening
½ c. sugar
½ c. light molasses
½ tblsp. vinegar
1 egg, beaten
3 c. sifted flour
½ tsp. baking soda
½ tsp. ground cinnamon
½ tsp. ground ginger
¼ tsp. salt

Combine shortening, sugar, molasses and vinegar in small saucepan. Bring mixture to a boil and remove from heat. Cool well and beat in egg.

Sift together flour, baking soda, cinnamon, ginger and salt. Gradually stir into molasses mixture. Cover and chill for 1 hour.

Divide dough in half. Roll on floured surface ⅛" thick. Cut into desired shapes with floured cookie cutters. Place 1" apart on greased baking sheets.

Bake in 375° oven 10 minutes, or until done. Remove from baking sheets. Cool on racks. Makes about 2½ dozen.

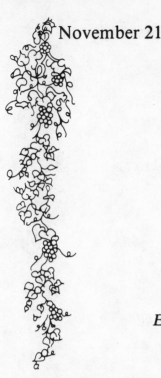

November 21

Lunch

Assorted Cheeses

Coolrise French Bread*

Fresh Fruit Salad

Chocolate Cupcakes

Tea   Milk

Dinner

<u>*Jambalaya*</u>

Buttered Broccoli

Endive and Sliced Radish Salad

Floating Island

Coffee   Milk

Jambalaya

6 slices bacon, chopped
1 c. chopped onion
2 medium green peppers, cut in strips
2 c. uncooked regular rice
2 cloves garlic, minced
1 (1-lb., 12-oz.) can tomatoes, cut up
2 c. chicken broth
1 tsp. salt
½ tsp. dried thyme leaves
¼ tsp. ground red pepper
1 lb. cooked, smoked ham, cut in strips
½ lb. cleaned, frozen shrimp, thawed
2 tblsp. chopped fresh parsley (optional)

Cook bacon in Dutch oven until crisp. Drain on paper towels. Add onion to bacon drippings and cook over low heat, stirring occasionally, 5 minutes. Add green pepper; continue cooking 3 minutes. Add rice; cook over moderately hot heat, stirring frequently, until rice becomes somewhat opaque. Add bacon, garlic, tomatoes, chicken broth, salt, thyme, red pepper and ham. Bring to a boil.

Cover and bake in 350° oven 15 minutes. Stir in shrimp; continue baking 20 to 25 minutes, or until rice is tender and liquid absorbed. Serve garnished with parsley, if desired. Makes 6 servings.

* See Index for recipe

Lunch

Herbed Tomato Juice in Mugs

Tuna Aspic Mold*

Baking Powder Biscuits

Yogurt with Crushed Pineapple

Tea   Milk

Dinner

Swiss Steak

Acorn Squash with Creamed Onions

Escarole and Sliced Avocado Salad

Mincemeat Tarts

Coffee   Milk

Acorn Squash with Creamed Onions

3 acorn squash
Salt
2 lb. small onions, peeled (about 4 c.)
½ c. light raisins
2 tblsp. butter or regular margarine
2 tblsp. flour
¼ tsp. salt
1½ c. milk
¼ tsp. ground nutmeg

Wash squash; cut in halves lengthwise, and remove seeds. Place squash, cut side down, in shallow baking pan; add a few tablespoons water to pan. Bake in 400° oven 30 minutes. Turn cut side up; sprinkle with salt and continue baking 25 to 30 minutes, until tender.

Cook onions in boiling salted water, covered, about 30 minutes, or until tender. Drain.

Simmer raisins in water to cover 10 minutes; drain.

Melt butter in saucepan; blend in flour and ¼ tsp. salt. Add milk all at once. Cook and stir until sauce is thickened. Blend in ¼ tsp. nutmeg. Gently stir in onions and raisins. Spoon into cooked squash halves; sprinkle with additional nutmeg. Makes 6 servings.

November 23

Lunch

Cheddar Cheese Soup

Bean Sprouts and Sliced Ham in Pita Bread

Crisp Cranberry Crumble

Tea   Milk

Dinner

Old World Sauerbraten*

Whipped Potatoes   Buttered Sliced Beets

Tossed Salad

Lemon-Frosted Spice Cake

Coffee   Milk

Crisp Cranberry Crumble

1 c. brown sugar, firmly packed
1 c. sifted flour
¾ c. quick-cooking rolled oats
1 tsp. ground cinnamon
½ c. melted butter or regular
  margarine
4 c. whole cranberries
1 c. sugar
2 tblsp. cornstarch
1 c. water
½ c. chopped walnuts
Whipped cream or ice cream

Combine brown sugar, flour, oats, cinnamon and butter in bowl; mix until crumbly. Press half of mixture in 9" square baking pan. Place cranberries in a layer over crust.

Combine sugar and cornstarch in small saucepan. Slowly stir in water. Cook over medium heat, stirring constantly, until thick and clear. Pour sauce over cranberries.

Add walnuts to remaining crumb mixture. Sprinkle over top.

Bake in 350° oven 1 hour, or until golden brown. Cut into squares and top with whipped cream or ice cream. Makes 6 to 9 servings.

*See Index for recipe

Lunch

Skillet Salmon Chowder
Corn Muffins
Honey-Dipped Apple Wedges Rolled in Sesame Seeds
Walnut-Stuffed Dates
Tea   Milk

Dinner

Broiled Sausage Patties
Buttered Peas and Small White Onions
Avocado Salad
Spicy Sugar Loaf*
Coffee   Milk

Skillet Salmon Chowder

6 slices bacon
½ c. chopped onion
1 (10½-oz.) can condensed chicken broth
1 (5½-oz.) pkg. au gratin potato mix
2 c. water
1½ c. milk
1 (1-lb.) can whole-kernel corn
⅛ tsp. pepper
1 (1-lb.) can salmon, drained and flaked
⅓ c. evaporated milk

Sauté bacon in 12″ skillet until crisp; drain on paper towels. Crumble. Reserve 2 tblsp. bacon fat. Sauté onion in fat until tender. Stir in chicken broth, au gratin potato mix (add both potatoes and sauce mix), water, milk, corn, pepper and bacon. Bring to a boil; reduce heat. Simmer for 15 minutes, stirring often.

Stir in salmon and evaporated milk. Simmer for 5 minutes. Makes 6 to 8 servings.

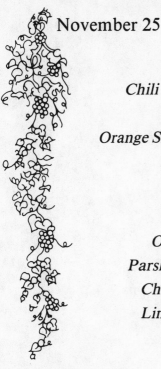

November 25

Lunch

Chili Topped with Crushed Taco Chips

Succotash Salad

Orange Sherbet and Vanilla Ice Cream Parfaits

Tea   Milk

Dinner

Oven-Barbecued Lamb Chops*

Parslied Rice   Sautéed Mushrooms

Chicory and Cherry Tomato Salad

Lime Gelatin with Banana Chunks

Coffee   Milk

Succotash Salad

1 (10-oz.) pkg. frozen cut green beans
1 (10-oz.) pkg. frozen corn
1 (4-oz.) jar sliced pimientos, drained
  and chopped
¾ c. chopped celery
2 tblsp. finely chopped onion
½ c. bottled French dressing with
  garlic

Cook beans and corn in boiling salted water in 2-qt. saucepan following package directions. Drain thoroughly and place vegetables in bowl. Stir in remaining ingredients. Cover and chill 4 hours or overnight, stirring occasionally. Makes 4 cups or 8 servings.

See Index for recipe

Lunch

Fresh Fruit Salad

Orange-Honey Dressing*

Hot Rolls

Chocolate Chip Cookies

Cocoa

Dinner

Roast Turkey

Bread-Sausage Dressing   Giblet Gravy

Whipped Potatoes   Steamed Butternut Squash

Cranberry Sauce in Lemon Shells

Watercress and Sliced Mushroom Salad

Pecan Meringue Pie

Coffee   Milk

Pecan Meringue Pie

1 c. sugar
⅓ c. flour
⅛ tsp. salt
2 c. milk
4 eggs, separated
1 tblsp. butter or regular margarine
2 tsp. vanilla
1½ c. finely chopped pecans
4 drops yellow food coloring
1 baked 10″ pie shell
⅛ tsp. cream of tartar
6 tblsp. sugar
1 tsp. vanilla

Combine 1 c. sugar, flour and salt in a medium saucepan. Slowly stir in milk. Cook over medium heat, stirring constantly, until thickened. Stir a small amount of hot mixture into beaten egg yolks. Stir back into remaining hot mixture. Cook, stirring, for 2 minutes. Remove from heat. Stir in butter, 2 tsp. vanilla, pecans and yellow food coloring. Cool well.

Pour mixture into pie shell.

Beat egg whites and cream of tartar until frothy. Gradually add 6 tblsp. sugar, beating until stiff glossy peaks form. Beat in 1 tsp. vanilla. Spread meringue over filling, sealing edges.

Bake in 400° oven 5 minutes, or until top is golden brown. Cool on rack. Makes 6 to 8 servings.

Lunch

Beef Bouillon

Peanut Butter, Chopped Almond and Raisin Sandwiches

Chewy Coconut Macaroons*

Hot Spiced Cocoa

Dinner

Broiled Knockwurst

Lemon-Glazed Carrots

Chow Mein Cabbage

Lettuce Wedges with Russian Dressing

Custard-Filled Cream Puffs

Coffee   Milk

Chow Mein Cabbage

3 c. shredded cabbage
1 c. diagonally cut celery
⅔ c. chopped green pepper
1 c. chopped onion (1 medium)
2 tblsp. butter or regular margarine
½ tsp. salt
Soy sauce

Combine vegetables.

Melt butter in skillet; add vegetables and salt. Cook 5 minutes, stirring constantly. Cover and cook until vegetables are tender-crisp, 3 to 5 minutes. Serve immediately, passing soy sauce. Makes 6 servings.

      *See Index for recipe

Lunch

Tomato Juice

Sliced Roast Beef   Swiss Cheese

Hot Mustard

Corn-Kernel Biscuits

Riced Cherry Gelatin

Tea   Milk

Dinner

Broiled Flounder Fillets

French Fried Potatoes   Sweet-Sour Green Beans*

Romaine and Sliced Black Olive Salad

Toasted Pound Cake

Coffee   Milk

Corn-Kernel Biscuits

3 c. biscuit mix
2 tsp. sugar
½ tsp. salt
2 tblsp. chopped onion
2 tblsp. chopped fresh parsley
1 c. whole-kernel corn
1 egg, beaten
½ c. milk
2 tblsp. salad oil
Milk

Combine biscuit mix, sugar, salt, onion, parsley and corn in large bowl.

Mix egg with milk and oil; add all at once to flour mixture. Stir with fork into a soft dough; beat about 30 seconds (dough should be stiff and a bit sticky).

Turn out on floured surface and knead lightly about 10 times. Roll to ½" thickness.

Cut with 3" floured biscuit cutter. Brush tops with milk. Bake on ungreased baking sheet in 450° oven 12 to 15 minutes. Makes 1 dozen.

*See Index for recipe

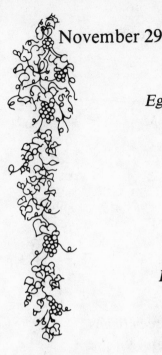

November 29

Lunch

Egg Salad and Salami Sandwiches

Sunflower Seeds   Dates

Tropical Fruit Shakes*

Dinner

Turkey Stuffing Casserole

Buttered Brussels Sprouts

Escarole and Grapefruit Salad

Hot Mincemeat Pie

Coffee   Milk

Turkey Stuffing Casserole

1 c. chopped onion
1 c. chopped celery
½ c. butter or regular margarine
8 c. soft bread cubes (½″)
1 tsp. salt
½ tsp. rubbed sage
½ tsp. poultry seasoning
¼ tsp. pepper
3 c. cubed, cooked turkey
3 tblsp. butter or regular margarine
3 tblsp. flour
½ tsp. salt
1 (13¾-oz.) can chicken broth
¾ c. water
2 eggs, well beaten
2 tblsp. chopped parsley

Sauté onion and celery in ½ c. melted butter until soft.

Combine bread cubes, 1 tsp. salt, sage, poultry seasoning and pepper in greased 3-qt. casserole. Add onion mixture; toss gently. Top with turkey.

Melt 3 tblsp. butter in saucepan, blend in flour and ½ tsp. salt. Add chicken broth and water; cook, stirring constantly, until mixture comes to a boil. Stir hot broth slowly into eggs; add parsley. Pour over turkey in casserole.

Cover and bake in 350° oven 30 minutes. Uncover and continue baking 15 minutes. Makes 8 servings.

     *See Index for recipe

Lunch

Snackers' Tomato Soup*

Grilled Cheese and Bacon on English Muffins

Vanilla Pudding with Chocolate Sauce and Pecans

Cocoa

Dinner

Broiled Lamb Steaks

Orange-Candied Sweet Potatoes

Broccoli with Toasted Almonds

Tossed Salad

Raspberry Sherbet with Crushed Raspberries

Coffee   Milk

Orange-Candied Sweet Potatoes

6 medium sweet potatoes, cooked and pared
1 small orange, peeled and cut in thin slices
⅔ c. brown sugar, firmly packed
1 tsp. salt
1 tblsp. grated orange rind
¼ c. butter or regular margarine

Cut sweet potatoes in ½" slices. Place half the slices in greased 2-qt. casserole. Top with orange slices, then half the brown sugar, salt and orange rind. Dot with half the butter. Add remaining sweet potatoes. Top with remaining brown sugar, salt, orange rind and butter.

Bake uncovered in 375° oven 30 minutes, or until glazed. Makes 6 servings.

December 1

Lunch

Herbed Omelets

Sour Cream Cinnamon Rolls

Green Grapes and Pineapple Cubes

Tea   Milk

Dinner

Broiled Pork Chops

Mushroom Pilaf*   Buttered Asparagus Spears

Butter Pecan Ice Cream

Espresso

Sour Cream Cinnamon Rolls

1 c. dairy sour cream
2 tblsp. shortening
½ c. sugar
¼ tsp. baking soda
1 tsp. salt
1 pkg. active dry yeast
¼ c. lukewarm water
1 egg
3 c. sifted flour
2 tblsp. soft butter or regular
    margarine
⅓ c. brown sugar, firmly packed
1 tsp. ground cinnamon
Confectioners' Sugar Icing (recipe
    follows)

Heat sour cream in saucepan until lukewarm. Combine sour cream, shortening, sugar, baking soda and salt in large bowl.

Sprinkle yeast on lukewarm water; stir to dissolve. Add yeast and egg to sour cream mixture. Gradually mix in enough flour to make a soft dough.

Turn out on floured surface and knead lightly for a minute. Form into a ball and let rest 5 minutes.

Roll into 13x9" rectangle. Spread with butter. Sprinkle with brown sugar and cinnamon. Roll up like jelly roll from long side. Cut into 12 slices. Place in greased 13x9x2" baking pan. Let rise until doubled, about 1½ hours.

Bake in 375° oven 22 minutes, or until golden brown. Remove from pan; cool on rack. While warm, drizzle with Confectioners' Sugar Icing. Makes 12 rolls.

Confectioners' Sugar Icing: Combine 1 c. sifted confectioners' sugar, 2 tblsp. light cream or milk and 1 tsp. vanilla; beat until smooth.

*See Index for recipe

Lunch

Mugs of Vegetable Beef Soup
Low-Cal Clam Dip*
Raw Cauliflowerets, Carrots and Green Peppers
Bread Sticks
Frozen Strawberries with Custard Sauce
Tea   Milk

Dinner

Mustard Ham Loaf
Buttered Noodles   Sautéed Cherry Tomatoes
Endive and Watercress Salad
Angel Food Cake with Black Cherry Ice Cream
Coffee   Milk

Mustard Ham Loaf

1½ lb. ground smoked ham
½ lb. ground fresh pork
1 c. milk
1 c. bread cubes (2 slices)
1 tblsp. dry mustard
½ c. brown sugar, firmly packed
¼ c. vinegar
2 tblsp. water

Combine meat, milk and bread cubes. Mix lightly; form into loaf. Place in shallow baking pan.

Combine remaining ingredients for sauce; pour over meat.

Bake in 375° oven 1½ hours, basting often with sauce in pan. Makes 8 to 10 servings.

December 3

Lunch

Swiss Cheese and Deviled Ham Sandwiches

Dill Pickles   Black Olives

Brown-Rim Butter Cookies*

Cocoa

Dinner

Crisp Oven-Fried Chicken

Baked Potatoes with Sour Cream and Chives

Honey-Glazed Carrots

Spinach Salad

Pineapple Upside-Down Cake

Coffee   Milk

Crisp Oven-Fried Chicken

1 c. crushed saltine crackers
¼ c. grated Parmesan cheese
1 tblsp. minced fresh parsley
½ tsp. salt
½ tsp. dried oregano leaves
½ tsp. dried crushed basil leaves
½ tsp. celery salt
½ tsp. onion salt
¼ tsp. paprika
¼ tsp. pepper
½ bay leaf, crushed
2 (3-lb.) broiler-fryers, cut up
½ c. evaporated milk
⅓ c. cooking oil

Combine saltine crackers, Parmesan cheese, parsley, salt, oregano, basil, celery salt, onion salt, paprika, pepper and bay leaf. Dip chicken pieces in evaporated milk and coat with crumbs.

Place in shallow roasting pan, skin side up. Bake in 375° oven 30 minutes. Brush with oil. Continue baking 30 minutes, or until golden brown and tender. Makes 8 servings.

*See Index for recipe

December 4

Lunch

Camembert Cheese and Green Grapes

Golden Sesame Braid

Blueberry Pie

Tea   Milk

Dinner

Glazed Beef Balls*

Sautéed Mushrooms   Steamed Cabbage Wedges

Romaine and Cucumber Salad

Butterscotch Pudding with Whipped Cream and Walnuts

Coffee   Milk

Golden Sesame Braid

1½ c. milk, scalded
¼ c. shortening
¼ c. sugar
1 tblsp. salt
1 pkg. active dry yeast
½ c. lukewarm water
3 eggs
7½ c. sifted flour
1 egg, beaten
1 tblsp. water
2 tblsp. sesame seeds

Combine milk, shortening, sugar and salt in large bowl. Cool to lukewarm.

Sprinkle yeast on lukewarm water; stir to dissolve. Add yeast, 3 eggs and 2 c. flour to milk mixture. Beat with electric mixer at medium speed until smooth, about 2 minutes, scraping bowl occasionally. Or beat with spoon until batter is smooth.

Gradually add enough remaining flour to make a soft dough that leaves the sides of the bowl. Turn out on floured surface and knead until smooth and satiny, about 8 to 10 minutes.

Place dough in lightly greased bowl; turn over to grease top. Cover and let rise in warm place until doubled, about 1 hour.

Divide dough into 6 parts. Roll each in 12" strip. Braid 3 strips together to form loaf and place on 2 greased baking sheets. Cover and let rise until doubled, about 45 minutes.

Brush braids with a glaze using 1 beaten egg and 1 tblsp. water. Sprinkle with sesame seeds.

Bake in 350° oven 30 minutes, or until loaves sound hollow when tapped. Remove from baking sheets; cool on racks. Makes 2 loaves.

*See Index for recipe

December 5

Lunch

Chicken Tostadas

Avocado and Grapefruit Salad

Lemon Pudding

Tea   Milk

Dinner

Tuna à la King on Biscuits

Green Peas Lorraine*   *Cranberry Sauce*

Marinated Artichoke Hearts on Lettuce

Chocolate Mousse

Coffee

Chicken Tostadas

12 corn tortillas, canned or frozen
  and thawed
Cooking oil
2 (15½-oz.) cans refried beans
2 c. shredded Monterey Jack cheese
  (8 oz.)
2 c. cubed, cooked chicken
3 c. shredded lettuce
2 medium tomatoes, chopped
1 avocado, cut in 12 slices
Bottled or canned taco sauce

Fry tortillas in ½ " hot oil in 8" skillet until crisp and golden brown, about 3 seconds. Hold top side of tortilla under fat with spatula during cooking. Drain on paper towels. (Tortillas can be fried in advance, stored airtight and heated in oven just before using.)

Heat beans; spread ⅓ c. over each fried tortilla. Sprinkle with cheese, chicken, lettuce and tomatoes. Garnish each with strip of avocado. Pass taco sauce. Makes 6 servings.

*See Index for recipe

Lunch

Sliced Ham and Lettuce Sandwiches

Baked Apples

Mexican Chocolate

Dinner

Broiled Chicken Livers

Danish Sugar-Browned Potatoes*

Brussels Sprouts with Lemon Butter

Tossed Salad

Vanilla Ice Cream Topped with

Crushed Peppermint Candies

Coffee   Milk

Mexican Chocolate

½ c. sugar
¼ c. baking cocoa
2 tsp. instant coffee
¾ tsp. ground cinnamon
Dash of salt
4 c. milk
1 tsp. vanilla

Combine sugar, cocoa, instant coffee, cinnamon and salt in heavy saucepan. Gradually add 1 c. milk, beating with wire whisk or rotary beater until smooth. Bring to a boil over low heat, stirring constantly. Add remaining milk; bring to a boil, stirring frequently. Add vanilla. Beat with rotary beater until frothy before serving. Makes 6 servings.

*See Index for recipe

December 7

Lunch

Scotch Chicken Soup*

Cream Cheese, Chopped Olive and Celery Sandwiches

Sesame Seeds   Dried Apricots

Coconut Cookies

Tea   Milk

Dinner

Timballo with Cheese Sauce

Broiled Tomato Halves   Buttered Broccoli Spears

Chicory and Sliced Radish Salad

Stewed Prunes and Apricots

Coffee   Milk

Timballo with Cheese Sauce

1 lb. spaghetti (break strands in half)
⅓ c. butter or regular margarine
1 lb. pork sausage
1 (4-oz.) can sliced mushrooms, drained
3 tblsp. finely chopped onion
⅓ c. sliced stuffed olives
½ c. grated Parmesan cheese
2 tblsp. chopped fresh parsley
½ tsp. salt
¼ tsp. pepper
¼ c. dry bread crumbs
2 eggs, well beaten
¼ lb. mozzarella cheese, shredded
Cheese Sauce (recipe follows)

Cook spaghetti for 10 minutes in boiling salted water. Drain. Toss with butter; coat well.

Sauté sausage in skillet until almost done. Pour off all fat except 2 tblsp. Add mushrooms and onion. Sauté in fat until tender (do not brown).

Toss together spaghetti, sausage mixture, olives, Parmesan cheese, parsley, salt and pepper.

Coat a buttered 9″ springform pan with bread crumbs; reserve some for top. Place half the spaghetti mixture in pan; pour eggs evenly over all. Sprinkle with mozzarella cheese; put remaining mixture on top. Sprinkle with remaining crumbs. Cover with aluminum foil; bake in 375° oven 40 minutes. Let stand for 5 minutes. Serve with Cheese Sauce. Makes 6 to 8 servings.

Cheese Sauce: Stir ¼ c. grated Parmesan cheese and 1 tblsp. chopped fresh parsley into 2 c. of medium white sauce.

*See Index for recipe

Lunch

Vegetable-Egg Combo*
Toasted English Muffins
Sliced Oranges and Bananas
Tea   Milk

Dinner

Corned Beef Hash
Lima Beans with Pimientos
French-style Turnips
Escarole and Sliced Avocado Salad
Spice Cake
Coffee   Milk

French-style Turnips

2½ lb. medium turnips (about 9)
¼ lb. bacon in one piece
⅔ c. minced onion
1 tblsp. flour
¾ c. canned beef bouillon
1 tsp. sugar
¼ tsp. rubbed sage
¼ tsp. pepper

Pare, quarter and cook turnips in 1″ boiling salted water 5 minutes. Drain.

Cut bacon in ¼″ cubes; you should have ¾ c. Cook bacon 4 minutes in skillet, stirring constantly. Add onion and cook 5 minutes (do not let brown). Blend in flour; add bouillon, sugar, sage and pepper. Cook 2 minutes, stirring constantly.

Add turnips; cover and simmer 15 to 20 minutes, or until turnips are tender. Makes 6 servings.

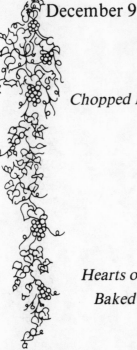

Lunch

Beef Bouillon

Chopped Bacon, Chive and Mayonnaise Sandwiches

Easy Rice Pudding*

Cider

Dinner

Turkey Drumstick Pie

Whipped Butternut Squash

Hearts of Lettuce with Tarragon French Dressing

Baked Custard Topped with Cranberry Sauce

Coffee   Milk

Turkey Drumstick Pie

4 turkey legs (about 3 lb.)
4 c. water
1½ tsp. salt
¼ tsp. pepper
1½ c. sliced pared carrots
1 c. cubed pared potatoes
½ c. chopped celery
½ c. chopped onion
1 c. frozen loose-pack peas
⅓ c. flour
1 c. water
1 tsp. salt
Biscuit Topping (recipe follows)

Combine turkey legs, 4 c. water, 1½ tsp. salt and pepper in large skillet. Cover and simmer 2 to 2½ hours, until turkey is tender. Remove turkey from broth; strip meat from bones. Discard skin and bones.

Add water to broth to make 3 c., if necessary. Add carrots, potatoes, celery and onion; simmer about 15 minutes, until vegetables barely are tender. Add peas and turkey meat.

Blend together flour, 1 c. water and 1 tsp. salt. Add to turkey mixture and cook, stirring constantly, until mixture comes to a boil.

Prepare Biscuit Topping.

Place bubbling, hot turkey mixture in greased 2½-qt. casserole. Top with biscuits. Bake in 450° oven 12 to 15 minutes, until biscuits are golden brown. Makes 8 servings.

Biscuit Topping: Sift together 2 c. flour, 3 tsp. baking powder and 1 tsp. salt. Cut in ¼ c. shortening until mixture resembles coarse crumbs. Stir in ¾ c. milk. Turn out on lightly floured surface. Knead 6 to 8 times. Roll dough to ½" thickness. Cut with floured cutter.

*See Index for recipe

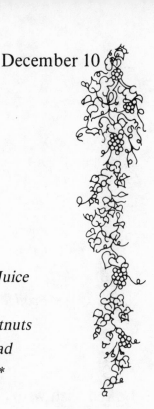

December 10

Lunch

Fresh Fruit Salad

Streusel Kuchen

Vanilla Yogurt

Tea   Milk

Dinner

Pork Sausages Cooked in Apple Juice

Cheesed Mashed Potatoes*

Brussels Sprouts with Water Chestnuts

Romaine and Sliced Onion Salad

3-Layer Lemon Meringue Pie*

Coffee   Tea   Milk

Streusel Kuchen

½ c. butter or regular margarine
1 c. sugar
1 tsp. salt
1 egg, separated
1 pkg. active dry yeast
⅓ c. lukewarm water
2 c. milk, scalded and cooled
7 c. sifted flour
¼ c. melted butter or regular
   margarine
Streusel Topping (recipe follows)

Cream together ½ c. butter and sugar in a large bowl until light and fluffy. Add salt and egg yolk, beating well.

Sprinkle yeast on lukewarm water; stir to dissolve. Combine yeast and milk. Add to creamed mixture alternately with flour, mixing well after each addition.

Beat egg white until stiff peaks form. Fold into mixture. Cover bowl with plastic wrap. Refrigerate 8 hours or overnight.

Divide dough in fourths. Pat dough in 4 greased 9″ pie plates. Cover; let rise in warm place until almost doubled, about 1 hour 30 minutes.

Brush with ¼ c. melted butter. Sprinkle with Streusel Topping.

Bake in 400° oven 20 minutes, or until golden. Makes 4 kuchens.

Streusel Topping: Combine ¼ c. flour, ½ c. sugar and 1 tsp. ground cinnamon. Cut in 3 tblsp. butter or regular margarine until mixture is crumbly. Add 1 tsp. vanilla and ¼ c. finely chopped walnuts; mix well.

*See Index for recipe

Autumn/287

December 11

Lunch

Creamed Eggs Supreme*

Cherry Tomatoes   Celery Sticks

Riced Lime Gelatin with Sliced Pears

Tea   Milk

Dinner

Baked Fish with Stuffing

Broiled Eggplant Slices   Steamed Spinach

Chocolate Eclairs

Coffee   Milk

Baked Fish with Stuffing

2 (1-lb.) pkg. frozen fish fillets
½ c. finely chopped celery
¼ c. finely chopped onion
3 tblsp. butter or regular margarine
4 c. dry bread cubes
1 tblsp. dried parsley flakes
½ tsp. salt
⅛ tsp. pepper
½ tsp. grated lemon rind
2 tblsp. lemon juice
1 tblsp. melted butter or
   regular margarine
¼ tsp. salt
Paprika

Partially thaw fish (about 2 hours at room temperature).

Cook celery and onion in 3 tblsp. butter in 2-qt. saucepan until soft. Combine with bread cubes, parsley, ½ tsp. salt, pepper, lemon rind and lemon juice.

Slice each block of partially thawed fish in half through the center, making 4 thin rectangular pieces about ½" thick. Place 2 pieces side by side in greased 12x8x2" (2-qt.) glass baking dish. Top with stuffing, then with remaining 2 pieces of fish. Brush with 1 tblsp. melted butter and sprinkle with ¼ tsp. salt.

Bake in 350° oven 25 to 30 minutes, or until fish flakes easily with fork. Sprinkle with paprika. Makes 6 servings.

*See Index for recipe

Lunch

Tuna-Macaroni Salad*
Sourdough Rolls
Cinnamon-Dusted Applesauce à la Mode
Tea   Milk

Dinner

Braised Short Ribs
Buttered Noodles   Julienne Beets
Marinated Artichoke and Chicory Salad
Blackberry Jam Cake
Coffee   Milk

Blackberry Jam Cake

1 c. butter or regular margarine
1 c. sugar
4 eggs
1 c. blackberry jam
3¼ c. sifted flour
1 tsp. baking soda
1 tsp. baking powder
1 tsp. ground cinnamon
1 tsp. ground nutmeg
1 tsp. ground allspice
¾ tsp. salt
1 c. buttermilk
1⅓ c. chopped walnuts

Cream together butter and sugar in large bowl until light and fluffy. Add eggs, one at a time, beating well after each addition. Stir in jam.

Sift together flour, baking soda, baking powder, cinnamon, nutmeg, allspice and salt. Add dry ingredients alternately with buttermilk, beating well after each addition. Stir in walnuts. Spread batter in greased and waxed paper-lined 9″ tube pan.

Bake in 325° oven 1 hour 30 minutes, or until cake tests done. Makes 10 servings.

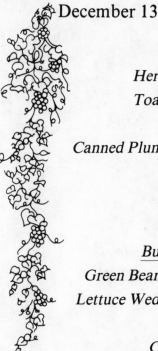

December 13

Lunch

*Herbed Onion Soup**

Toasted Garlic Bread

Tossed Salad

Canned Plums with Camembert Cheese

Tea   Milk

Dinner

Bulgarian Chicken

Green Beans with Toasted Almonds

Lettuce Wedges with Russian Dressing

Peach Melba

Coffee   Milk

Bulgarian Chicken

5 c. coarsely chopped cabbage
1 (1-lb.) can sauerkraut
½ c. uncooked regular rice
¾ c. water
1 c. chopped onion
3 tblsp. cooking oil
2 (1-lb.) cans tomatoes, cut up
2 (2½-lb.) broiler-fryers, cut in
   serving pieces
½ tsp. salt
⅛ tsp. pepper

Place cabbage in bottom of small roasting pan or 13x9x2″ (3-qt.) glass baking dish. Top with layers of sauerkraut and rice. Pour water over cabbage mixture.

Sauté onion in hot oil in skillet until tender (do not brown). Arrange layers of sautéed onion and tomatoes in baking dish.

Season chicken with salt and pepper. Place chicken, skin side up, on vegetables.

Bake in 375° oven 1 hour 30 minutes, until chicken is tender and golden brown. Makes 8 servings.

See Index for recipe

Lunch

Cream of Asparagus Soup
Grilled Muenster Cheese Sandwiches
Oliebollen
Cinnamon-Spiced Cocoa

Dinner

Roasted Pork Shoulder

Baked Sweet Potatoes

Buttered Peas and Small White Onions

Cauliflower-Olive Salad*

Tapioca Pudding with Crushed Raspberries

Coffee   Milk

Oliebollen

1 pkg. active dry yeast
½ tsp. sugar
¾ c. warm milk
2 c. sifted flour
2 tblsp. sugar
⅛ tsp. salt
2 eggs, beaten
½ c. raisins
½ c. diced pared apple
3 tblsp. chopped, mixed candied fruit
1 tsp. grated lemon rind
Cooking oil
Confectioners' sugar

Sprinkle yeast and ½ tsp. sugar on milk; stir to dissolve. Let stand 10 minutes.

Sift together flour, 2 tblsp. sugar and salt into bowl. Make a well in the center. Add yeast and eggs; mix just until blended. Stir in raisins, apple, candied fruit and lemon rind. Cover and let rise in warm place until doubled, about 1 hour.

Drop batter by heaping tablespoonfuls into deep, hot oil (350°), frying until golden brown, about 3 minutes. Drain on paper towels. Dust with confectioners' sugar. Makes 15.

*See Index for recipe

December 15

Lunch

Sliced Egg and Bacon Sandwiches
Celery Stuffed with Cream Cheese and Grated Carrots
Apple Turnovers
Orange Cider Punch

Dinner

Cheese Soufflé
Steamed Broccoli with Quick Mustard Sauce*
Romaine and Cucumber Salad
Butterscotch Cream Pie
Coffee   Milk

Orange Cider Punch

1 qt. apple cider
2 c. orange juice
½ c. lemon juice
¼ c. sugar

Combine all ingredients in 2-qt. pitcher. Cover and chill in refrigerator, or serve over ice. Makes about 6½ cups.

*See Index for recipe

Lunch

Mugs of Chili Bean Soup

Golden Sausage Boats*

Gingersnaps

Tea   Milk

Dinner

Scandinavian Hash

Steamed Cabbage Wedges   Buttered Diced Beets

Spinach and Mushroom Salad

Vanilla Ice Cream Topped with Chopped Cashews

Coffee   Milk

Scandinavian Hash

¾ c. chopped onion
½ c. butter or regular margarine
3 c. diced, cooked potatoes
3 c. ground, cooked beef
Salt
Pepper
1½ c. light cream
3 tblsp. chopped fresh parsley

Sauté onion in melted butter in 10″ skillet until tender (do not brown). Add potatoes and beef; sauté until browned. Season with salt and pepper as needed. Pour cream over all and heat well over low heat. Serve sprinkled with parsley. Makes 6 servings.

December 17

Lunch

Vegetable Soup

Tuna Fish Sandwiches

Sunflower Refrigerator Cookies

Tea   Milk

Dinner

Polynesian-style Liver*

Buttered Noodles   Mixed Vegetables

Lettuce, Parmesan Cheese and Black Olive Salad

Chocolate Layer Cake

Coffee   Milk

Sunflower Refrigerator Cookies

½ c. butter or regular margarine
½ c. sugar
½ c. brown sugar, firmly packed
1 egg
1 tsp. vanilla
1½ c. quick-cooking rolled oats
¾ c. stirred whole-wheat flour
¼ c. wheat germ
½ tsp. baking soda
¼ tsp. salt
¾ c. dry-roasted sunflower seeds

Cream together butter and sugars in large bowl. Add egg and vanilla; beat thoroughly.

Stir together rolled oats, whole-wheat flour, wheat germ, soda and salt. Stir into creamed mixture. Stir in sunflower seeds.

Divide dough in half and form two rolls about 2" in diameter. Wrap tightly in waxed paper and chill at least 4 hours. Cut in ¼" slices and place 2" apart on ungreased baking sheets.

Bake in 375° oven 10 to 12 minutes, or until lightly browned. Cool on racks. Makes about 4 dozen.

*See Index for recipe

Lunch

Midwestern Turkey-Cheese Sandwiches*

Carrot Curls   Radishes

Riced Cherry Gelatin with Banana Chunks

Cocoa

Dinner

New-style Salmon Soufflé

Sautéed Mushrooms   Buttered Peas

Watercress and Avocado Salad

Mocha-Frosted Vanilla Cupcakes

Coffee   Milk

New-style Salmon Soufflé

1 (7¾-oz.) can pink salmon
2 tblsp. butter or regular margarine
¼ c. finely chopped onion
2 tblsp. flour
¾ c. milk
½ tsp. salt
¼ tsp. dill weed
⅛ tsp. pepper
3 egg yolks, beaten
1 c. creamed cottage cheese
3 egg whites, stiffly beaten

Place salmon with liquid in bowl; remove all bones. Mash salmon into liquid.

Melt butter in saucepan; add onion and cook until soft. Blend in flour. Add milk and cook, stirring constantly, until mixture comes to a boil. Stir in salt, dill weed and pepper.

Beat together egg yolks and cottage cheese; stir in hot mixture and salmon. Fold in egg whites. Turn into a 1½-qt. casserole.

Bake in 300° oven 60 to 70 minutes, or until knife inserted halfway between center and edge comes out clean. Makes 5 to 6 servings.

Lunch

Green Bean Soup
Toasted Garlic Bread
Coconut Cream Pudding Topped with Fruit Cocktail
Tea   Milk

Dinner

Chicken Fricassee
Baked Almond Rice*   Buttered Broccoli
Escarole and Bean Sprout Salad
Pecan Meringue Pie*
Coffee   Tea   Milk

Green Bean Soup

1 meaty ham bone (about 2 lb.)
2 qt. water
4 c. cut-up green beans (1″ pieces)
3 c. cubed pared potatoes
2 medium onions, sliced
¼ c. chopped fresh parsley
1 tsp. dried savory
1 tsp. salt
¼ tsp. pepper
1 c. light cream

Cook ham bone in water in 6-qt. saucepan until tender, for about 1½ hours. Remove meat from bone and cut in chunks. Return to soup base.

Add green beans, potatoes, onions, parsley, savory, salt and pepper. Bring to a boil; reduce heat and simmer, covered, for 20 minutes, or until vegetables are tender. Skim off excess fat.

Just before serving, stir in light cream. Makes about 3½ quarts.

Lunch

Corned Beef and Pickle Sandwiches

Tangy Slaw*

Chocolate Chip Cookies

Tea   Milk

Dinner

Beef Florentine Casserole

Tossed Salad with Marinated Artichokes

Lime Sherbet Topped with Grated Lime Rind

and Crystallized Ginger

Coffee   Milk

Beef Florentine Casserole

1½ lb. ground beef
1 medium onion, chopped
1 clove garlic, minced
1 (10-oz.) pkg. frozen chopped
   spinach
Water
1 (l-lb.) can spaghetti sauce
1 (6-oz.) can tomato paste
1 (8-oz.) can tomato sauce
½ tsp. salt
¼ tsp. ground red pepper
1 (7-oz.) pkg. shell macaroni,
   cooked and drained
1 c. shredded sharp Cheddar cheese
   (4 oz.)
½ c. soft bread crumbs
2 eggs, well beaten
2 tblsp. salad oil

Cook ground beef, onion and garlic in large skillet until meat is lightly browned; drain off excess fat.

Cook spinach by package directions; drain, saving liquid. Add water to spinach liquid to make 1 c. Combine spinach liquid, spaghetti sauce, tomato paste, tomato sauce, salt and red pepper; stir into meat mixture. Simmer 10 minutes.

Combine spinach with macaroni, cheese, crumbs, eggs and oil. Spread in 13x9x2" baking pan. Top with meat mixture.

Bake in 350° oven 30 minutes. Let stand 10 minutes before serving. Makes about 10 servings.

Breakfast

Sliced Pears in Pineapple Juice

Shrimp Omelet Supreme

Graham Muffins*   *Citrus Honey**

Mexican Chocolate*

Shrimp Omelet Supreme

6 eggs
2 tsp. soy sauce
¼ tsp. dried tarragon leaves
1 (4½-oz.) can medium shrimp,
   drained and rinsed
1 (4-oz.) can sliced mushrooms,
   drained
½ c. bean sprouts, drained
½ c. water chestnuts, sliced
1 tblsp. butter or regular margarine
2 tblsp. butter or regular margarine

Combine eggs, soy sauce and tarragon; beat well. Add shrimp, mushrooms, bean sprouts and water chestnuts to 1 tblsp. melted butter in 10" skillet. Heat mixture, stirring occasionally.

Melt 2 tblsp. butter in 10" omelet pan or heavy skillet. When butter is hot, add egg mixture. Cook slowly over low heat. As egg mixture starts to set around edges, gently pull it toward center, tilting pan so that uncooked egg will run to edges. When all of mixture seems set, spoon the shrimp-vegetable filling over half of omelet; fold other half of omelet over filling and brown slightly. Serve immediately. Makes 3 or 4 servings.

Brunch

Easy Spinach Soufflé*

Mustard Ham Loaf*   *Glazed Apricots*

Sunflower Wheat Muffins*

Coffee   *Milk*

Glazed Apricots

1 (1-lb.) can apricot halves
2 tblsp. butter or regular margarine
1 tblsp. brown sugar
1 stick cinnamon
⅛ tsp. nutmeg
¼ tsp. vanilla

Drain apricots, reserving ½ c. syrup. Combine syrup, butter, sugar, cinnamon, nutmeg and vanilla in 1-qt. saucepan; boil 5 minutes. Gently add apricots; reduce heat and simmer 5 minutes. Makes 6 servings.

Breakfast

Mugs of Hot Buttered Tomato Juice

Mushroom and Sausage Omelets

<u>Hot Breakfast Bread</u>

Coffee   Milk

Hot Breakfast Bread

1 (1-lb.) loaf white bread
¼ c. butter or regular margarine
⅔ c. sugar
1 tsp. cinnamon
½ c. sifted confectioners' sugar
1½ to 2 tblsp. light cream
2 tblsp. finely chopped nuts

Spread bread slices on one side with softened butter; sprinkle with combined sugar and cinnamon. Put back in shape of loaf. If desired, cut in half lengthwise and tie with string. Wrap loaf securely in foil and heat in 375° oven 20 to 25 minutes. Unwrap, cut and remove string. Make glaze from confectioners' sugar and cream; pour glaze over top and sprinkle with nuts. Serve piping hot. Makes 10 to 12 servings.

Brunch

Spiced Fruit Cocktail

Creamed Chicken and Ham à la King in Patty Shells

Cottage Cheese Rolls*   Black Raspberry Jelly

Coffee   Milk

Spiced Fruit Cocktail

2 (1-lb. 1-oz.) cans fruit for salad
  or fruit cocktail
1 (1-lb. 1-oz.) can light cherries
2 tblsp. lemon juice
1 (6″ piece) stick cinnamon
1 tsp. whole cloves
⅛ tsp. salt

Drain syrup from fruit into saucepan. Add lemon juice, cinnamon and cloves (tied in cheesecloth bag) and salt. Boil 5 minutes. Remove spices. Pour over fruit. Cover and chill several hours or overnight.

Serve in sherbet glasses. Garnish each serving with a sprig of mint. Makes 6 servings.

*See Index for recipe

Shortcuts & Seasonings

• For a quick Baked Alaska, top packaged frozen brownies with a slice of ice cream and cover with a meringue. Pop into a 450° oven for 3 to 5 minutes—just long enough to delicately brown the meringue.

• Don't throw out the pickle juice from your dill or sweet pickles; make pickled carrot sticks. First, cook carrot sticks until tender. Then, heat the pickle juice and pour over carrots. Store in refrigerator in a covered jar. Keeps up to a month.

• For a weekend eye-opener, combine equal parts of tomato and clam juice. Season to taste with minced onion, garlic salt and freshly ground pepper and chill well.

• Here's a refreshing, healthful appetizer: Dip Bartlett pear cubes in a mixture of equal parts orange juice and lemon juice. Spear on toothpicks, alternating with cubes of cheese, and serve cold.

• Next time you mix your favorite punch, make and freeze "punch cubes" at the same time. As they melt, they won't dilute the punch.

• To make a quick no-cook relish for meats or poultry, combine a 16-oz. can of whole cranberry sauce with ½ c. seedless raisins, ½ c. chopped, cored, unpared apples, ½ c. chopped celery and 1 tsp. ground ginger. Mix well, cover and chill. Serve as a main-dish accompaniment, or combine with cream cheese to make a tasty cranapple-cheese sandwich.

• For a variation on marinated olives, add a dash of curry powder to Italian salad dressing, pour over black or green olives in a bowl, and marinate for several hours. Drain olives well before serving.

Winter

December 21 -
March 19

W I N T E R

Winter opens on a joyous note—the Christmas season is in full swing with trim-the-tree parties, caroling suppers and all the special delights of the holidays.

To help you celebrate this merry season with friends and neighbors, we feature an assortment of delicacies. Fruit Preserves Cake is a rich yet practical fruitcake made with cherry, apricot and pineapple preserves instead of the luxury-priced candied citron and cherries that take so long to snip into small pieces. When friends drop in to say "happy holidays," offer them a tray of Christmas Jewel Cookies—little buttery nuggets filled with jelly that look and taste as though they came straight from a fancy French bakery. On Christmas Eve, you might want to make lefse, a flat Norwegian bread that's popular among Scandinavian-American farm families; or do as many Wisconsin women do, and serve it all through the Christmas season.

When the holidays are over and the weather settles into bitter cold days, chase the chill with homemade soups, breads, hearty main dishes and delectable pies.

These are the days to serve Chili Chicken Stew, Tuna Bisque, Maine Corn Chowder, Pasta and Bean Soup or Chicken Vegetable Soup tinged with saffron and served with a fat dollop of sour cream. Each of these soup recipes makes a generous amount, so there'll be plenty to fill a lunch box thermos the next day.

For sharpened winter appetites, there are rib-sticking main dishes such as New England Boiled Dinner, Pot Roast with Vegetable Gravy, Old World Sauerbraten, and Chicken and Stuffing Pie made with an herb-seasoned stuffing mix crust.

When you're expecting company for dinner, try our recipe for Danish Pork Roast—it's a real beauty. Stuffed with apples, raisins and prunes, glazed with jelly and rolled in crumbs, this roast is a gourmet recipe worth every minute of the preparation time. The Baked Chicken Breasts with Almond Sauce is an economical entrée that tastes just heavenly.

Winter vegetables can be both interesting and appealing. Our Corn Custard Pudding is a delicious blend of corn niblets in a smooth-as-silk custard—a great dish to tempt youngsters who don't care for milk. Easy Spinach Soufflé is just what it promises—a snap to prepare—and it features two kinds of cheese for a double helping of protein.

Those bright red cranberries are a good buy throughout the season, and they offer lots of opportunities to brighten winter meals. Salads such as Spiced Cranberry Mold or Ruby Cranberry Crunch Salad will add a bright color note to any table, and Frosted Cranberry Squares and Cottage Cheese-Cranberry Mold are special enough to serve for an important company dinner.

When it comes time for dessert, splurge and forget the calories with our French Chocolate Pie, or offer a foretaste of spring with Raspberry Parfait Pie.

This section also features recipes to help you keep the cookie jar full. When the kids come home with wet, soggy mittens and cold, rosy cheeks, warm them up with a big mug of cocoa and a plate of Peanut Butter Fingers, Old-Fashioned Filled Cookies, Chewy Coconut Macaroons or spicy Cinnamon Jumbles.

With the help of these menus and recipes, your family will be so well-fed throughout the long winter months that they might even be sorry to see winter end!

Lunch

Black Bean Soup

Guacamole Burgers*

Vanilla Pudding with Diced Oranges

Hot Cider

Dinner

Baked Ham Slice*

Whipped Potatoes   Buttered Zucchini

Escarole Salad with Garlic Croutons

Fruit Preserves Cake

Coffee   Milk

Fruit Preserves Cake

3 c. sifted flour
1 tsp. baking soda
½ tsp. ground cinnamon
½ tsp. ground nutmeg
½ tsp. ground cloves
¾ c. butter or regular margarine
2 c. brown sugar, firmly packed
4 eggs, separated
1 tsp. vanilla
½ c. buttermilk
⅔ c. cherry preserves
⅔ c. apricot preserves
⅔ c. pineapple preserves
1 c. chopped walnuts

Sift together flour, baking soda, cinnamon, nutmeg and cloves in bowl.

Cream together butter and brown sugar in large bowl until light and fluffy. Add egg yolks; beat well. Add vanilla.

Add dry ingredients alternately with buttermilk, beating well after each addition. Stir in preserves and walnuts.

Beat egg whites until stiff. Fold into batter. Pour batter into greased 10″ tube pan.

Bake in 350° oven 1 hour 30 minutes, or until cake tests done. Cool for 10 minutes. Remove from pan. Cool on rack. Makes 12 servings.

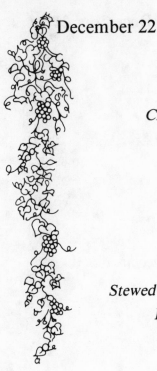

December 22

Lunch

Mugs of Chicken Broth

Cream Cheese on Toasted Bagels

Country-style Beet Salad

Chocolate Doughnuts

Tea   Milk

Dinner

Baked Codfish Cakes

Stewed Tomatoes   Buttered Green Beans

Endive and Diced Apple Salad

Poppy Seed Salad Dressing*

Herbed Garlic Bread

Lime Sherbet

Coffee   Milk

Country-style Beet Salad

¼ c. vinegar
1 small onion, chopped
1 (1-lb.) can or jar sliced beets
Crisp salad greens
½ c. grated Cheddar cheese
Bottled French dressing

Combine vinegar, onion and ¼ c. liquid drained from beets; pour over drained beets. Cover and chill at least 1 hour.

Put generous helpings of drained beets on salad greens and sprinkle with cheese. Pass French dressing. Makes 6 servings.

See Index for recipe

Lunch

Egg Salad and Sliced Cucumber Sandwiches

Black Olives

Sliced Pineapple

<u>*Christmas Jewel Cookies*</u>

Coffee   Milk

Dinner

Roast Veal with Sweet Onions*

Cauliflower in White Sauce

Buttered Brussels Sprouts with Tarragon

Avocado and Chicory Salad

Cherry Tarts

Coffee   Milk

Christmas Jewel Cookies

1 c. butter or regular margarine
½ c. sugar
3 hard-cooked egg yolks
1 tsp. vanilla
2 c. sifted flour
Strawberry or currant jelly

Cream together butter and sugar in mixing bowl until light and fluffy. Break up egg yolks and beat into creamed mixture; blend well. Add vanilla.

Gradually stir in flour. Cover and chill for 1 hour. Shape dough into 1″ balls and place 1″ apart on ungreased baking sheets. Make a small dent in top of each cookie with finger.

Bake in 375° oven 10 minutes. Remove from oven and fill dents with jelly. Return to oven and bake 1 or 2 more minutes to set jelly. If you wish, top with your favorite glaze while still warm. Remove from baking sheets. Cool on racks. Makes 5 dozen.

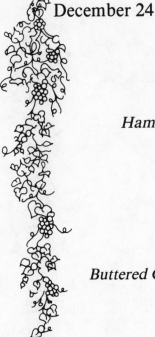

December 24

Lunch

Oyster Stew*

<u>*Lefse*</u>

Ham, Swiss Cheese and Romaine Salad

Figs   Assorted Nuts

Cocoa

Dinner

Broiled Pork Chops

Buttered Corn Niblets   Baked Tomato Halves

Tossed Salad

Raspberry-Vanilla Cloud*

Coffee   Milk

Lefse

2 lb. baking potatoes (4 large), pared
    and quartered
1 tsp. salt
¼ c. butter or regular margarine,
    melted
¼ c. half-and-half
2¼ c. sifted flour

Cook potatoes with salt in boiling water in saucepan until tender. Drain well. Rice potatoes using a potato ricer. Cool slightly. Cover and chill in refrigerator 8 hours, or overnight.

Firmly pack chilled riced potatoes into measuring cup. You will need 3½ c. Return to bowl. Add melted butter and half-and-half. Mix until smooth, using large spoon.

Add flour, a little at a time, mixing until dough forms. Shape mixture into 12" roll. (Be sure to remove all air from mixture when shaping into roll.) Divide roll into 12 pieces.

Roll out each piece of dough very thinly on well-floured pastry cloth to 12" circle, using stockinet-covered rolling pin. The lefse should be very thin, about ¹⁄₁₆" thick. Carefully roll lefse around rolling pin so it can be transferred to griddle.

Bake lefse, one at a time, on ungreased very hot griddle or in 12" skillet (475°). When small brown spots appear on the underside of the lefse, turn over, using a long metal spatula. When browned on both sides, fold into fourths, using spatula. Remove from griddle. Place on a dish towel (do not use terry towels). Cover with another towel. Bake another lefse, fold, and place on top of first one, placing point of wedge in opposite direction. Re-cover with towel. Continue in this way until all lefse are prepared. Cool lefse to room temperature. Makes 12 lefse.

* See Index for recipe

Lunch

Western Omelets

Toasted Bran Muffins   *Orange Marmalade*

Minted Fruit Cup*

Tea   Milk

Dinner

Roast Turkey

Sage Dressing   Giblet Gravy

Pecan Sweet Potatoes   Creamed Onions

Cranberry Sauce

Light Puffy Rolls*

Hot Mincemeat Pie with Rum-Flavored Hard Sauce

Espresso

Pecan Sweet Potatoes

6 medium sweet potatoes, cooked and
  pared
½ c. brown sugar, firmly packed
⅓ c. chopped pecans
1 tblsp. grated orange rind
1 c. orange juice
2 tblsp. butter or regular margarine
½ tsp. salt

Slice potatoes and put one layer deep in greased 13x9x2″ baking pan. Sprinkle with brown sugar, nuts and orange rind. Pour orange juice over all. Dot with butter and sprinkle with salt.

Bake in 350° oven 1 hour. Makes 8 servings.

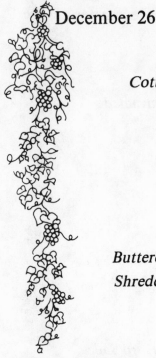

December 26

Lunch

Cottage Cheese and Sliced Pear Salad

Delicious Date Walnut Loaf

Butter Pecan Ice Cream

Tea   Milk

Dinner

Lamb Chop Marinade*

Buttered Noodles   Minted Carrot Slices

Shredded Lettuce and Green Pepper Salad

Riced Peach Gelatin

Coffee   Milk

Delicious Date Walnut Loaf

2 c. sifted flour
1½ tsp. salt
1 tsp. baking powder
1 tsp. baking soda
2 c. chopped dates
1 c. chopped walnuts
⅓ c. shortening
1 c. boiling water
⅓ c. cold water
¾ c. brown sugar, firmly packed
1 tsp. vanilla
1 egg

Sift together flour, salt, baking powder and baking soda in small bowl.

Combine dates, walnuts and shortening in bowl. Add boiling water and beat with a wooden spoon until shortening breaks into small lumps. Add cold water.

Stir in brown sugar, vanilla and egg; mix well. Add dry ingredients; beat well. Pour into greased 9x5x3″ loaf pan.

Bake in 350° oven 1 hour and 15 minutes, or until bread tests done. Cool in pan on rack 10 minutes. Remove from pan; cool on rack. Makes 1 loaf.

* See Index for recipe

Lunch

Cream of Potato Soup*
Deviled Ham and Sliced Egg Sandwiches
Gingerbread Cookies
Tea   Milk

Dinner

Sweet-and-Sour Turkey
Hot Fluffy Rice   Buttered Lima Beans
Spinach and Sliced Mushroom Salad
Lemon Mousse
Coffee   Milk

Sweet-and-Sour Turkey

1 (20-oz.) can pineapple chunks
½ c. brown sugar, firmly packed
¼ c. cornstarch
½ tsp. ground ginger
½ c. cider vinegar
¼ c. soy sauce
1¼ c. green pepper strips
1 c. sliced onion
1 c. sliced carrots
2 c. cubed cooked turkey
Hot fluffy rice

Drain pineapple; reserve juice. Add water to juice to make 3 c.

Combine brown sugar, cornstarch and ginger in saucepan. Stir in pineapple juice, vinegar and soy sauce. Bring mixture to a boil, stirring constantly. Add green pepper, onion, carrots and turkey. Cover; simmer 10 minutes, or until vegetables are tender-crisp. Serve with rice. Makes 6 servings.

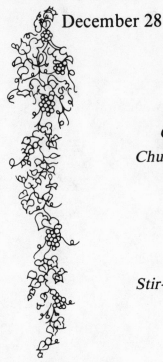

December 28

Lunch

Chili

Toasted Corn Muffins

Carrot Curls and Green Olives

Chunky Cider Applesauce* à la Mode

Tea   Milk

Dinner

Clove-Studded Baked Ham

Stir-Fried Broccoli with Sesame Seeds

Scalloped Potatoes Supreme

Chocolate Meringue Pie

Espresso

Scalloped Potatoes Supreme

4 c. thinly sliced, pared potatoes
  (about 6 medium)
1 c. coarsely diced ham
¾ c. chopped onion
1 (10½-oz.) can condensed cream of
  celery soup
¼ c. milk
¼ tsp. salt
⅛ tsp. pepper
1 c. shredded Cheddar cheese
Paprika

Combine potatoes, ham and onion in 2-qt. casserole.

Mix together soup, milk, salt and pepper. Pour over potato mixture. Cover and bake in 350° oven 1 hour.

Uncover and top with cheese. Sprinkle with paprika. Continue baking 30 more minutes, or until potatoes are tender and top is golden brown. Makes 6 servings.

*See Index for recipe

Lunch

Turkey Salad

Frosty Tomato Cup*

Vanilla-Glazed Cupcakes

Tea   Milk

Dinner

Meat Loaf with Barbecue Sauce

Buttered Peas   Whipped Turnips

Lettuce Wedges with Oil and Vinegar Dressing

Almond Rice Pudding

Coffee   Milk

Almond Rice Pudding

1¼ c. uncooked regular rice
⅔ c. sugar
1 tsp. salt
6 c. milk
⅓ c. cream sherry
3 tsp. vanilla
1⅓ c. toasted, slivered almonds
2 c. heavy cream
Raspberry Sauce (recipe follows)

Combine rice, sugar, salt and milk in 3-qt. saucepan. Bring mixture to a boil. Reduce heat; simmer, uncovered, 25 minutes, stirring frequently. Remove from heat.

Pour mixture into 13x9x2″ (3-qt.) glass baking dish. Cool slightly. Stir in sherry, vanilla and almonds.

Whip cream until soft peaks form. Fold into rice mixture. Cover and chill several hours. Serve with Raspberry Sauce. Makes 12 servings.

Raspberry Sauce: Combine 2 (10-oz.) pkg. frozen raspberries, completely thawed, 2 tblsp. cornstarch and 2 tsp. lemon juice in a saucepan. Bring to a boil, stirring constantly. Boil 1 minute. Remove from heat. Strain. Cool.

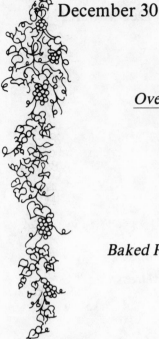

December 30

Lunch

Minestrone
Oven-Fried Oysters on Toasted Buns
Peanut Butter Cookies*
Tea   Milk

Dinner

Succulent Sirloin Steak*
Baked Potatoes with Sour Cream and Chives
Buttered Sliced Beets
Coleslaw
Poppy Seed Torte*
Coffee   Milk

Oven-Fried Oysters

1½ c. flour
1¼ tsp. salt
¼ tsp. pepper
24 large oysters
2 eggs, slightly beaten
Fine bread crumbs
Salad oil
Lemon wedges

Combine flour, salt and pepper in bowl.

Roll oysters in flour; dip in eggs, then roll in bread crumbs. Sprinkle both sides of oysters with oil. Place in shallow pan.

Bake in 400° oven about 15 minutes, until brown. Serve with lemon wedges. Makes 6 servings.

*See Index for recipe

Lunch

Mushroom Omelets

Marinated Green Beans

Coconut Crown Coffee Cake

Cocoa

Dinner

Beef Stew

Cottage Cheese Rolls*

Tossed Salad

Orange Frost*

Coffee   Milk

Coconut Crown Coffee Cake

5 to 5½ c. sifted flour
2 pkg. active dry yeast
½ c. sugar
1 tsp. salt
¾ c. milk
½ c. water
½ c. butter or regular margarine
2 eggs
½ tsp. grated lemon rind
Brown Sugar Syrup (recipe follows)
1 c. flaked coconut
½ c. chopped pecans

Combine 1¾ c. of the flour, dry yeast, sugar and salt in bowl.

Heat milk, water and butter in saucepan to very warm (120-130°). Add to flour-yeast mixture with eggs and lemon rind. Beat with electric mixer at low speed ½ minute. Beat at high speed 3 minutes.

Gradually stir in enough flour to make a soft dough. Knead until smooth. Let rest 20 minutes.

Prepare Brown Sugar Syrup.

Shape dough into 1¼″ balls. Sprinkle 2 tblsp. coconut in greased 10″ tube pan. Drizzle with ¼ c. Brown Sugar Syrup. Arrange one half of dough balls in layer. Top with half of coconut, Syrup and pecans. Arrange remaining dough balls in a layer, topping with remaining coconut, Syrup and pecans. Cover; let rise until doubled, about 1 hour.

Bake in 375° oven 20 minutes. Cover with foil. Bake 40 minutes more, or until golden brown. Remove from pan; cool on rack, top side up. Drizzle with your favorite confectioners' icing.

Brown Sugar Syrup: Combine 1½ c. brown sugar (firmly packed), 6 tblsp. evaporated milk, 6 tblsp. butter and 2 tblsp. light corn syrup in saucepan. Heat, stirring constantly, until sugar is dissolved.

*See Index for recipe

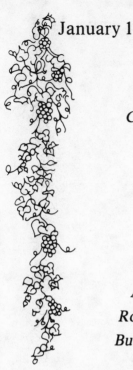

January 1

Lunch

Welsh Rarebit
Cherry Tomatoes and Cucumber Strips
Gingersnaps
Cinnamon-Spiced Cocoa

Dinner

Roast Lamb with Mint Sauce
Roasted Potatoes
Acorn Squash with Creamed Onions*
Romaine Salad with Lemon Juice and Oil
Butterscotch Sundaes with Toasted Pecans
Coffee   Milk

Welsh Rarebit

1 lb. shredded, sharp Cheddar cheese
2 tblsp. flour
1 c. beer
2 tblsp. butter or regular margarine
2 tsp. Worcestershire sauce
1 tsp. dry mustard
¼ tsp. cayenne pepper
12 slices bread, toasted and cut in
   triangles

Combine cheese with flour in heavy 2-qt. saucepan. Add beer, butter, Worcestershire sauce, mustard and cayenne pepper; mix well. Cook over medium heat, stirring constantly, until cheese is melted and mixture is smooth (about 15 minutes).

Pour cheese sauce over hot toast, allowing 2 slices of toast per serving. If you wish, you can place Welsh rarebit under the broiler before serving. Place 2 slices toast in each oven-proof shallow baking dish or 8″ pie plate. Pour cheese sauce over all. Place under broiler, 4″ from source of heat and broil 1½ minutes, or until top is lightly browned and cheese is bubbly. Makes 6 servings.

See Index for recipe

Lunch

Famous Clam Chowder*
Oyster Crackers
Riced Strawberry Gelatin and Green Grapes
Tea   Milk

Dinner

Pork Sausages Poached in Cider
Sautéed Green Peppers and Mushrooms
Red and Green Cabbage Salad
Amish Vanilla Pie
Coffee   Milk

Amish Vanilla Pie

½ c. brown sugar, firmly packed
1 tblsp. flour
¼ c. dark corn syrup
1½ tsp. vanilla
1 egg, beaten
1 c. water
1 c. unsifted flour
½ c. brown sugar, firmly packed
½ tsp. cream of tartar
½ tsp. baking soda
⅛ tsp. salt
¼ c. butter or regular margarine
1 unbaked 9″ pie shell

Combine ½ c. brown sugar, 1 tblsp. flour, corn syrup, vanilla and egg in 2-qt. saucepan. Slowly stir in water. Cook over medium heat, stirring constantly, until mixture comes to a boil. Let cool.

Combine 1 c. flour, ½ c. brown sugar, cream of tartar, baking soda, salt and butter; mix until crumbly. Pour cooled mixture into pie shell; top with crumbs.

Bake in 350° oven 40 minutes, or until golden brown. Cool on rack. Makes 6 to 8 servings.

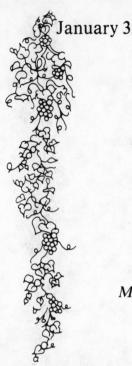

January 3

Lunch

Chicken Noodle Soup

Assorted Cold Cuts

Cranberry Muffins

Coffee Milk Shakes

Dinner

Roast Beef Hash

Sliced Carrots   Herbed Spinach*

Marinated Artichoke and Escarole Salad

Honey-Glazed Baked Pears

Coffee   Milk

Cranberry Muffins

2¼ c. sifted flour
¼ c. sugar
¾ tsp. baking soda
¼ tsp. salt
1 egg, slightly beaten
¾ c. buttermilk
¼ c. cooking oil
1 c. chopped raw cranberries
½ c. sugar

Sift together flour, ¼ c. sugar, baking soda and salt into bowl.

Combine egg, buttermilk and oil in bowl; blend well. Add all at once to dry ingredients, stirring just enough to moisten. Combine cranberries and ½ c. sugar; stir into batter.

Spoon into greased 2½″ muffin-pan cups, filling two-thirds full.

Bake in 400° oven 20 minutes or until golden brown. Makes 12.

*See Index for recipe

Lunch

Tomato Bouillon*

Grilled Muenster Cheese and Salami Sandwiches

Fruit Cocktail

Tea   Milk

Dinner

Chicken and Stuffing Pie

Buttered Italian Green Beans   Cranberry Sauce

Tossed Salad

Orange Sherbet Garnished with Grated Coconut

Coffee   Milk

Chicken and Stuffing Pie

1 (8-oz.) pkg. herb-seasoned stuffing
  mix
¾ c. chicken broth
½ c. melted butter or regular
  margarine
1 egg, beaten
1 (4-oz.) can mushrooms
2 tsp. flour
½ c. chopped onion
1 tblsp. butter or regular margarine
1 (10½-oz.) can chicken giblet gravy
3 c. cubed, cooked chicken
1 c. peas
2 tblsp. diced pimientos
1 tblsp. dried parsley flakes
1 tsp. Worcestershire sauce
½ tsp. dried thyme leaves
4 slices process American cheese

Mix together stuffing mix, chicken broth, ½ c. butter and egg. Press into greased 10″ pie plate.

Drain mushrooms. Combine mushroom liquid with flour; set aside.

Sauté mushrooms and onion in 1 tblsp. melted butter in saucepan until tender (do not brown). Stir in chicken giblet gravy, chicken, peas, pimientos, parsley flakes, Worcestershire sauce, thyme and mushroom liquid. Heat thoroughly.

Turn mixture into crust. Bake in 375° oven 20 minutes. Cut each cheese slice into 4 strips. Place in lattice design on pie. Bake 5 more minutes. Makes 6 servings.

January 5

Lunch

Beef Consommé

Cauliflower Salad Bowl

Toasted Garlic Bread

Tapioca Pudding with Chopped Dates

Tea   Milk

Dinner

Baked Spareribs

Buttered Noodles   Buttered Lima Beans

Chocolate Pecan Sponge Cake*

Coffee   Milk

Cauliflower Salad Bowl

1 medium head cauliflower
10 ripe olives, sliced
1 tblsp. minced onion
½ c. diced sharp Cheddar cheese
7 anchovy fillets, cut in small pieces
  (optional)
1 tsp. salt
¼ tsp. pepper
3 tblsp. olive or salad oil
1 tblsp. vinegar
Lettuce
Cherry tomatoes or tomato wedges

Wash and trim cauliflower. Break into small flowerets. Cook in boiling salted water until tender-crisp, 8 to 10 minutes. Drain, cover and chill.

Combine cauliflower with remaining ingredients, except lettuce and tomatoes. Cover and chill at least 30 minutes. Serve in lettuce-lined bowl garnished with cherry tomatoes or tomato wedges. Makes 6 servings.

*See Index for recipe

Lunch

Maine Corn Chowder

Whole-Wheat Crackers

Endive and Sliced Radish Salad

Poached Prunes

Tea   Milk

Dinner

Cheese Soufflé with Chives

Stir-Fried Celery and Peas

Waldorf Variation Salad*

Vanilla-Glazed Mincemeat Pie

Espresso

Maine Corn Chowder

5 slices bacon, chopped
2 medium onions, sliced
3 c. diced pared potatoes
2 c. water
1 tsp. salt
⅛ tsp. pepper
1 (1-lb. 1-oz.) can cream-style corn
2 c. milk

Cook bacon in Dutch oven until crisp. Remove and drain on paper towels. Set aside.

Sauté onions in bacon drippings until soft. Add potatoes, water, salt and pepper. Bring to a boil. Reduce heat; cover and simmer 12 to 15 minutes, or until potatoes are tender.

Add corn and milk; heat thoroughly. Garnish with bacon. Makes about 9 cups.

January 7

Lunch

Deviled Ham and Cream Cheese Sandwiches

Assorted Pickles   Olives

Spicy Raisin Cupcakes*

Chocolate Milk

Dinner

New England Boiled Dinner

Cucumber and Escarole Salad

Coconut Cream Pudding

Coffee   Milk

New England Boiled Dinner

1 (3- to 4-lb.) corned brisket of beef
3 qt. water
2 bay leaves
¼ tsp. peppercorns
6 whole cloves
6 whole medium potatoes, pared
6 whole carrots, pared
4 parsnips, pared and cut in halves
  crosswise
3 onions, peeled and cut in halves
  crosswise
1 turnip, pared and quartered
1 head cabbage, cut in 6 wedges

Place meat in deep kettle. Cover with water. Add bay leaves, peppercorns and cloves. Cover, bring to a boil; reduce heat and simmer until tender, about 3 hours.

Add potatoes, carrots, parsnips, onions and turnip. Simmer 30 minutes. Add cabbage and continue cooking until all vegetables are tender, about 20 minutes.

Place meat in center of platter, and surround with vegetables. Makes 6 servings.

* See Index for recipe

Lunch

Liverwurst Reubens

Kidney Bean Salad*

Canned Peach Halves Filled with Green Grapes

Tea   Milk

Dinner

Broiled Lamb Chops

Parslied Rice

Frosted Cranberry Squares

Whipped Cream-Filled Eclairs

Coffee   Milk

Frosted Cranberry Squares

2 (3-oz.) pkg. strawberry flavor
  gelatin
1½ c. boiling water
1 (1-lb.) can whole cranberry sauce
1½ c. ginger ale
1 c. chopped walnuts
1 c. chopped, unpared apple
1 (8½-oz.) can crushed pineapple,
  drained
1 small banana, diced
1 tblsp. grated orange rind
1 c. heavy cream
1 (3-oz.) pkg. cream cheese, softened

Dissolve gelatin in boiling water. Add cranberry sauce, stirring until dissolved. Stir in ginger ale. Cover and chill until thick and syrupy.

Fold in walnuts, apple, pineapple, banana and orange rind. Pour into lightly oiled 8" square baking dish. Cover and chill until set.

Combine heavy cream and cream cheese. Beat until cream is whipped and mixture is thick. Spread over gelatin. Cover and chill at least 1 hour. To serve, cut in squares. Makes 9 servings.

January 9

Lunch

Special Chef's Salad*

Crusty Rolls

Pineapple Cubes Rolled in Coconut

Tea   Milk

Dinner

English Fish and Chips

Coleslaw with Grated Green Peppers

Riced Cherry Gelatin with Bing Cherries

Coffee   Milk

English Fish and Chips

3 lb. potatoes, pared
Cooking oil
2 c. sifted flour
2 eggs, separated
¼ c. beer
½ tsp. salt
6 tblsp. milk
6 tblsp. water
2 lb. white fish fillets, such as
    haddock, sole or flounder
Salt

Several hours before serving, cut potatoes in ⅜″ slices and then in lengthwise strips ⅜″ wide. Wash in very cold water; dry well between paper towels. Fry in deep, hot oil (370°) until tender but not brown, about 5 minutes. Drain on paper towels in baking pan. Cover with waxed paper; set aside until just before mealtime.

Combine flour, egg yolks, beer and ½ tsp. salt in bowl; mix well. Gradually add milk and water; stir until batter is smooth. Let stand 30 minutes.

Beat egg whites until stiff peaks form. Fold into batter.

Cut fish fillets into 5x3″ pieces. Coat fish with batter. Fry several pieces at a time in deep, hot oil (375°) until golden brown and tender, about 5 minutes. Turn fillets frequently to keep them from sticking. Drain on paper towels. Keep warm in 300° oven.

Brown precooked potatoes in deep, hot oil (390°) until crisp and brown. Drain on paper towels; sprinkle with salt. Keep warm in 300° oven. Makes 6 servings.

*See Index for recipe

Lunch

Tomato-Rice Soup

Thinly Sliced Provolone Cheese

Four-Grain Bread

Brown Sugar-Glazed Baked Apples

Tea   Milk

Dinner

Creamed Chipped Beef on Toasted Corn Bread

Parslied Carrots

Tossed Salad

Streusel Pear Pie*

Tea   Milk

Four-Grain Bread

1¾ c. milk
¼ c. honey
2 tblsp. shortening
2 tsp. salt
1 c. all-purpose flour
1 c. rye flour
½ c. buckwheat flour
2 pkg. active dry yeast
1 egg
¾ c. wheat germ
¾ c. quick-cooking oats
2 c. stirred whole-wheat flour

In saucepan heat milk, honey, shortening and salt until warm, stirring to melt shortening.

In large mixer bowl, stir together all-purpose flour, rye flour, buckwheat flour and yeast. Add warm milk mixture and egg. Beat at low speed ½ minute, scraping sides and bottom of bowl constantly. Beat at high speed 3 minutes, scraping bowl occasionally.

By hand, stir in wheat germ, oats, and enough whole-wheat flour to make a moderately stiff dough. Turn out on lightly floured surface and knead until smooth and elastic, about 10 minutes.

Place in greased bowl, turning to grease all sides. Cover and let rise in warm place until doubled, about 1 hour 15 minutes.

Punch down. Divide dough in half, cover and let rise 10 minutes. Shape each half into a loaf. Place in 2 greased 8½x4½x2½″ loaf pans. Cover and let rise in warm place until doubled, about 1 hour.

Bake in 375° oven 40 to 45 minutes, or until loaves sound hollow when tapped. Remove from pans; cool on racks. Makes 2 loaves.

*See Index for recipe

January 11

Lunch

Meatball and Lentil Soup
Sourdough Bread
Chocolate Chip Cookies
Tea   Milk

Dinner

Braised Pork Steaks
Whipped Potatoes   Buttered Asparagus Spears
Romaine and Sliced Mushroom Salad
Date and Apricot Bars*
Coffee   Milk

Meatball and Lentil Soup

1 lb. lentils, rinsed and drained
2 tsp. salt
1 bay leaf
2½ qt. water
Meatballs (recipe follows)
1 c. chopped onion
⅓ c. bacon drippings
1 (1-lb.) can stewed tomatoes
½ tsp. dried marjoram leaves
½ tsp. salt
⅛ tsp. pepper
1 c. sliced carrots, ½ " thick
1 c. sliced celery, ½ " thick

Combine lentils, salt, bay leaf and water in 6-qt. kettle. Bring to a boil; reduce heat and simmer, covered, for 45 minutes. Do not drain. Meanwhile, prepare Meatballs.

Sauté onion in bacon drippings. Stir in tomatoes, marjoram, salt and pepper; bring to a boil. Add tomato mixture, Meatballs, carrots and celery to cooked lentils. Bring to a boil; reduce heat and simmer, covered, for 30 minutes. Makes 3½ quarts.

Meatballs: Combine 1 lb. ground beef, ½ c. dry bread crumbs, 2 beaten eggs, ¼ c. milk, 2 tblsp. finely chopped onion, 2 tblsp. finely chopped parsley, 1 minced garlic clove, ¾ tsp. salt, ½ tsp. marjoram and ⅛ tsp. pepper. Mix lightly and shape into 15 meatballs. Brown meatballs in ¼ c. hot oil in 8″ skillet. Drain and set aside.

* See Index for recipe

Lunch

Thinly Sliced Boiled Ham

Corn-Kernel Biscuits*

Strawberry Milk Shakes

Dinner

Spicy Oven-Barbecued Chicken

Buttered Noodles   Buttered Brussels Sprouts

Endive and Sliced Radish Salad

Coffee-Frosted Spice Cake

Coffee   Milk

Spicy Oven-Barbecued Chicken

½ c. chopped onion
½ c. chopped celery
2 tblsp. cooking oil
1 (10½-oz.) can condensed tomato
  soup
1 c. ketchup
½ c. water
¼ c. lemon juice
3 tblsp. Worcestershire sauce
3 tblsp. brown sugar, firmly packed
2 tblsp. vinegar
2 tblsp. prepared mustard
1½ tsp. salt
¼ tsp. pepper
2 drops Tabasco sauce
2 (2½-lb.) broiler-fryers, quartered

Sauté onion and celery in hot oil in saucepan until tender (do not brown). Add tomato soup, ketchup, water, lemon juice, Worcestershire sauce, brown sugar, vinegar, mustard, salt, pepper and Tabasco sauce. Bring mixture to a boil; reduce heat. Simmer, uncovered, for 30 minutes.

Meanwhile, place chicken in shallow roasting pan. Bake in 400° oven 40 minutes. Baste with barbecue sauce. Continue baking and basting with sauce until chicken is crisp and tender. Makes 8 servings.

January 13

Lunch

Coney Island Hot Dogs

Grandmother's Best Potato Salad*

Oatmeal Cookies

Cocoa

Dinner

Cheese-Stuffed Pasta Shells with Tomato Sauce

Steamed Spinach   Swedish Rutabagas*

Shredded Lettuce and Carrot Salad

Fruit Cocktail

Coffee   Milk

Coney Island Hot Dogs

1 (15-oz.) can chili con carne
1 (6-oz.) can tomato paste
1 tsp. prepared mustard
10 frankfurters
10 frankfurter buns, split

Combine chili con carne, tomato paste and mustard in saucepan; heat.

Heat frankfurters in hot water, but do not boil.

Toast split buns. Place frankfurter on each bun and spoon sauce over. Makes 10 servings.

*See Index for recipe

Lunch

*Lima Bean Chowder**
Buttered Pumpernickel Bread
Blueberry Turnovers
Tea   Milk

Dinner

Broiled Veal Shoulder Chops
Corn Fritters   Steamed Cabbage Wedges
Cottage Cheese-Cranberry Mold
Lemon Sherbet with Ladyfingers
Coffee   Tea   Milk

Cottage Cheese-Cranberry Mold

1 (3-oz.) pkg. raspberry flavor gelatin
¾ c. boiling water
2 tblsp. orange juice
1 tsp. grated orange rind
⅛ tsp. salt
1 (1-lb.) can whole cranberry sauce
1 c. large curd cottage cheese
½ c. dairy sour cream

Dissolve gelatin in boiling water in bowl. Stir in orange juice, orange rind and salt. Cover and chill until thick and syrupy.

Blend in cranberry sauce, cottage cheese and sour cream. Pour into lightly oiled 4-c. mold. Cover and chill until set. Makes 4 to 6 servings.

January 15

Lunch

Sliced Turkey Roll and Crisp Bacon Sandwiches

Coleslaw with Slivered Green Pepper

Orange Cupcakes*

Tea   Milk

Dinner

Pot Roast with Vegetable Gravy

Hot Fluffy Rice   Buttered Broccoli Spears

Escarole and Avocado Salad

Pumpkin Pie with Whipped Cream

Coffee   Milk

Pot Roast with Vegetable Gravy

3 lb. boned beef rump roast
½ tsp. salt
¹/₈ tsp. pepper
1 tblsp. cooking oil
1 c. chopped celery
½ c. chopped onion
½ c. diced carrots
1 clove garlic, minced
1 beef bouillon cube
1 c. water
1 (8-oz.) can tomato sauce
½ tsp. dried oregano leaves
2 tblsp. cornstarch
½ c. water

Season meat with salt and pepper. Brown well in hot oil in Dutch oven. Remove meat. Add celery, onion, carrots and garlic to hot oil; sauté until tender (do not brown). Add bouillon cube, 1 c. water, tomato sauce and oregano. Bring to a boil. Return meat to Dutch oven. Cover. Bake in 325° oven 2 hours 30 minutes, or until tender.

Remove meat and keep warm. Skim off excess fat. Slowly stir combined cornstarch and ½ c. water into pan juices. Bring to a boil; boil for 1 minute. Makes 6 to 8 servings.

*See Index for recipe

Lunch

Bologna and Egg Salad Sandwiches
Dilly Cheese-Stuffed Celery*
Riced Raspberry Gelatin
Tea   Milk

Dinner

Baked Ham Slices with Mustard Glaze
Country Potato Patties   Whipped Butternut Squash
Rice Pudding with Chocolate Sauce
Coffee   Milk

Country Potato Patties

6 medium potatoes (1½ lb.)
2 tblsp. chopped onion
2 tblsp. chopped pimiento or parsley
2 tblsp. flour
1 tsp. salt
3 tblsp. bacon drippings, butter or regular margarine

Parboil unpared potatoes 15 to 20 minutes (they will still be hard in the center). Turn at once into a colander and cool under running water.

As soon as they can be handled, pare potatoes and shred with a coarse grater. Toss with onion, pimiento, flour and salt, using 2 forks to mix ingredients.

Shape into patties, using about ½ c. for each; brown in hot bacon drippings about 5 minutes on each side. Makes 6 servings.

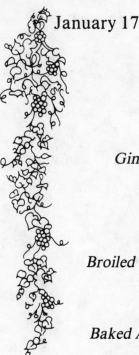

January 17

Lunch

Black Bean Soup
*American-style Enchiladas**
Watermelon Pickles
Gingerbread Topped with Vanilla Yogurt
Coffee   Milk

Dinner

Broiled Chicken Livers and Green Pepper Kabobs
Buttered Noodles   Succotash
Vegetable Confetti Mold
Baked Apples Stuffed with Raisins and Almonds
Coffee   Milk

Vegetable Confetti Mold

2 (3-oz.) pkg. lemon flavor gelatin
½ tsp. salt
2 c. boiling water
1 c. mayonnaise
3 tblsp. vinegar
⅛ tsp. Tabasco sauce
1 c. cold water
½ c. chopped celery
½ c. chopped radishes
½ c. chopped green pepper
½ c. shredded carrot
2 tblsp. minced onion
Lettuce

Dissolve gelatin and salt in boiling water. Combine mayonnaise, vinegar and Tabasco sauce in bowl. Gradually add gelatin to mayonnaise mixture, mixing well. Stir in cold water. Cover and chill until thick and syrupy.

Whip gelatin mixture with rotary beater until fluffy. Fold in celery, radishes, green pepper, carrot and onion. Pour into lightly oiled 9" square baking pan. Cover and chill until set.

Cut into 9 squares and serve on lettuce leaves. Makes 9 servings.

*See Index for recipe

Lunch

Tomato Cheeseburgers*

Shredded Carrot and Green Pepper Salad

Vanilla Milk Shakes

Dinner

Danish Pork Roast

Roasted Potatoes   Peas with Pimiento Strips

Marinated Artichokes in Lettuce Cups

Deep-Dish Plum Pie*

Coffee   Milk

Danish Pork Roast

½ tsp. salt
½ tsp. ground cinnamon
½ tsp. ground allspice
½ tsp. pepper
¼ tsp. ground cloves
¼ tsp. ground mace
3 to 3½ lb. boned pork loin
12 pitted prunes
2 medium apples, pared, cored
  and cut in sixths
2 tblsp. raisins
¼ tsp. ground cinnamon
¼ c. brandy or apple juice
1½ tblsp. currant jelly, melted
1 c. fresh bread crumbs
¼ c. melted butter or
  regular margarine

Combine salt, ½ tsp. cinnamon, allspice, pepper, cloves and mace. Rub in surface of roast. Cover and refrigerate overnight.

Combine prunes, apples, raisins, ¼ tsp. cinnamon and brandy. Cover and refrigerate overnight.

Cut a long, deep pocket the length of the roast. Stuff with fruit. Sew closed with large needle; tie with kitchen twine. Place roast on rack in roasting pan. Brush roast with liquid left over from fruit.

Roast in 325° oven 1 hour. Remove from oven; brush with jelly. Roll in bread crumbs. Baste with butter; roast 1 hour 30 minutes more, or until meat thermometer reads 170°. Let stand 15 minutes before carving. Makes 6 servings.

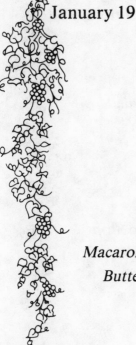

January 19

Lunch

Tuna Bisque

Crackers   Swiss Cheese

Raisin Cookies

Tea   Milk

Dinner

Broiled Lamb Chops with Thyme

Macaroni and Cheese   Baked Tomato Halves*

Butterscotch Pudding with Whipped Cream

and Chocolate Curls

Coffee   Milk

Tuna Bisque

1 (10½-oz.) can condensed tomato
  soup
1 (10½-oz.) can condensed pea soup
2 (6- to 7-oz.) cans tuna, drained and
  flaked
2 c. milk
½ c. light cream
1½ tsp. lemon juice

Mix soups in 3-qt. saucepan until smooth. Add tuna, milk and cream. Heat. Add lemon juice. Simmer a few minutes before serving. Makes 6 to 8 servings.

*See Index for recipe

Lunch

Shrimp Salad

Garlic Breadsticks

Walnut Applesauce Cake*

Tea   Milk

Dinner

Pork Curry

Rice Mixed with Chutney   Buttered Beets

Red and Green Cabbage Salad

Baked Custard Topped with Plums

Coffee   Milk

Pork Curry

4 tblsp. butter or
   regular margarine
1 medium onion, finely chopped
1 tart apple, pared and diced
¾ tsp. salt
⅛ tsp. pepper
1 tblsp. curry powder
3 tblsp. flour
2 c. chicken broth
¾ lb. cooked pork roast,
   cut into thin strips
2 tblsp. raisins

In a heavy saucepan over medium heat, melt butter and sauté onion and apple until golden.

Stir in salt, pepper and curry powder and simmer a few minutes. Stir in flour to make a smooth paste. Gradually stir in chicken broth. Cook and stir over medium heat until sauce is thickened.

Add pork pieces and raisins. Cook for 5 minutes more, or until pork is heated through. Makes 6 servings.

January 21

Lunch

Minestrone

Wheat Germ Molasses Muffins

Cream Cheese and Chopped Bacon Spread

Riced Orange Gelatin Topped with Orange Yogurt

Tea   Milk

Dinner

Broiled Flank Steak

Whipped Turnips with Chopped Pecans

Green Beans with Garlic Dressing*

Tossed Salad

3-Layer Lemon Meringue Pie*

Coffee   Milk

Wheat Germ Molasses Muffins

1¾ c. sifted flour
1 c. toasted wheat germ
¼ c. sugar
1 tsp. salt
1 tsp. baking powder
½ tsp. baking soda
½ tsp. ground cinnamon
1 egg, beaten
½ c. milk
½ c. light molasses
¼ c. cooking oil

Combine flour, wheat germ, sugar, salt, baking powder, baking soda and cinnamon in a bowl.

Combine egg, milk, molasses and oil. Add to dry ingredients, stirring just enough to moisten.

Spoon into greased 2½″ muffin-pan cups, filling two-thirds full.

Bake in 400° oven 15 to 18 minutes, or until done. Makes 12.

*See Index for recipe

Lunch

Turkey Noodle Soup
Sliced Cucumber and Salami Sandwiches
Slimmers' Deviled Eggs*
Ice Cream Sandwiches
Tea   Milk

Dinner

Baked Chicken Breasts with Almond Sauce
Brown Rice   Peas with Water Chestnuts
Jelly Roll with Crushed Raspberry Sauce
Coffee   Milk

Baked Chicken Breasts with Almond Sauce

1 clove garlic, minced
¼ c. butter or regular margarine
1 tblsp. paprika
1 tblsp. lemon juice
¼ tsp. salt
4 whole chicken breasts, split
1 (10¾-oz.) can condensed cream of
   mushroom soup
¼ c. milk
1 (4-oz.) can mushroom stems and
   pieces, drained
½ tsp. Worcestershire sauce
½ c. dairy sour cream
½ c. toasted slivered almonds
2 tblsp. flour
¼ c. water

Sauté garlic in melted butter in small skillet until tender (do not drain). Remove from heat. Add paprika, lemon juice and salt. Coat chicken breasts on all sides in butter mixture. Place chicken, skin side up, in 13x9x2" (3-qt.) glass baking dish.

Bake in 350° oven 30 minutes.

Meanwhile, combine soup, milk, mushrooms, Worcestershire sauce and sour cream in bowl. Mix well. Spoon mixture over chicken. Sprinkle with almonds. Return to oven. Bake 30 more minutes, or until chicken is tender. Remove chicken; place on serving platter. Keep warm.

Pour drippings into 2-qt. saucepan. Combine flour and water; blend well. Stir into drippings. Cook over medium heat, stirring constantly, until mixture thickens. Pour over chicken. Makes 6 servings.

*See Index for recipe

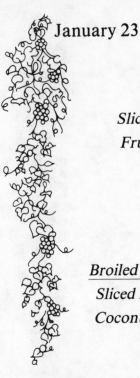

January 23

Lunch

Double Dairy Salad*

Sliced Peperoni   Sesame Bread Sticks

Fruit Cocktail with Grated Lemon Rind

Tea   Milk

Dinner

Sautéed Flounder Fillets

Broiled Mushrooms   Buttered Broccoli Spears

Sliced Avocado and Grapefruit in Lettuce Cups

Coconut Cream Pudding with Hot Maple Syrup

Coffee   Tea   Milk

Broiled Mushrooms

18 fresh mushrooms
¼ c. butter or regular margarine
Salt
Pepper
Lemon juice

Remove stems from mushrooms.

Place mushroom caps, tops down, in shallow baking pan. In cavities of upturned mushrooms place butter (about ½ tsp. for each mushroom cap) and sprinkle with salt, pepper and lemon juice. Brush with melted butter and broil 6 to 8 minutes. Makes 6 servings.

Lunch

Hearty Split Pea Soup
Sourdough Bread with Garlic Butter
Poached Oranges and Pears
Tea   Milk

Dinner

Chicken à la King
Hot Fluffy Rice   Puffy Carrot Soufflé*
Romaine Salad with Blue Cheese Dressing
Brownies
Coffee   Milk

Hearty Split Pea Soup

3 ham hocks (1½ lb.)
1 lb. dried split peas
1¼ c. chopped carrots (¼" cubes)
½ c. sliced onion
8 c. water
1 tsp. salt
4 whole peppercorns
4 whole allspice
1 bay leaf

Combine ham hocks, peas, carrots, onion, water and salt in Dutch oven. Cover. Bring to a boil.

Meanwhile, tie peppercorns, allspice and bay leaf in a small piece of cheesecloth. Add spice bag to pea mixture. Reduce heat and simmer 45 minutes, or until peas are tender. Discard spice bag.

Remove ham hocks from soup mixture. Remove meat from bones. Discard bones. Cut ham into chunks and add back to soup mixture. Makes 2 quarts or 6 servings.

January 25

Lunch

*Tuna-Macaroni Salad**

Crusty Rolls

Sugar Cookies

Pineapple Juice Spritzers

Dinner

Ham with Vegetables

Spinach, Chopped Egg and Bacon Salad

Sliced Bananas in Peach Gelatin

Coffee   Tea   Milk

Ham with Vegetables

1 (2- to 3-lb.) smoked pork shoulder
  butt
1 (1-lb.) can sauerkraut (2 c.)
2 c. apple juice
6 medium potatoes, pared
3 onions, halved
6 carrots, pared

Place pork butt in large Dutch oven or kettle. Add sauerkraut and apple juice. Cover and bring to a boil. Reduce heat and simmer 45 minutes.

Add potatoes, onions and carrots. Continue simmering until tender, 45 minutes to 1 hour. Makes 6 servings.

*See Index for recipe

Lunch

Espanola Valley Soup*
Whole-Wheat Crackers
Tossed Salad
Chocolate Cupcakes
Coffee   Tea   Milk

Dinner

Broiled Cod Fillets
Whipped Potatoes and Turnips
Ruby Cranberry Crunch Salad
Vanilla Ice Cream Garnished with Toasted Coconut
Coffee   Milk

Ruby Cranberry Crunch Salad

2 (3-oz.) pkg. cherry flavor gelatin
2 c. boiling water
1 c. cold water
2 tblsp. lemon juice
1 (1-lb.) can whole cranberry sauce
1 c. finely diced celery
½ c. chopped walnuts

Dissolve gelatin in boiling water in bowl. Stir in cold water and lemon juice. Cover and chill until thick and syrupy.

Fold cranberry sauce, celery and walnuts into gelatin mixture. Pour into lightly oiled 2-qt. mold. Cover and chill until set. Makes 8 to 10 servings.

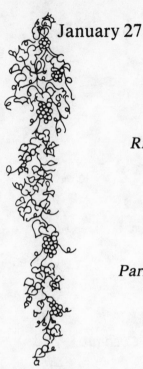

January 27

Lunch

Smothered Burgers

Carrot Curls

Rice Pudding with Raisins and Honey

Cocoa

Dinner

Broiled Chicken Livers

Parmesan-Topped Baked Tomato Halves

Savory Green Beans*

Apple Crisp with Whipped Cream

Coffee   Milk

Smothered Burgers

1 egg
⅓ c. water
3 slices bread, cubed
¼ c. finely chopped onion
1 tsp. salt
¼ tsp. pepper
1 tsp. Worcestershire sauce
1 lb. ground beef
2 tblsp. salad oil
1 (10¾-oz.) can condensed cream
   of mushroom soup
2 tblsp. water
3 hamburger buns

Beat egg in bowl. Thoroughly mix in ⅓ c. water, bread cubes, onion, salt, pepper, Worcestershire sauce and ground beef. Form into 6 patties. Brown on both sides in large skillet in hot oil. Remove meat. Drain off excess fat.

Combine soup and 2 tblsp. water in same skillet. Heat, stirring and scraping brown particles from bottom of skillet. Return patties to skillet; spoon some of the sauce over them. Cover and simmer 20 minutes.

Serve on buns, split and toasted. Makes 6 open-face sandwiches.

*See Index for recipe

Lunch

Chili-Topped Frankfurters in Toasted Buns
Potato Salad
Luscious Blueberry Cake*
Coffee   Milk

Dinner

Company-Special Veal
Broccoli with Toasted Almonds
Escarole Salad with Garlic Croutons
Napoleons
Espresso

Company-Special Veal

½ lb. fresh mushrooms, sliced
2 tblsp. butter or
   regular margarine
½ c. flour
1½ tsp. salt
¼ tsp. pepper
1 tsp. paprika
1½ lb. boneless veal, cut in
   ½ x ½ x 1″ strips
¼ c. butter or regular margarine
1 clove garlic, minced
1 green pepper, cut in strips
1 onion, thinly sliced
1½ c. chicken broth
1½ c. processed rice, cooked
   (about 6 c.)
⅓ c. sliced pimiento-stuffed olives

Brown mushrooms in 2 tblsp. butter. Remove from skillet and reserve.

Combine flour, salt, pepper and paprika in paper bag. Shake veal in seasoned flour. Melt ¼ c. butter in skillet. Brown veal on both sides in melted butter. Add minced garlic; sauté 1 minute. Add green pepper, onion and 1 c. chicken broth; cover and simmer 30 minutes, or until veal is tender.

Blend remaining ½ c. chicken broth with 3 tblsp. flour from paper bag. (If not enough seasoned flour is left, add enough flour to make 3 tblsp.) Add to veal mixture and cook, stirring until thickened. Add mushrooms to veal. Serve over hot rice, cooked following package directions, with sliced pimiento-stuffed olives folded into the rice. Makes 8 servings.

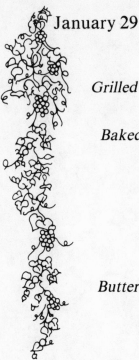

January 29

Lunch

Grilled Ham and Mozzarella Cheese Sandwiches
Cabbage-Onion Salad
Baked Pears Topped with Frozen Raspberries
Tea   Milk

Dinner

Broiled Herbed Lamb Chops
Broiled Potato Slices
Buttered Lima Beans with Small White Onions
Chicory and Sliced Radish Salad
Poppy Seed Torte*
Coffee   Milk

Cabbage-Onion Salad

8 c. shredded cabbage (1 large head)
2 large onions, thinly sliced and
　　separated in rings
1 c. sugar
1 c. vinegar
1 tsp. salt
1 tsp. celery seeds
1 tsp. dry mustard
¼ tsp. pepper
1 c. salad oil

Alternate layers of cabbage and onions in bowl, ending with onions.

Combine sugar, vinegar, salt, celery seeds, mustard and pepper in 2-qt. saucepan. Bring to a boil. Remove from heat; add salad oil.

Drip the hot mixture over cabbage and onions; do not stir. Cover and refrigerate 24 hours or longer before serving. Toss salad before serving. Makes about 8 cups.

      *See Index for recipe

Winter

Company treats: Roast Loin of Pork
(p. 355) with Fried Apple Rings
(p. 254); Baked Onions (p. 216); and
Lemon Sponge Pie (p. 249).

Home baking makes any menu special.
From top: Cranberry Muffins (p. 318);
Coconut Crown Coffee Cake (p. 315);
Old-Fashioned Filled Cookies (p. 362).

Jewel-bright accents for meats or
baked goods: Cranberry Honey
(p. 385), delicious spooned over pork,
and Citrus Honey (p. 390), made from
oranges and lemons.

A traditional holiday food is Lefse
(p. 308), a thin Norwegian bread. Serve it
with butter and sugar as a snack or
with meatballs as a main dish.

Lunch

Clam and Tomato Juice
Vegetable-Egg Combo*
Bread Sticks
Chocolate-Covered Ice Cream Bars
Tea   Milk

Dinner

Linguini with Sliced Sausages, Oil and Garlic
Polka Dot Carrots
Romaine and Sliced Mushroom Salad
Marble Cake
Coffee   Milk

Polka Dot Carrots

6 medium carrots
¼ c. butter or regular margarine
1 tblsp. minced onion
½ tsp. salt
½ tsp. sugar
⅛ tsp. pepper
½ c. sliced pimiento-stuffed
  green olives

Pare carrots and cut in ¼″ slices. Cook in boiling salted water until tender; drain.

Meanwhile, melt butter. Add onion and cook until onion is soft. Add to carrots along with remaining ingredients. Heat thoroughly and serve. Makes 6 servings.

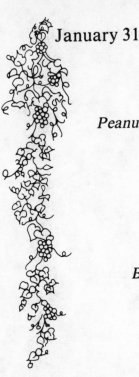

January 31

Lunch

Vegetable Soup

Peanut Butter and Chopped Bacon Sandwiches

<u>*Apricot Snowdrifts*</u>

Tea   Milk

Dinner

Teriyaki Steak*

Buttered Rice   Stir-Fried Broccoli

Curly Endive Salad

Lemon Sherbet with Kumquats

Tea   Milk

Apricot Snowdrifts

⅔ c. dried apricots
1 c. sifted flour
¼ c. sugar
½ c. butter or regular margarine
⅓ c. sifted flour
½ tsp. baking powder
¼ tsp. salt
2 eggs
1 c. brown sugar, firmly packed
½ c. chopped walnuts
½ tsp. vanilla
Confectioners' sugar
Candied cherries

Cook apricots in boiling water for 10 minutes; drain. Cool and cut up. Set aside.

Combine 1 c. flour, sugar and butter; mix until crumbly. Press into greased 9" square pan. Bake in 350° oven 18 minutes.

Sift together ⅓ c. flour, baking powder and salt into small bowl.

Beat eggs well. Slowly beat in brown sugar, blending well. Add flour mixture; stir well. Add apricots, nuts and vanilla. Spread over baked layer.

Bake in 350° oven 25 minutes, or until golden brown. Cool in pan on rack. Cut into bars with a wet knife. Roll in confectioners' sugar. Decorate each bar with candied cherry half. Makes 32 (2x1") bars.

*See Index for recipe

Lunch

Cream of Shrimp Soup
Luscious Pumpkin Bread*
Whipped Cream Cheese with Grated Orange Rind
Tapioca Pudding Layered with Cranberry Sauce
Tea   Milk

Dinner

Old World Sauerbraten
Buttered Noodles with Poppy Seeds
Steamed Hubbard Squash Cubes
Tossed Salad
Coconut Layer Cake
Coffee   Milk

Old World Sauerbraten

3 to 4 lb. boned beef rump roast
1 c. cider vinegar
1 c. water
¼ c. brown sugar, firmly packed
2 tsp. salt
¼ tsp. pepper
¼ tsp. ground cloves
1 bay leaf
1 c. chopped onion
1 c. sliced carrots
1 c. sliced celery
2 tblsp. flour
3 tblsp. cooking oil
¼ c. gingersnap crumbs
½ c. dairy sour cream

Place meat in large bowl. Combine vinegar, water, brown sugar, salt, pepper and cloves. Pour over meat, turning meat to coat all sides. Add bay leaf, onion, carrots and celery. Cover. Refrigerate meat for 2 days, turning meat several times.

Remove meat from marinade. Pat dry with paper towels. Roll meat in flour. Brown well in hot oil in Dutch oven. Add marinade and vegetables; bring to a boil. Reduce heat. Cover. Simmer for 3 hours, or until meat is tender.

Remove meat and keep warm. Skim off fat. Strain liquid. Press vegetables through a sieve and return to liquid. Stir in gingersnap crumbs. Cook over medium heat, stirring constantly, until gravy thickens slightly. Blend in sour cream. (Do not boil.) Serve with sliced meat. Makes 6 to 8 servings.

*See Index for recipe

February 2

Lunch

Chicken Vegetable Soup
Tuna and Chopped Apple Sandwiches
Dried Figs   Toasted Almonds
Cider

Dinner

Herbed Baked Fish Fillets
Sliced Beets   Buttered Corn Niblets
Escarole, Celery and Sesame Seed Salad
Frozen Pumpkin Pie*
Coffee   Milk

Chicken Vegetable Soup

1 (3-lb.) broiler-fryer, quartered
2 qt. water
4 medium onions, quartered
4 stalks celery, cut in 3″ chunks
3 medium carrots, cut in 3″ chunks
10 sprigs chopped fresh parsley
1 tblsp. salt
1 clove garlic
1 bay leaf
½ tsp. dried thyme leaves
2 whole cloves
¼ tsp. pepper
1/16 tsp. powdered saffron
1 c. sliced carrot
1 c. sliced celery
2 eggs, well beaten
1 tblsp. lemon juice
Sliced green onions and tops
Dairy sour cream

Place first 13 ingredients in 6-qt. Dutch oven. Bring to a boil; reduce heat. Cover; simmer 1 hour 15 minutes. Strain broth. Place broth back into Dutch oven; boil, uncovered, 15 minutes. Add 1 c. carrot and 1 c. celery. Cover; simmer 10 minutes, or until vegetables are tender. Remove chicken from broth. Cool slightly. Remove meat from bones and cut in chunks. Add to broth.

Remove from heat. Let stand 10 minutes. Gradually add 2 c. hot broth to eggs, stirring vigorously. Slowly add mixture into Dutch oven, stirring constantly. Add lemon juice. Serve in bowls topped with green onions and sour cream. Makes 2 quarts.

* See Index for recipe

Lunch

Cauliflower-Cheese Soup*
Pumpernickel Bread with Chive Butter
Molasses Cookies
Cocoa

Dinner

Meat Loaf

Rancho Mashed Potatoes   *Herbed Buttered Carrots*

Hard-Cooked Eggs on a Bed of Lettuce

Peach Melba

Coffee   Tea   Milk

Rancho Mashed Potatoes

9 medium potatoes, pared
1 clove garlic
¼ c. melted butter or regular
   margarine
2 egg yolks
½ c. heavy cream
½ tsp. salt
¼ tsp. pepper
1 (4-oz.) can mushroom slices,
   drained
2 tblsp. butter or regular margarine
¼ c. finely chopped fresh parsley

Cook potatoes in salted water with clove of garlic in Dutch oven until just tender. Drain; remove garlic.

Mash potatoes with ¼ c. butter. Blend in egg yolks, cream, salt and pepper.

Cook mushrooms in 2 tblsp. butter in small skillet; add with parsley to potatoes and mix.

Place potato mixture in 3-qt. casserole. Bake in 375° oven 35 minutes. Makes 8 servings.

February 4

Lunch

Oyster Stew

Buttered Baking Powder Biscuits

Currant Jelly

Baked Custard

Tea   Milk

Dinner

Macaroni with Broiled Sausages and Cheese

Broiled Eggplant Slices   French-style Green Beans

Endive and Sliced Cucumber Salad

Lace-Crusted Apples*

Coffee   Milk

Oyster Stew

3 qt. milk
4 tblsp. flour
3 tsp. salt
¼ tsp. pepper
¼ c. water
2 pt. shucked stewing oysters in own liquor
3 tblsp. butter or regular margarine

Pour milk into 5-qt. Dutch oven. Heat over medium heat until scalded. Meanwhile, combine flour, salt, pepper and water in small jar. Cover and shake until blended.

Pour oysters with liquor in 3-qt. saucepan. Slowly stir in flour mixture. Cook just a few minutes over low heat, stirring constantly, until mixture thickens and oysters begin to curl around the edges. Pour oyster mixture into hot milk. Add butter. Heat and serve immediately. Makes about 4 quarts or 16 (1-c.) servings.

* See Index for recipe

Lunch

*Chicken Tostadas**

Refried Beans

Ambrosia

Tea   Milk

Dinner

Broiled Herbed Lamb Chops

Easy Spinach Soufflé   Broiled Mushroom Caps

Tossed Salad

Sponge Cake with Sliced Strawberries

Coffee   Milk

Easy Spinach Soufflé

2 c. cream-style cottage cheese

½ c. shredded Cheddar cheese

3 eggs

⅓ c. flour

¼ c. melted butter or regular margarine

¾ tsp. salt

¼ tsp. ground nutmeg

⅛ tsp. pepper

2 (10-oz.) pkg. frozen chopped spinach, thawed and drained

Place cottage cheese, Cheddar cheese, eggs, flour, butter, salt, nutmeg and pepper in a blender. Blend at high speed for 1 minute. Mix with spinach. Turn into greased 2-qt. soufflé dish. Set dish in a pan of hot water.

Bake in 350° oven 1 hour, or until mixture is set. Makes 6 to 8 servings.

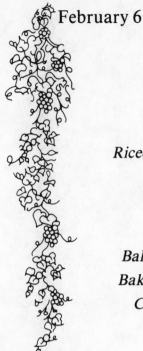

February 6

Lunch

Beef Bouillon

Swiss Salmon Sandwiches*

Watermelon Pickles

Riced Cherry Gelatin with Whipped Cream

Tea   Milk

Dinner

Baked Mustard-Glazed Canadian Bacon

Baked Potatoes   Baked Acorn Squash

Cabbage and Sliced Ripe Olive Salad

Creamy Cheesecake

Coffee   Milk

Creamy Cheesecake

3 c. cream-style cottage cheese,
    drained
5 eggs, slightly beaten
¼ tsp. salt
1 tsp. vanilla
¼ tsp. almond extract
1 c. sugar
¾ c. sifted flour
1½ c. milk
Tangy Jam Sauce (recipe follows)
Whipped cream

Press cottage cheese through sieve into large bowl. Add eggs, salt, vanilla and almond extract to cheese; blend thoroughly.

Combine sugar and flour; slowly blend into cheese mixture. Add milk; blend well. Pour into buttered 9″ square baking dish. Set dish in pan of water.

Bake in 350° oven 1 hour, or until knife inserted halfway between side and center comes out clean. (Surface may be pale.) Cool on rack. Cut in squares and serve with Tangy Jam Sauce and whipped cream. Makes 6 to 8 servings.

Tangy Jam Sauce: Combine ½ c. strawberry jam, ½ tsp. lemon juice, ¼ tsp. vanilla; blend thoroughly.

*See Index for recipe

Lunch

Green Pepper and Onion Omelets

Quick Cinnamon Rolls

Chocolate Pudding with Sour Cream and Brown Sugar

Tea   Milk

Dinner

Rolled Stuffed Flank Steak*

Honey-Glazed Baked Sliced Sweet Potatoes

Brussels Sprouts with Grated Lemon Rind

Mincemeat Tarts with Brandy-Flavored Whipped Cream

Coffee   Milk

Quick Cinnamon Rolls

2 pkg. active dry yeast
3 tblsp. sugar
1 tsp. salt
1 c. light cream
1 c. water
5 c. sifted flour
1½ c. brown sugar, firmly packed
1 c. chopped walnuts
¼ c. melted butter or regular
　margarine
1½ tsp. ground cinnamon
⅛ tsp. salt
Vanilla Glaze (recipe follows)

Combine yeast, sugar and 1 tsp. salt. Add light cream and water. Gradually add enough flour, a little at a time, to make a soft dough that leaves the sides of the bowl. Turn on-to lightly floured surface and knead for 5 minutes.

Combine brown sugar, walnuts, melted butter, cinnamon and ⅛ tsp. salt.

Divide dough in half. Roll each half into 15x8″ rectangle. Sprinkle with half of brown sugar mixture. Roll up like jelly roll, starting at long side. Cut each roll into 12 slices. Arrange in 2 greased 9″ square baking pans. Let rise until doubled (about 1 hour).

Bake in 425° oven 18 to 20 minutes, or until golden brown. Remove from pans. Cool on racks. Frost with Vanilla Glaze. Makes 24 rolls.

Vanilla Glaze: Combine 1 c. sifted confectioners' sugar, 1½ tblsp. milk and ½ tsp. vanilla; beat until smooth.

February 8

Lunch

Sloppy Joes on Toasted Buns

Potato Chips

Chewy Coconut Macaroons

Cocoa

Dinner

Fish Piquant*

Whipped Turnips   Buttered Sliced Beets

Pecan Pie Garnished with Whipped Cream and Pecans

Coffee   Milk

Chewy Coconut Macaroons

⅓ c. sifted flour
¼ tsp. baking powder
⅛ tsp. salt
2 eggs
1 tsp. vanilla
¾ c. sugar
1 tblsp. butter or regular margarine, melted
2⅔ c. flaked coconut

Sift together flour, baking powder and salt into small bowl; set aside.

Beat together eggs and vanilla in bowl until foamy, using electric mixer at high speed. Gradually beat in sugar. Continue beating at high speed until thick and lemon-colored. Blend in butter.

Gradually add dry ingredients to egg mixture, using electric mixer at low speed. Fold in coconut. Drop mixture by rounded teaspoonfuls, about 2″ apart, on greased baking sheets.

Bake in 325° oven 15 minutes, or until golden brown around the edges. Remove from baking sheets; cool on racks. Makes 2½ dozen.

*See Index for recipe

Lunch

Chicken Salad on Toasted Frankfurter Buns
Mixed Vegetable Marinade*
Cherry Turnovers
Coffee   Tea

Dinner

Roast Loin of Pork
Warm Applesauce   Steamed Potatoes and Carrots
Tossed Salad
Orange-Frosted Layer Cake
Espresso

Roast Loin of Pork

5 lb. pork loin roast
Salt
Pepper
Apricot preserves, orange marmalade
  or red currant jelly

Rub surface of pork roast with salt and pepper. Place roast on rack in roasting pan. Insert a meat thermometer in thickest part of roast. (Be sure it doesn't touch a bone.)

Roast in 325° oven until done, allowing 30 minutes per pound. (Meat thermometer should read 170°.) During the last 30 minutes of roasting, brush pork loin frequently with melted preserves. (Heat preserves in small saucepan until melted.) Remove from oven. Let roast stand 20 minutes before carving. Makes 8 servings.

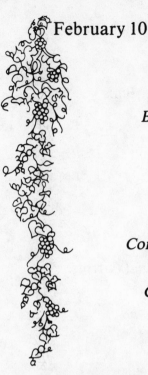

February 10

Lunch

Shortcut Beef-Vegetable Soup
Bran Muffins with Cream Cheese
Fresh Sliced Pears
Coffee   Tea   Milk

Dinner

Corned Beef Hash with Poached Eggs
Sweet-Sour Green Beans*
Chicory and Sliced Radish Salad
Raspberry Sherbet
Coffee   Milk

Shortcut Beef-Vegetable Soup

6 beef bouillon cubes
5 c. water
1 c. chopped onion
¾ c. chopped celery
1 medium carrot, sliced
1 medium potato, pared and cubed
1 clove garlic, minced
1 (1-lb. 12-oz.) can tomatoes, cut up
1½ tsp. salt
¼ tsp. dried oregano leaves
⅛ tsp. pepper
1 lb. ground beef
1 (10-oz.) pkg. frozen peas

Combine bouillon cubes and water in large kettle or Dutch oven. Bring to a boil, stirring until cubes are dissolved. Add onion, celery, carrot, potato, garlic, tomatoes and seasonings. Cover and simmer 20 minutes.

Meanwhile, brown beef in skillet; pour off excess fat. Add beef and peas to soup. Continue simmering 10 minutes. Makes 3 quarts.

* See Index for recipe

Lunch

Hot Dog Curls*

Potato Sticks

Lettuce Wedges with Russian Dressing

Butterscotch Pudding Garnished with Toasted Coconut

Tea   Milk

Dinner

Baked Ham Slices

Corn Custard Pudding   Whipped Squash

Endive and Sliced Mushroom Salad

Baked Apples with Cream

Coffee   Milk

Corn Custard Pudding

1 (1-lb.) can cream-style corn
2 tblsp. flour
2 tblsp. melted butter or regular
  margarine
1 tblsp. minced onion
1 tblsp. chopped pimientos
2 tblsp. sugar
1 tsp. salt
3 eggs, slightly beaten
2½ c. milk

Combine corn, flour, butter, onion, pimientos, sugar and salt in bowl. Beat together eggs and milk. Stir into corn mixture. Turn into greased 8″ square baking dish.

Bake in 300° oven 1 hour, or until knife comes out clean. Place under broiler a few minutes to brown top. Makes about 8 servings.

February 12

Lunch

Roast Beef and Escarole Sandwiches

Watermelon Pickles

Carrot and Raisin Salad

<u>*Coffee-Iced Brownies*</u>

Tea   Milk

Dinner

Grated Vegetable Meat Loaf*

Broiled Potato Slices   Succotash

Spinach Salad with Chopped Bacon

Lemon-Filled Jelly Roll

Coffee   Milk

Coffee-Iced Brownies

⅔ c. sifted flour
¼ c. baking cocoa
2 eggs
1 c. sugar
⅓ c. butter or regular margarine
1 tsp. vanilla
½ c. chopped pecans
Coffee Icing (recipe follows)

Sift together flour and baking cocoa into small bowl; set aside.

Beat together eggs and sugar in bowl until thick and lemon-colored, using electric mixer at high speed for 2 minutes. Add butter and vanilla; beat well.

Blend in dry ingredients. Stir in pecans. Spread batter in greased 8″ square baking pan.

Bake in 350° oven 25 minutes, or until done. Cool in pan on rack. Frost with Coffee Icing. Cut into 2″ squares. Makes 16.

Coffee Icing: Combine 1¾ c. sifted confectioners' sugar, 1 tblsp. baking cocoa, 1 tblsp. butter or regular margarine, 2 tblsp. strong hot coffee and 1 tsp. vanilla in bowl. Beat with spoon until frosting is smooth.

See Index for recipe

Lunch

Skillet Salmon Chowder*
Toasted Corn Muffins
Vanilla Ice Cream with Crushed Peanut Brittle
Tea   Milk

Dinner

Oven-Barbecued Lamb Chops
Buttered Noodles
Brussels Sprouts with Water Chestnuts
Chicory and Sliced Grapefruit Salad
Spice Cake
Coffee   Milk

Oven-Barbecued Lamb Chops

6 shoulder lamb chops (about 2½ lb.)
1 tsp. salt
¼ tsp. pepper
¼ c. cooking oil
½ c. chopped onion
3 tblsp. chili sauce
1½ tblsp. vinegar
1 tblsp. Worcestershire sauce
1½ tsp. ground ginger
1½ tsp. dry mustard
¼ tsp. garlic salt
¼ c. water

Season chops with salt and pepper. Brown in hot oil in large skillet. Remove from skillet. Place in 13x9x2" baking pan.

Sauté onion in hot oil until tender (do not brown). Stir in chili sauce, vinegar, Worcestershire sauce, ginger, mustard, garlic salt and water. Bring to a boil. Pour over chops.

Bake in 350° oven 40 minutes, or until meat is tender, basting occasionally. Makes 6 to 8 servings.

February 14

Lunch

Midwestern Turkey-Cheese Sandwiches

Cranberry Sauce

Heart-Shaped Sugar Cookies

Cocoa

Dinner

Succulent Sirloin Steak*

Herbed Rice   Buttered Italian Beans

Tomato Aspic in Heart-Shaped Molds

Strawberry Sundaes

Coffee   Milk

Midwestern Turkey-Cheese Sandwiches

12 slices bacon
12 slices buttered rye bread
Sliced, cooked turkey
Salt
8 oz. Swiss cheese, thinly sliced
6 c. shredded lettuce
3 c. Easy Thousand Island Dressing
(recipe follows)
12 tomato wedges (optional)

Cut bacon in half crosswise; pan-fry until crisp. Drain on paper towels; set aside.

On each of 6 plates, place 2 slices buttered bread, side by side. Make open-face sandwiches as follows: Cover bread slices with turkey. Sprinkle with salt; cover with cheese slices. Mound 1 c. lettuce over cheese; spoon ½ c. Easy Thousand Island Dressing over lettuce. Top each with 4 half slices cooked bacon. Garnish with tomato wedges, if desired. Makes 6 servings.

Easy Thousand Island Dressing: Combine 3 c. mayonnaise or salad dressing, 3 hard-cooked eggs, finely chopped, ⅓ c. chili sauce, 3 tblsp. chopped dill pickle and 2 tsp. grated onion. Cover and refrigerate several hours to blend flavors. Makes 5 cups.

* See Index for recipe

Lunch

Mexican Cheeseburgers*
Toasted Taco Chips
Poached Apple Slices with Raisins
Hot Cocoa Topped with Marshmallows

Dinner

Roast Duckling

Whipped Turnips   *Braised Red Cabbage*

Escarole and Sliced Apple Salad

Frozen Pumpkin Pie*

Espresso

Braised Red Cabbage

¼ c. chopped onion
3 tblsp. butter or regular margarine
1 medium red cabbage, shredded
  (about 2 lb.)
¼ c. water
¼ c. vinegar
2 apples, pared and sliced
1 tsp. sugar
1 tsp. salt

Sauté onion in melted butter in 10″ skillet until tender (do not brown). Add cabbage, water, vinegar, apples, sugar and salt. Cover and simmer for 30 minutes, or until cabbage is tender. Makes 6 servings.

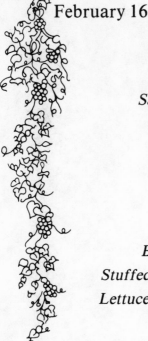

February 16

Lunch

Chicken Noodle Soup

Salami and Dill Pickle Sandwiches

Cherry Tomatoes

Old-Fashioned Filled Cookies

Tea   Milk

Dinner

Broiled Liver and Braised Onions

Stuffed Baked Potatoes   Buttered Carrots

Lettuce Wedges with Mock Russian Dressing*

Sponge Cake

Coffee   Milk

Old-Fashioned Filled Cookies

2½ c. sifted flour
1 tsp. salt
1 c. butter or regular margarine
1 c. sugar
2 eggs
1 tsp. vanilla
Apricot Filling (recipe follows)

Sift together flour and salt.

Cream together butter and sugar in bowl until light and fluffy, using electric mixer at medium speed. Add eggs, one at a time, beating well after each addition. Beat in vanilla.

Gradually stir dry ingredients into creamed mixture, mixing well. Cover and refrigerate dough overnight, or until firm enough to roll out.

Divide dough in half. Use one half of dough, keeping remaining dough in refrigerator. Roll out on floured surface to ⅛" thickness. Cut 30 rounds, using floured 2" cookie cutter. Place, about 2" apart, on ungreased baking sheets. Place 1 tsp. Apricot Filling in center of each.

Roll out remaining dough. Cut 30 (2") rounds. Cut out center of each, using ¾" cookie cutter. Place over filled rounds. Press edges of each cookie with floured fork.

Bake in 400° oven 8 minutes, or until golden. Remove from sheets; cool on racks. Makes 2½ dozen.

Apricot Filling: Combine 1 (6-oz.) pkg. dried apricots (1 c.) and 1 c. water in saucepan. Bring to a boil over medium heat. Simmer 5 minutes. Remove from heat. Purée apricots with cooking liquid in blender until smooth. Stir in ½ c. sugar and 2 tblsp. butter; cool completely. Makes enough filling for 2½ dozen cookies.

*See Index for recipe

Lunch

Potato-Bacon Omelet*

Marinated Green Beans

Gingerbread

Cocoa

Dinner

Toad-in-the-Hole

Corn Niblets   Buttered Asparagus Spears

Tossed Salad

Honey-Glazed Broiled Grapefruit

Coffee   Milk

Toad-in-the-Hole

1 lb. small, fresh pork sausage links
2 tblsp. water
2 eggs
1 c. milk
1 c. sifted flour
½ tsp. salt
⅛ tsp. pepper

Place sausages and water in 10″ skillet. Cover and cook over low heat 3 minutes. Remove cover; increase heat to medium. Continue cooking sausages, turning them frequently, until the water evaporates and sausages begin to brown.

Meanwhile, prepare batter. Beat eggs with rotary beater. Add milk; blend well. Add flour, salt and pepper, beating until batter is smooth.

Pour ¼ c. sausage drippings in bottom of 12x8x2″ (2-qt.) glass baking dish. Arrange sausage links in bottom of dish. Pour batter over all.

Bake in 425° oven 30 minutes. Makes 6 servings.

*See Index for recipe

February 18

Lunch

Cottage Cheese and Chopped Ham with Sour Cream

Whole-Wheat Raisin Bread

Cinnamon-Dusted Sugar Cookies

Tea   Milk

Dinner

Broiled Fish Fillets

Buttered Broccoli   Creamed Onions

Endive and Sliced Mushroom Salad

Rainbow Parfaits*

Coffee   Milk

Whole-Wheat Raisin Bread

2 c. boiling water
2 c. raisins
1 c. sifted flour
2 c. stirred whole-wheat flour
2 tsp. baking powder
2 tsp. baking soda
1 tsp. salt
2 eggs
1½ c. sugar

Pour boiling water over raisins in small bowl. Let stand until cooled.

Stir together flour, whole-wheat flour, baking powder, baking soda and salt.

Beat together eggs and sugar in mixing bowl until light and lemon-colored, using electric mixer at medium speed. Stir in raisin mixture. Add dry ingredients all at once, stirring just until moistened. Pour mixture into 5 greased (1-lb.) vegetable cans.

Bake in 350° oven 40 minutes, or until cake tester or wooden pick inserted in center comes out clean. Remove from cans; cool on racks. Makes 5 small loaves.

*See Index for recipe

Lunch

Liverwurst and Sliced Cucumber Sandwiches

Cabbage Salad Bowl

Blueberry Turnovers

Tea   Milk

Dinner

Veal Loaf*

Parslied Rice   French-style Green Beans

Chicory and Black Olive Salad

Sliced Apples and Brie

Coffee   Milk

Cabbage Salad Bowl

½ c. light raisins
¼ c. orange juice
1 medium head cabbage, shredded
1 carrot, shredded
2 tblsp. sugar
½ tsp. salt
¼ c. mayonnaise
2 tblsp. tarragon vinegar

Soak raisins in orange juice while preparing other ingredients. Combine cabbage, carrot, sugar and salt in salad bowl. Blend mayonnaise and vinegar. Add to cabbage along with raisins and orange juice.

Toss lightly. Makes 8 servings.

* See Index for recipe

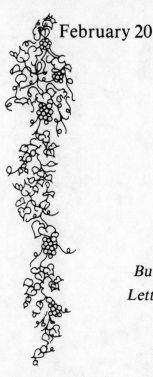

February 20

Lunch

Grilled Tortilla Sandwiches*
Fresh Fruit Salad
Cocoa

Dinner

Broiled Lamb Chops
Whipped Sweet Potatoes
Buttered Peas with Toasted Almonds
Lettuce Salad with Green Pepper Rings
<u>*Individual Schaum Tortes*</u>
Coffee   Milk

Individual Schaum Tortes

8 egg whites
½ tsp. cream of tartar
2 c. sugar
1 tsp. vanilla
1 tsp. vinegar
2 qt. fresh strawberries, sliced and
   sweetened, or 3 (10-oz.) pkg.
   frozen strawberries, thawed
2 c. heavy cream, whipped and
   sweetened

Beat egg whites with electric mixer at high speed until frothy. Add cream of tartar. Beat until egg whites are almost dry.

Slowly add sugar, 2 tblsp. at a time, beating well after each addition. (Total beating time: 20 minutes.) Add vanilla and vinegar; beat 2 minutes. (Mixture should be very stiff and glossy.) Drop mixture by spoonfuls onto greased baking sheets, making 10 tortes.

Bake in 250° oven 1 hour 15 minutes, or until tortes are pale brown and crusty. Remove from baking sheets; cool on racks.

Spoon strawberries over each torte and top with whipped cream. Makes 10 servings.

*See Index for recipe

Lunch

Chili Chicken Stew

Tossed Salad

Riced Lemon Gelatin with Plums

Tea   Milk

Dinner

Broiled Ham Slices

Buttered Lima Beans   Fried Apple Rings*

Avocado and Tomato Salad

Pineapple Upside-Down Cake

Coffee   Milk

Chili Chicken Stew

1 (4½-lb.) stewing chicken, cut in
  pieces
2 qt. water
1 tsp. salt
1 (1-lb.) can tomatoes, cut up
4 c. sliced, pared potatoes
1 c. diced, pared carrots
1 c. chopped onion
1 c. ketchup
⅓ c. parboiled rice
2 tblsp. lemon juice
1 tblsp. chili powder
2 tsp. salt
1 tsp. pepper
1 tsp. Worcestershire sauce
1 tsp. dried marjoram leaves
1 bay leaf

Cook chicken in water and 1 tsp. salt in Dutch oven until tender (about 2 hours). Chicken can also be cooked in pressure cooker according to manufacturer's directions.

Add tomatoes, potatoes, carrots, onion, ketchup, rice, lemon juice, chili powder, 2 tsp. salt, pepper, Worcestershire sauce, marjoram and bay leaf. Simmer, covered, for 1 hour, or until vegetables are tender. Makes 6 servings.

*See Index for recipe

February 22

Lunch

Hot Buttered Tomato Soup
Cottage Cheese Sandwiches*
Lemon Yogurt and Ladyfingers
Tea   Milk

Dinner

Baked Turkey Thighs
Sage Stuffing   Steamed Butternut Squash Cubes
Spiced Cranberry Mold
Cherry Cobbler
Coffee   Milk

Spiced Cranberry Mold

1 (3-oz.) pkg. orange flavor gelatin
1 c. boiling cranberry juice
¾ c. cold cranberry juice
1½ tsp. Worcestershire sauce
1 tsp. ground cinnamon
¼ tsp. ground nutmeg
1 (1-lb.) can sliced peaches, drained
   and chopped
½ c. chopped walnuts

Dissolve gelatin in boiling cranberry juice in bowl. Stir in cold cranberry juice, Worcestershire sauce, cinnamon and nutmeg. Cover and chill until thick and syrupy.

Fold in peaches and walnuts. Pour into lightly oiled 4-c. mold. Cover and chill until set. Makes 6 servings.

*See Index for recipe

Lunch

Black Bean Soup

Bologna and Lettuce Sandwiches

Coconut Custard Pie

Cocoa

Dinner

Broiled Sweet Italian Sausage

Eggplant Parmesan*   *Garlic Bread*

Romaine and Black Olive Salad

Raspberry Sherbet

Coffee   Milk

Coconut Custard Pie

3 eggs
1½ c. sugar
½ c. melted butter or regular
  margarine
1 tblsp. lemon juice
2 tsp. vanilla
¹/₁₆ tsp. salt
1⅓ c. flaked coconut
1 unbaked 9″ pie shell

Beat eggs in bowl until lemon-colored. Beat in sugar, butter, lemon juice, vanilla and salt. Stir in coconut. Pour into pie shell.

Bake in 350° oven 40 minutes, or until knife inserted halfway between edge and center of custard comes out clean. (Center will be soft.) Cool on rack. Makes 6 to 8 servings.

*See Index for recipe

February 24

Lunch

*Tuna Carrot Salad**

Bread Sticks

Sliced Pears

Coffee Milk Shakes

Dinner

Red Flannel Hash

Buttered Green Beans

Escarole and Sliced Mushroom Salad

Banana Splits

Tea   Milk

Red Flannel Hash

¾ c. chopped onion

2 tblsp. melted butter or regular margarine

3 c. chopped, cooked potatoes

2 c. finely chopped corned beef

1½ c. chopped, cooked beets or 1 (1-lb.) can chopped beets, drained

½ c. dairy sour cream

1 tsp. salt

¼ tsp. pepper

Sauté onion in melted butter in small skillet until soft. Combine with potatoes, corned beef, beets, sour cream, salt and pepper. Spoon mixture into greased 2-qt. casserole. Smooth out top.

Bake in 350° oven 35 minutes. Or fry mixture slowly in 3 tblsp. butter or bacon drippings in 12″ skillet until bottom is crusty. Invert platter over skillet and turn out, crusty side up. Makes 6 servings.

*See Index for recipe

Lunch

Cheese-Stuffed Frankfurters

Baked Kidney Beans

Baked Custard

Orange Spritzers

Dinner

Sautéed Chicken Livers

Brown Rice

Spinach and Grated Turnip Salad

Lemon Sponge Pie*

Espresso

Baked Kidney Beans

2 (1-lb.) cans red kidney beans
1 large onion, finely chopped
½ c. ketchup
3 tblsp. brown sugar, packed
2 slices bacon

Combine beans, onion, ketchup and sugar in greased 2-qt. casserole. Top with bacon.

Bake in 400° oven 1¼ hours. Makes 6 servings.

February 26

Lunch

Beef Noodle Soup

Waldorf Salad with Poppy Seed Salad Dressing*

Buttered Rolls

Brownies

Tea   Milk

Dinner

Beef and Cabbage Scallop

Broiled Tomato Halves

Marinated Artichoke Hearts

Bread Pudding Dusted with Nutmeg

Coffee   Milk

Beef and Cabbage Scallop

1 lb. ground beef
1 c. chopped celery
½ c. chopped onion
2 tblsp. flour
1 (1-lb. 12-oz.) can tomatoes, cut up
1 (8-oz.) can tomato sauce
1½ tsp. salt
1 tsp. dried oregano leaves
¼ tsp. pepper
4 c. coarsely chopped cabbage
2 c. thinly sliced, pared potatoes
2 c. bread cubes (½ ")
2 tblsp. melted butter or regular
   margarine

Brown ground beef in large skillet. When meat begins to brown, add celery and onion. Cook for 5 minutes. Stir in flour, tomatoes, tomato sauce, salt, oregano and pepper. Bring mixture to a boil; remove from heat.

Place alternate layers of meat mixture, cabbage and potatoes in 3-qt. casserole. Combine bread and butter; sprinkle on top. Cover.

Bake in 375° oven 1 hour, or until vegetables are tender. Makes 6 to 8 servings.

*See Index for recipe

Lunch

Chicken Bouillon

Marinated Sausage Sandwiches*

Blueberry Turnovers

Tea   Milk

Dinner

Barbecued Spareribs

Noodles Parmesan   Buttered Sliced Beets

Tossed Salad

Broiled Peach Halves Filled with Vanilla Ice Cream

Coffee   Milk

Noodles Parmesan

1 (8-oz.) pkg. thin noodles
6 tblsp. butter or regular margarine
½ c. dairy half-and-half
1 c. grated Parmesan cheese
½ c. dairy half-and-half

Cook noodles according to package directions; drain.

Melt butter in skillet; cook over low heat until lightly browned. Stir in ½ c. half-and-half; heat until bubbly. Add noodles and toss with two forks. Add cheese and ½ c. half-and-half in three additions, tossing after each. Makes 8 servings.

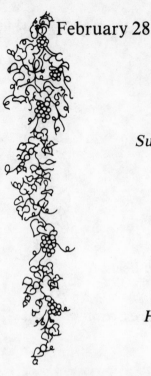

February 28

Lunch

Mexican Salad Bowl*
Toasted Pumpernickel Bread
Sunflower Seeds   Dried Apricots
Cocoa

Dinner

Cheese and Ham Soufflé
Buttered Brussels Sprouts
Carrot-Walnut Bread
Honey-Glazed Broiled Grapefruit
Coffee   Milk

Carrot-Walnut Bread

1½ c. sifted flour
1 tsp. baking soda
½ tsp. ground cinnamon
¼ tsp. ground nutmeg
¼ tsp. salt
1 c. sugar
¾ c. cooking oil
2 eggs
1½ c. shredded, pared carrots
½ c. chopped walnuts

Sift together flour, baking soda, cinnamon, nutmeg and salt into small bowl; set aside.

Combine sugar, oil and eggs in mixing bowl. Beat with electric mixer at medium speed 2 minutes. Add dry ingredients, stirring just until moistened. Stir in carrots and walnuts. Pour into greased 9x5x3" loaf pan.

Bake in 350° oven 1 hour, or until cake tester or wooden pick inserted in center comes out clean. Cool in pan on rack 10 minutes. Remove from pan; cool on rack. Makes 1 loaf.

*See Index for recipe

Lunch

Shrimp Salad

Refrigerator Bran Muffins*

Sliced Bananas and Yogurt Topped with Brown Sugar

Coffee   Tea

Dinner

Swiss Steak with Onions

Baked Potato Sticks   Buttered Lima Beans

Romaine and Cucumber Salad

Pound Cake

Coffee   Milk

Baked Potato Sticks

6 medium potatoes
1 tsp. salt
1 tsp. parsley flakes
1 tsp. instant minced onion
¼ tsp. pepper
¾ c. dairy half-and-half or light cream
3 tblsp. butter or regular margarine
½ c. grated process American cheese

Pare potatoes and cut in lengthwise strips as for French fries. Place in greased 2-qt. casserole. Sprinkle with salt, parsley, onion and pepper. Pour half-and-half over. Dot with butter and sprinkle with cheese.

Cover; bake in 425° oven 50 minutes, or until potatoes are tender. Makes 6 servings.

Lunch

Pasta and Bean Soup
Whole-Wheat Crackers
Sliced Apples   Walnuts   Muenster Cheese
Tea   Milk

Dinner

Corned Beef Hash
Broiled Pineapple Slices   Buttered Broccoli
Avocado and Watercress Salad
Apricot Pie à la Mode*
Coffee   Milk

Pasta and Bean Soup

1 lb. dry great northern beans
2 qt. water
2½ tsp. salt
1 large whole carrot
6 strips bacon
½ c. chopped onion
½ c. chopped celery
1 small clove garlic, minced
1 (1-lb.) can stewed tomatoes, cut up
½ bay leaf
½ tsp. dried oregano leaves
½ tsp. salt
¼ tsp. pepper
¼ c. water
1 c. ditalini or small elbow macaroni

Soak beans 8 hours or overnight. Rinse well and drain. Combine beans, 2 qt. water, 2½ tsp. salt and carrot; simmer in 6-qt. pot for 2 hours, or until beans are tender.

Fry bacon in skillet until crisp. Remove and drain on paper towels. Reserve ¼ c. bacon drippings. Add onion, celery and garlic. Sauté until tender (do not brown). Stir in tomatoes, bay leaf, oregano, ½ tsp. salt, pepper and ¼ c. water. Bring to a boil; reduce heat. Simmer 30 minutes.

Cook macaroni according to package directions. Drain.

Purée half of the beans. Cube carrot. Crumble bacon. Combine all ingredients. Makes 3½ quarts.

*See Index for recipe

Lunch

Sliced Liverwurst   Deviled Eggs

Delicious Health Bread

Riced Orange and Raspberry Gelatin

Vanilla Milk Shakes

Dinner

Turkey Fricassee with Parslied Dumplings

Hot Spiced Beets*

Escarole and Sliced Orange Salad

Poached Pears with Custard Sauce

Coffee   Milk

Delicious Health Bread

1 c. raisins
1 c. boiling water
1 egg
¾ c. sugar
½ tsp. salt
1 c. graham flour
1 c. quick-cooking oats
1 c. whole bran cereal
1 tsp. baking soda
1 c. buttermilk
2 tblsp. wheat germ

Simmer raisins in boiling water for 5 minutes. Cool well.

Beat together egg, sugar and salt in large bowl. Add graham flour, oats, bran cereal, baking soda and buttermilk. Stir just until mixture is moistened. Stir in raisins and liquid. Pour batter into 2 greased 8½x4½x2½" loaf pans. Sprinkle tops with wheat germ.

Bake in 350° oven 1 hour, or until breads test done. Remove from pans. Cool on racks. Makes 2 loaves.

*See Index for recipe

March 4

Lunch

Vegetable Beef Soup

Cream Cheese, Olive and Grated Carrot Sandwiches

Jellied Fruit Compote*

Tea   Milk

Dinner

Broiled Flounder Fillets

Broiled Eggplant Slices   Peas with Toasted Almonds

Arizona Green Salad

Strawberry Ice Cream with Crushed Strawberries

Coffee   Milk

Arizona Green Salad

1 medium head romaine
2 tblsp. lemon juice
1 ripe avocado, pared and sliced
1 (16-oz.) can grapefruit sections,
   drained and chilled
1 red onion, thinly sliced and
   separated in rings
Oil-Vinegar Dressing (recipe follows)

Tear romaine in bite-size pieces. Sprinkle lemon juice on avocado slices to prevent discoloration.

Add avocado, grapefruit and onion rings to romaine. Toss with Oil-Vinegar Dressing. Cover and chill 30 minutes before serving. Makes 6 to 8 servings.

Oil-Vinegar Dressing: Put ½ c. salad oil, ¼ c. wine vinegar, 1 tblsp. lemon juice, 2¼ tsp. seasoned salt and ¼ tsp. seasoned pepper in pint jar with screw-type lid. Shake well. Makes ¾ cup.

* See Index for recipe

Lunch

Sliced Tongue and Grated Cheese Sandwiches
Spinach-Mushroom Vinaigrette*
Spice Cupcakes
Tea   Milk

Dinner

Sautéed Calves' Liver and Bacon
Corn with Pimientos   Whipped Butternut Squash
Chicory and Sliced Radish Salad
French Chocolate Pie
Coffee   Tea   Milk

French Chocolate Pie

½ c. butter or regular margarine, softened
¾ c. sugar
2 (1-oz.) squares unsweetened chocolate, melted and cooled
2 eggs
2 c. frozen whipped topping, thawed
1 (9″) baked graham cracker crust

Combine butter, sugar and cooled chocolate in large mixing bowl. Beat with electric mixer at medium speed until well blended, about 1 to 2 minutes. Beat in eggs, one at a time, beating well after each addition. Fold in whipped topping. Pour into graham cracker crust.

Cover and chill 4 hours, or until set. Makes 6 to 8 servings.

*See Index for recipe

March 6

Lunch

Turkey Club Sandwiches

Assorted Pickles

Peanut Butter Cookies*

Cocoa

Dinner

Pork with Apples and Potatoes

Sauerkraut with Caraway Seeds

Vanilla Pudding with Chopped Walnuts

Coffee   Tea   Milk

Pork with Apples and Potatoes

1½ lb. boneless pork shoulder, cut in
   1″ cubes
4 c. water
1 tblsp. salt
⅛ tsp. pepper
1 bay leaf
6 medium potatoes, pared and cut in
   eighths
4 medium, tart red apples, pared,
   cored and cut in eighths

Place pork cubes, water, salt, pepper and bay leaf in Dutch oven. Cover and bring to a boil. Reduce heat and simmer 1 hour 30 minutes, or until meat is tender. Add potatoes; cook 10 minutes. Add apples and cook 20 minutes, or until apples are tender. Makes 4 to 6 servings.

*See Index for recipe

Lunch

Oyster Stew*

Sliced Ham

Special Corn Meal Muffins

Canned Plums and Peaches   Molasses Cookies

Tea   Milk

Dinner

Chicken Supreme*

Herbed Rice   Sautéed Cherry Tomatoes

Tossed Salad

Lemon Sherbet Topped with Cranberry Sauce

Coffee   Milk

Special Corn Meal Muffins

1¼ c. sifted flour
1 c. yellow corn meal
2 tblsp. sugar
4 tsp. baking powder
½ tsp. salt
1 egg, beaten
1 c. milk
¼ c. cooking oil
1 tblsp. chopped pimientos
1 tblsp. chopped green pepper

Sift together flour, corn meal, sugar, baking powder and salt into small bowl; set aside.

Combine egg, milk and oil. Add to dry ingredients, stirring just until moistened. Stir in pimientos and green pepper.

Spoon into greased 2½" muffin-pan cups, filling two-thirds full.

Bake in 425° oven 20 to 25 minutes, or until done. Makes 12.

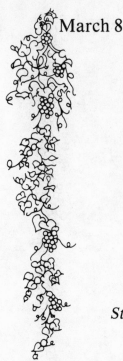

March 8

Lunch

<u>Russian Meatball Soup</u>

Crusty Rolls

Muenster Cheese

Sugar-Frosted Grapes

Tea   Milk

Dinner

Veal Patties*

Potatoes au Gratin

Stir-Fried Julienne Carrots and Green Beans

Escarole and Hearts of Palm Salad

Ladyfingers Filled with Strawberry Jam

Espresso

Russian Meatball Soup

4 c. water
1 pkg. onion soup mix
1 carrot, sliced
1 c. finely shredded cabbage
1 medium potato, pared and diced
2 slices bread, torn in small pieces
1 egg
½ c. milk
½ tsp. salt
⅛ tsp. pepper
½ lb. ground beef
2 c. water
½ tsp. salt
1 (8-oz.) can chopped beets
Dairy sour cream

Combine 4 c. water, onion soup mix and carrot in kettle or Dutch oven. Bring to a boil; reduce heat, cover and simmer, 10 minutes. Add cabbage and potato; simmer 15 minutes longer.

Meanwhile, soak bread pieces several minutes in mixture of egg, milk, ½ tsp. salt and pepper. Add ground beef and mix until blended. Shape in tiny balls, using a rounded half-teaspoon of mixture for each.

In medium saucepan heat 2 c. water and ½ tsp. salt to simmering. Add half the meatballs. Cover; simmer 5 minutes. Remove with slotted spoon. Simmer remaining meatballs 5 minutes. Add meatballs with cooking broth and undrained beets to soup. Heat thoroughly. Pass sour cream to spoon on top. Makes 2½ quarts.

*See Index for recipe

Lunch

Salmon Salad Sandwiches

Cauliflower-Olive Salad

Cinnamon-Dusted Sliced Bananas

Tea   Milk

Dinner

Pork Kabobs*

Buttered Noodles   Lemon-Glazed Whole Beets

Shredded Lettuce and Sliced Tomato Salad

Gingerbread with Whipped Cream

Coffee   Milk

Cauliflower-Olive Salad

½ c. olive oil
¼ c. lemon juice or white wine
  vinegar
½ tsp. salt
Dash freshly ground pepper
2 Bermuda onions, thinly sliced and
  separated in rings
½ small head cauliflower, broken
  into flowerets and sliced (about
  3 c.)
½ c. sliced pimiento-stuffed olives
½ c. crumbled blue cheese
1 medium head iceberg lettuce, torn
  in bite-size pieces

Combine oil, lemon juice, salt and pepper in bowl. Add onions, cauliflower and olives to mixture. Cover and chill in refrigerator at least 30 minutes.

Sprinkle cheese over lettuce in salad bowl. Add marinated mixture and toss gently. Makes 6 servings.

*See Index for recipe

Lunch

*Barbecued Beef Buns**

Green Pepper Strips   Celery Sticks

Baked Custard with Maple Syrup

Tea   Milk

Dinner

Cheese Soufflé with Shrimp Sauce

Steamed Broccoli   Broiled Mushrooms

Endive and Watercress Salad

Raspberry Parfait Pie

Coffee   Milk

Raspberry Parfait Pie

1 (3-oz.) pkg. raspberry flavor gelatin
¼ c. sugar
1¼ c. boiling water
1 (10-oz.) pkg. frozen raspberries
1 tblsp. lemon juice
1 (3-oz.) pkg. cream cheese
⅓ c. confectioners' sugar
¼ tsp. salt
1 tsp. vanilla
1 c. heavy cream, whipped
1 baked 10" pie shell

Dissolve gelatin and sugar in boiling water in bowl. Add raspberries and lemon juice; stir until thawed. Cover; chill until slightly thickened.

Beat together cream cheese, confectioners' sugar, salt and vanilla until smooth. Fold in whipped cream.

Spread half of the cheese mixture in pie shell. Top with half of raspberry mixture. Repeat layers. Cover and chill well. Makes 8 servings.

Lunch

Chicken Bouillon

Sliced Ham

Cranberry Honey

Orange Gelatin Cubes with Yogurt and Nutmeg

Coffee   Tea   Milk

Dinner

Buttermilk Stroganoff*

Crumb-Topped Broiled Tomato Halves

Chicory with Garlic Croutons

Pineapple Sherbet*

Coffee   Milk

Cranberry Honey

2 c. cranberry cocktail
3 c. sugar
1 tsp. grated orange rind
1 c. honey
½ bottle fruit pectin

Bring first 3 ingredients to a boil in 3-qt. saucepan; simmer 10 minutes. Add honey. Bring to a rapid boil; boil 1 minute. Remove from heat.

Add pectin; skim. Pour into sterilized jelly glasses. Seal. Makes 5 (6-oz.) glasses.

*See Index for recipe

March 12

Lunch

Roast Beef and Watercress Sandwiches

Radish Roses   Olives

Lemon Slices*

Cocoa

Dinner

Cabbage with Polish Sausage

Parslied Boiled Potatoes with Lemon Butter

Tossed Salad

Chocolate Mousse

Coffee   Milk

Cabbage with Polish Sausage

1 c. chopped onion
2 tblsp. butter or regular margarine
2 tblsp. flour
1 c. water
¼ c. white vinegar
¾ tsp. salt
½ tsp. sugar
¼ tsp. pepper
3 qt. shredded cabbage
6 Polish sausages, cut in 1″ slices

Cook onion in butter in Dutch oven until soft and lightly colored. Blend in flour. Add water and vinegar, and cook, stirring constantly, until mixture comes to a boil. Blend in salt, sugar and pepper. Stir in cabbage and sausage.

Cover and simmer about 20 minutes, or until cabbage is tender. Stir occasionally. Makes 6 servings.

*See Index for recipe

Lunch

Sliced Salami and Lettuce

Italian-Tomato Dressing*

Bran Muffins

Pecan-Stuffed Baked Apples

Tea   Milk

Dinner

Broiled Sirloin Steak

Peas with Water Chestnuts

Herb-Stuffed Mushroom Caps

Spinach Salad

Party Angel Food Cake

Coffee   Milk

Party Angel Food Cake

1 c. plus 2 tblsp. sifted cake flour
¾ c. sugar
1⅔ c. egg whites (about 12)
1½ tsp. cream of tartar
½ tsp. salt
1 c. sugar
1 tsp. vanilla
½ tsp. almond extract
10 red maraschino cherries, cut up
½ c. chopped pecans
Maraschino cherries (optional)

Sift together cake flour and ¾ c. sugar in bowl 4 times; set aside.

Beat egg whites, cream of tartar and salt in large mixing bowl until foamy, using electric mixer at high speed. Gradually add 1 c. sugar, 2 tblsp. at a time, beating until stiff glossy peaks form. Blend in vanilla and almond extract.

Add flour mixture in 4 parts, folding about 15 strokes after each addition. Fold in cut-up cherries and pecans. Turn batter into ungreased 10″ tube pan. Pull metal spatula through batter once to break up air bubbles.

Bake in 350° oven 45 minutes, or until top springs back when lightly touched with finger. Invert tube pan on funnel or bottle to cool. When completely cooled, remove from pan. Frost with your favorite fluffy white frosting and decorate with red maraschino cherries with stems, if you wish. Makes 12 servings.

*See Index for recipe

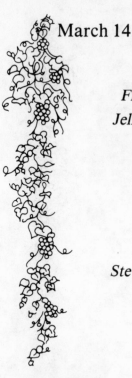

March 14

Lunch

Fish Sticks on Toasted Frankfurter Buns
Jellied Cucumber Mold with Dill Dressing*
Chocolate-Frosted Brownies
Tea   Milk

Dinner

Baked Swiss Fondue
Stewed Tomatoes   Buttered Lima Beans
Romaine and Black Olive Salad
Poached Pears and Apricots
Coffee   Milk

Baked Swiss Fondue

8 slices bread
6 (1-oz.) slices process Swiss cheese
3 eggs, beaten
2 c. milk
½ tsp. salt
⅛ tsp. white pepper
½ tsp. instant minced green onion

Trim crusts from bread; cut in halves diagonally. Arrange 8 halves in pin-wheel pattern in greased round pan (or in 1½ qt. casserole). Cover bread with cheese slices cut in halves for easy placement. Top with remaining bread like first layer.

Combine beaten eggs, milk, salt and pepper in bowl; blend with rotary beater. Pour over bread and cheese. Sprinkle with onion.

Bake in 325° oven until puffy and golden brown, about 1 hour. Serve at once. Makes 6 servings.

See Index for recipe

Lunch

Hot Frank Potato Salad*

Watermelon Pickles

Tapioca Pudding with Chopped Peanuts

Cocoa

Dinner

Braised Duckling

Rice with Grated Orange Rind   *Braised Red Cabbage*

Lettuce Wedges with Oil and Vinegar Dressing

Cinnamon Jumbles

Coffee   *Tea*   *Milk*

Cinnamon Jumbles

1 c. butter or regular margarine
2 c. sugar
2 eggs
2 tsp. vanilla
4 c. sifted flour
1 tsp. baking soda
1 tsp. salt
1½ c. buttermilk
½ c. sugar
2 tsp. ground cinnamon

Cream together butter and 2 c. sugar in large bowl until light and fluffy. Add eggs, one at a time, beating well after each addition. Beat in vanilla.

Sift together flour, baking soda and salt. Add dry ingredients alternately with buttermilk to creamed mixture, beating well after each addition. Cover and refrigerate dough overnight.

Drop by rounded teaspoonfuls 2″ apart on greased baking sheets. Combine ½ c. sugar and cinnamon; sprinkle mixture on each cookie.

Bake in 400° oven 8 to 10 minutes, or until golden brown. Remove from baking sheets. Cool on racks. Makes about 5 dozen.

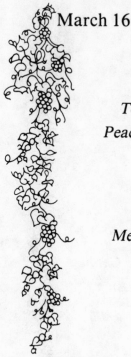

March 16

Lunch

Clam Chowder

Toasted Corn Muffins <u>*Citrus Honey*</u>

Peach Gelatin Cubes in Canned Peach Halves

Tea   Milk

Dinner

Meat Loaf Frosted with Whipped Potatoes

Corn 'n' Celery Sauté*

Watercress and Endive Salad

Pineapple Upside-Down Cake

Coffee   Milk

Citrus Honey

3 medium-size lemons
1 medium-size orange
1 c. sugar
2 c. honey
½ c. water
½ bottle fruit pectin

Peel rind from fruit; reserve fruit sections. Cut rind into ½″ thin strips. Combine rind, sugar, ½ c. honey and water in a small saucepan. Bring to a boil. Cover. Simmer 10 minutes, stirring occasionally.

Meanwhile, remove all membrane from fruit sections; dice fruit. Add fruit and juice to cooked mixture; bring to boil. Simmer, covered, 20 minutes. You should have 2 c. of fruit mixture; if not, add enough water to make 2 c.

Turn into large saucepan; stir in 1½ c. honey. Bring to a rapid boil, stirring constantly. Boil 1 minute. Remove from heat.

Add pectin; stir and skim 5 minutes. Pour into sterilized jelly glasses. Seal. Makes 4 (6-oz.) glasses.

*See Index for recipe

Lunch

Green Soup*

Egg Salad Sandwiches

Gingerbread

Cocoa

Dinner

Golden Noodle Bake

Steamed Spinach   Buttered Shredded Beets

Marinated Sliced Tomatoes

Luscious Lime Pie* Garnished with

Whipped Cream Shamrocks

Coffee   Milk

Golden Noodle Bake

¼ c. finely chopped onion
3 tblsp. melted butter or
  regular margarine
1 c. dairy sour cream
1 lb. cream-style cottage cheese
½ c. milk
2 tblsp. sugar
1 tsp. salt
8 oz. wide noodles, cooked
  and drained
1 c. crushed corn flakes
3 tblsp. melted butter or
  regular margarine
Chopped fresh parsley

Sauté onion in 3 tblsp. melted butter in small skillet until tender (do not brown).

Combine sour cream, cottage cheese, milk, sugar, salt and sautéed onion in a large bowl; mix well. Add noodles and mix well. Turn noodle mixture into greased 12x8x2″ (2-qt.) glass baking dish.

Combine corn flakes and 3 tblsp. melted butter. Sprinkle over noodle mixture.

Bake in 350° oven 50 minutes, or until hot and bubbly. Cut into squares. Serve sprinkled with parsley. Makes 12 servings.

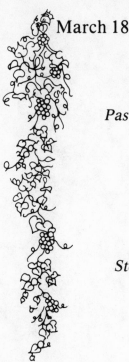

March 18

Lunch

Mugs of Hot Beef Bouillon
Pastrami Strips and Chick Peas in Pita Bread
Peanut Butter Fingers
Tea   Milk

Dinner

*Gingered Chicken with Grapes**
Steamed Brown Rice with Toasted Pecans
Parslied Carrot Slices
Escarole and Sliced Scallion Salad
Cream Puffs
Coffee   Milk

Peanut Butter Fingers

½ c. butter or regular margarine
½ c. sugar
½ c. brown sugar, firmly packed
1 egg
⅓ c. peanut butter
½ tsp. vanilla
1 c. sifted flour
½ tsp. baking soda
¼ tsp. salt
1 c. quick-cooking oats
1 (6-oz.) pkg. semi-sweet chocolate
  pieces
½ c. confectioners' sugar
¼ c. peanut butter
2 to 4 tblsp. milk

Cream together butter and sugars in large bowl until light and fluffy. Add egg; beat well. Beat in ⅓ c. peanut butter and vanilla.

Sift together flour, baking soda and salt. Stir dry ingredients and oats gradually into creamed mixture. Spread mixture in greased 13x9x2″ baking pan.

Bake in 350° oven 20 to 25 minutes. Sprinkle top with chocolate pieces. Let stand for 5 minutes. Spread melted chocolate over top. Combine confectioners' sugar, ¼ c. peanut butter and enough milk to make a thin icing. Drizzle over melted chocolate. Cool in pan on rack. Cut into 3x1″ bars. Makes about 3 dozen.

*See Index for recipe

Lunch

Mexican Tomato-Corn Soup
Avocado Salad Wrapped in Tortillas
Cold Poached Orange Slices
Tea   Milk

Dinner

Baked Ham   Glazed Apricots
Steamed Brussels Sprouts with Toasted Almonds
Orange-Candied Sweet Potatoes*
Tossed Salad
Banana Cream Pie
Coffee   Milk

Mexican Tomato-Corn Soup

2 (13¾-oz.) cans chicken broth
1 (1-lb.) can tomatoes, cut up
1 (12-oz.) can corn
¼ tsp. dried oregano leaves
¼ tsp. salt
⅛ tsp. pepper

Combine all ingredients in large saucepan. Bring to a boil. Reduce heat; cover and simmer 10 minutes. Makes about 2 quarts.

Breakfast

Hot Apple Juice with Cinnamon Stick Stirrers

Poached Eggs on Broiled Ham Slices

Poppy Seed Coffee Cake

Coffee   Milk

Poppy Seed Coffee Cake

3 c. sifted flour
1½ tsp. baking soda
1 tsp. salt
3 eggs
2 c. sugar
1 c. cooking oil
1 (13-oz.) can evaporated milk
⅓ c. poppy seeds
½ c. chopped walnuts
Sifted confectioners' sugar

Sift together flour, baking soda and salt in small bowl.

Combine eggs, sugar and oil in mixing bowl. Beat with electric mixer at medium speed 3 minutes.

Add dry ingredients alternately with evaporated milk to egg mixture, beating well after each addition. Stir in poppy seeds and walnuts. Pour batter into ungreased 10″ tube pan.

Bake in 325° oven 1 hour 25 minutes, or until done. Cool in pan on rack. Dust with confectioners' sugar before serving. Makes 16 servings.

Brunch

Tomato Bouillon*

Creamed Crab Meat over Avocado Halves

Marinated Green Beans

High-Protein Muffins*   *Honey Nut Butter*

Coffee   Tea   Milk

Honey Nut Butter

3 tblsp. vegetable oil
3 tblsp. honey
½ c. roasted peanuts
¼ c. roasted salted sunflower seeds
¼ c. sesame seeds

Place all ingredients in blender container. Blend at high speed until smooth, stopping blender frequently to scrape sides. Makes about ¾ cup.

Breakfast

Chilled Fruit Cocktail in Orange Cups

<u>*Frozen Wheat Waffles*</u>   *Melted Raspberry Jelly*

Broiled Sausages and Chicken Livers en Brochette

Coffee

Frozen Wheat Waffles

1 c. sifted all-purpose flour
¾ c. stirred whole-wheat flour
1 tsp. baking powder
1 tsp. baking soda
½ tsp. salt
2 eggs
⅓ c. vegetable oil
2 c. buttermilk

In large bowl, stir together all-purpose flour, whole-wheat flour, baking powder, baking soda and salt. Make well in dry ingredients. Add eggs, oil and buttermilk. Beat until well-blended.

Bake in preheated waffle iron; cool. Place waxed paper between waffles, wrap and freeze.

To serve, heat frozen waffles in toaster. Or place on baking sheet and bake, uncovered, in 325° oven 15 minutes. Makes 3 (10") square waffles or 7 (7") round waffles.

Brunch

Baked Canadian Bacon

<u>*Quick Mustard Sauce*</u>

Scrambled Eggs with Chives

Popovers*

Jelly

Coffee

Quick Mustard Sauce

1 pt. dairy sour cream
3 tblsp. prepared horseradish
½ c. prepared mustard

Combine ingredients. Serve cold, or heat until mixture simmers and serve warm. Makes 2½ cups.

*See Index for recipe

Shortcuts
& Seasonings

• For an almost instant mousse, dissolve a 4-oz. pkg. of strawberry-flavored gelatin in 1 c. boiling water. Stir in a little grated lemon or orange rind and a pint of strawberry ice cream, pour into sherbet glasses and chill for about 30 minutes.

• To perk up your favorite salad dressing, substitute grapefruit juice for the vinegar.

• If you must slice lots of onions for a big batch of stew, begin by dropping them into boiling water for about 5 minutes; the skins will then slide off easily.

• Put leftover vegetables to good use in a nutritious soup. First, whirl cooked carrots, cauliflower and broccoli in a blender until smooth; then stir in 2 c. cream of mushroom soup.

• Add 1 c. of finely chopped, pared apple to your favorite pancake batter and top off the pancakes by drizzling them with a dash of brandy-flavored extract.

• To freshen day-old biscuits or muffins, put them in a well-dampened paper bag, twist closed and heat in a 300° oven for about 10 minutes.

• To transform plain whipped potatoes into Chantilly Potatoes, add 1 tsp. lemon juice and a dash of nutmeg to 3 c. hot whipped potatoes and place in a shallow buttered baking dish. Whip ½ c. heavy cream and fold ¼ c. grated Swiss cheese into the cream. Spread over whipped potatoes, and brown briefly under the broiler.

• For super-crunchy coleslaw, start by cutting a cabbage in half and soaking it in ice water for about 30 minutes. Drain well and slice into shreds with a sharp knife.

Index